3/14

LAST HOURS ON EVEREST

GRAHAM HOYLAND

LAST HOURS ON EVEREST

The Gripping Story of Mallory & Irvine's Fatal Ascent

Collins

First published in 2013 by Collins

An imprint of HarperCollins*Publishers*
77–85 Fulham Palace Road
Hammersmith, London W6 8JB

www.harpercollins.co.uk

1 3 5 7 9 10 8 6 4 2

A catalogue record for this book is
available from the British Library.

HB ISBN 978-0-00-745575-1
TPB ISBN 978-0-00-748186-6

Printed and bound in Great Britain by
Clays Ltd, St Ives plc

MIX
Paper from
responsible sources
FSC™ **FSC® C007454**
www.fsc.org

FSC™ is a non-profit international organisation established to promote
the responsible management of the world's forests. Products carrying the
FSC label are independently certified to assure consumers that they come
from forests that are managed to meet the social, economic and
ecological needs of present and future generations,
and other controlled sources.

Find out more about HarperCollins and the environment at
www.harpercollins.co.uk/green

Contents

Preface

Mount Everest has been my arena. I have spent over two years of my life on the mountain, returning there again and again. I am drawn back because I see there the extremes of human experience played out in the most dramatic surroundings: greed and betrayal, loyalty and courage, endurance and defeat. It is a moral crucible in which we are tested, and usually found wanting. It has cost me my marriage, my home and half my possessions. Twice Everest has nearly killed me. But I find it utterly addictive. And so did George Mallory.

This volume is going to add to the vast pile of books about Mount Everest, a pile that must now must be higher than the mountain. I make no apology for this, for I think I have finally solved the mystery of what happened there on 8 June 1924, when Mallory and his young companion Sandy Irvine disappeared into clouds, climbing strongly towards the top.

My family had a unique relationship with Everest, and this helped me to climb the mountain and to find clues to what happened to Mallory, its most famous opponent. I spent a long time looking for his body, and then I spent a long time trying to prove that he climbed his nemesis before it killed him.

This is going to be a personal story, a detective thriller, a biography and a history book.

I hope it will set the record straight about how Mallory was found. It is about other things, too, such as why we believe in gods and mountains.

Most of all, though, it is about my life-long hunt for an answer to the greatest mystery in mountaineering: who first climbed Mount Everest?

Prologue

Dawn broke fine on that fatal day. A couple of thousand feet above the tiny canvas tent the summit of the world's highest mountain stood impassively, waiting for someone to have the courage to approach.

Inside the ice-crusted shelter, two forms lay as still as death. Then there was a groan, a stirring, and eventually the slow scratch of match against sandpaper. Low voices shared the high-altitude agonies of waking, the heating of water and the struggle with frozen boots.

As the sun rose through wisps of cloud beyond the Tibetan hills to the east, one of the men emerged through the tent flaps. It was a fine morning for the attempt, with only a few clouds in the sky. The two of them stood for a while, shuffling their feet and blowing into their hands. Inside the tent lay a mess of sleeping bags and food. The men lifted oxygen sets onto their backs, then turned towards the mountain and stamped off into history.

Seventy years later, above the Hillary Step on the other side of the mountain, I was teetering along the narrow icy summit ridge between Nepal and Tibet, between life and death. The sun was intensely bright and the sky was that deep blue-black of very high altitudes. All around were the icy fins of the world's highest mountains. And somewhere along that ridge I experienced one of those existential moments that gives you the reason for gambling with your life. The intenseness of the now, the sharp savour of living wholly in the present moment: no past, no worries. The chop of the ice axe, the crunch of the crampons, the hiss of breath – this is the very essence of life. Eventually I saw a couple of figures just above me, a couple of steps … and I was there.

I can't remember much. Now it all seems a sort of vivid dream: bright sunlight, a tearing wind, a long flag of ice particles flying downwind of us. A vast drop of two miles into Tibet. We could see across a hundred miles of tightly packed peaks, and we could see the curvature of the earth. Contorted faces shouting soundlessly, lips blue with oxygen starvation. Doctors prove with blood samples that climbers are in the process of dying up there on the summit, but I would say that is where I started to live.

As I stumbled down the mountain one thought kept recurring to me. If I, a very average climber, could stand on this summit, how could the legendary George Mallory have failed to do so?

I

Start of an Obsession

Mountaineering is in my blood. My father started taking me out into the hills of Arran when I was five, and I can still remember the moment when we scrambled to the top of the island's highest mountain. I saw the sea laid out almost three thousand feet beneath us like a polished steel floor. Down there was Brodick Bay, with the ferry steaming in from the mainland like a toy boat.

Climbing was filled with sensation: the sheer agony of panting up steep slopes in the summer sun, the sharp smell of my father's sweat as we lay resting in the heather, the hard coldness of a swim in the burn. Then the gritty feel of the granite under your fingers, and the blast of wind in your face as you breasted the summit.

It must have been a double-edged pleasure for my father, though. His brother, John Hoyland had been killed on Mont Blanc in 1934. Jack Longland, a famous climber of the day who was on the 1933 Everest expedition, described John as 'potentially the best mountaineer of his generation ... there was no young English climber since George Mallory of whom it seemed safe to expect so much'.[1]

John had hoped to go on the next expedition to Everest, but his death at the age of nineteen had put paid to those hopes. Even I could feel the loss at thirty years' distance.

My father told me about another climbing hero in our family, a man who had been close to the summit of Mount Everest in 1924. He called him 'Uncle Hunch', and Dad said that one day

I would meet him. He said he'd been a close friend of George Mallory, and again that name was mentioned. Mallory, the paragon of climbers. My young mind took it all in.

I lived and dreamed mountains on those summer holidays. To me Goat Fell, the highest of the Arran hills, looked uncannily like Mount Everest when viewed from the south; indeed it does to me even now. And it is almost exactly a tenth of Everest's height. I remember cricking my neck back and back on the Strabane shore and trying to count out ten Goat Fells standing on top of each other. I couldn't imagine anything so impossibly vast. How could anyone climb so high?

Eventually, when I was 13 and he was 81, I met Uncle Hunch.

We were at the memorial service of my great-aunt Dolly, who was one of the Quaker Cadburys. She was wealthy and lived in a large country mansion. I remember her house had a wide, open, red-carpeted spiral staircase for the family, inside of which was an enclosed stone staircase for the servants. I would race up the outer stairs past glass-cased model steam engines and then clatter down the inner, hidden stairs. We, the poor relations, used to receive a huge box of Cadbury's chocolates every Christmas from Aunt Dolly, and I was particularly fond of her for her gentleness and the P. G. Wodehouse books she used to pass on to me.

Her death was a shame, I thought, a further distancing from a more romantic past. But oddly enough, I was about to be more firmly connected with that past.

I remember standing on the lawn outside Verlands and looking up at Uncle Hunch – the legendary Howard Somervell, who was actually a cousin, not an uncle.

He really was an extraordinarily gifted man: a double first at Cambridge, a talented artist (his pictures of Everest are still on the walls of the Alpine Club) and an accomplished musician (he transcribed the music he heard in Tibet into Western notation). He served as an army surgeon during the First World War and was one of the foremost alpinists of the day when he was invited to join the 1922 Mount Everest expedition. He took part in the first serious attempt to climb the mountain, and his oxygen-free height record stood for over 50 years. General C. G. Bruce, the expedition leader, described his strength on the mountain: 'Stands by himself ... an extraordinary capacity for going day after day.'[2]

Furthermore, the great explorer Sir Francis Younghusband said that of all the Everest men he met he liked Somervell the best.[3]

At that stage in my life I knew nothing about this, I was only interested in the incredible story he was telling me. He was a stout old man by then, with the slight stoop that gave him his family name, but his voice still contained the excitement of his twenties youth.

'Norton and I had a last-ditch attempt to climb Mount Everest, and we got higher than any man had ever been before. I really couldn't breathe properly and on the way down my throat blocked up completely. I sat down to die, but as one last try I pressed my chest hard' – and here the old man pushed his chest to demonstrate to his fascinated audience – 'and up came the blockage. We got down safely. We met Mallory at the North Col on his way up. He said to me that he had forgotten his camera, and I lent him mine. So, if my camera was ever found,' said Uncle Hunch to me, 'you could prove that Mallory got to the top.' It was a throw-away comment that he probably had made a hundred times in the course of telling this story, but this time it found its mark.

Gripped by Uncle Hunch's story, I discussed it endlessly with my father. The mystery seemed simple enough. Mallory and his young companion Sandy Irvine, on their desperate last attempt to climb Mount Everest in 1924, had just disappeared into the clouds. No one knew whether they had succeeded or not. When a British expedition finally got two men to the top in 1953 they looked for signs of the pair but found nothing. The only way of proving their success would be to find Somervell's camera on a dead body, develop the film and discover a photograph of them on the summit. The story of Mallory and Irvine gripped my imagination. I read all the climbing books I could lay my hands on, and dreamed of being a mountaineer.

I had an idyllic boyhood in some ways. We were living in Rutland then, a rural part of England where rolling hills modulate into the flat lands of the Fens. This, the smallest of all the counties, is a secret Cotswolds of golden limestone villages, Collyweston stone slate roofs and fine churches. Our home was an archetypal English village, with a beautiful squire's hall, a spired church and a huge vicarage dominating a cluster of alms cottages, pubs and farm houses. I went to a Victorian primary school that taught Victorian religion.

My brother Denys and I once scrambled on to the church roof in an attempt to climb the steeple with its conveniently placed stone croquets, intricately carved ornamental bosses about four feet apart. The reason for our climb was a village legend that a drinker in the Boot and Shoe public house had one evening wagered that he could shin up the slender steeple and bring down the weathercock from the very top. He had done so, and had then returned it to its place. The thought of climbing to that ultimate stone point, up there in the pale moonlight, filled me with excitement and dread. We had to try! After getting up a drainpipe in a corner we crossed the lead roof and started up the square tower on the east side. About ten feet up I grasped a stone corbel – and it came off in my hand. We hastily rammed it back into place. The climb was over.

Years later I found out that George Mallory had climbed the roof of his father's parish church in Cheshire in a very similar way. Boys will be boys.

This idyll ended when I was sent to a local public school. The headmaster was an ex-Guards officer and, like Mallory, I was drafted into the Officer Training Corps as soon as I could polish a pair of boots. I got into trouble because my army boot toe-caps were scuffed by the Scottish heather.

Denys and my father had started taking me out climbing in the summer holidays on the Isle of Arran around the time we moved to Rutland. George Mallory went to Arran in August 1917 to climb with his friend David Pye and test a healing ankle. It was the first time he had walked in the Scottish hills and he enjoyed it:

> The mountains themselves are so lovely, and when one gets high ... the view of the islands and peninsulas in these parts is like being in some enchanting country – nothing I have seen beats it for colour.[4]

He stayed in Corrie, a small village on the east coast of the island, from which some of my ancestors came. My Scottish mother was brought up on Arran, and our family decamped to the island every summer holiday to stay with my grandmother. We didn't live in the Front House, her solid sandstone terraced house in Brodick, but camped in the Back, a tiny, two-roomed cottage with wooden cabins behind it in another, recessive Back. Grandmother came with us, as well. From here, in an atmosphere of paraffin lamps and the smell of damp, come my oldest memories of the island.

The reason for my grandmother's seasonal move was to make room for 'the Folk'. Nearly everyone in Arran seemed to let their houses to holiday-makers from Glasgow. Lying in a dominant position in the Firth of Clyde made the island an attractive holi-day destination from the late 19th century, but somehow its very popularity blinds people to the fact that it is one of the real gems of the British Isles.

The Scottish poet Robert Burns seemed indifferent to Arran, too. He must have seen its hills from the inland Ayrshire farms where he spent his youth, but he fails to mention the island in any of his writings. I became curious about this: could it be that a love of mountain beauty was just not fashionable in his time and place? Today Burns's omission seems unaccountable; arriving at the dismal town of Ardrossan to catch the ferry it's hard not to be impressed by the view across 14 miles of sea – if it is not raining. Then you might just see a dirty, grey smudge. But on a clear day, the island floats there in all her glory.

Arran is ancient. It was an island before the mainland of Britain parted company with Europe, and the mountains here were once as high as the Himalayas, which are youngsters by comparison at only 55 million years old. Now Goat Fell has worn down to just under 3,000ft, and so it is not even big enough to qualify as a Munro, a Scottish mountain over that height. This serves to point out the absurdity of a system based on size.

2

Getting the Measure
of the Mountain

As a schoolboy I had become curious about how the height of Mount Everest was calculated. You could hardly bore a hole in the summit and drop a tape measure from the top until you hit the bottom. So how was it done? I found the answer in Aunt Dolly's 1920s *Encyclopaedia Britannica*, and I found it even more amazing than the story of the attempts to climb the mountain.

The British in the 19th century were fascinated by exploring their world, measuring its features and naming them. They were making an inventory of their empire, but perhaps they were also trying to make sense of a planet of rock and sea whirling through the universe. They were particularly captivated by India. My missionary grandfather and his medical cousin Somervell – and I in turn – all fell in love with the sub-continent, and my father was born in Nagpur. India is a great, exotic, bohemian mother of our imagination, and the England of my childhood seems a pale reflection of her culture and peoples.

The Great Trigonometrical Survey was commissioned by the East India Company to survey all their lands in the sub-continent. The survey started in 1802, and it was initially estimated it would take just five years to complete the work. In the end, it took more than sixty years, and cost the Company a fortune.

Imaginary triangles were to be drawn all over India, starting at the southern end and eventually reaching the Himalayas over 1,500 miles away. A great arc of 20° would be drawn along the earth's surface. This would also establish how much the earth flattened towards the poles. The measurements had to be extremely accurate otherwise errors would build up by the time they reached the Himalayas.

The precision the surveyors attained was remarkable. A baseline between two points visible to each other about seven miles apart would be carefully measured with 100ft chains. Later, special metal bars that compensated for the expansion due to temperature were used. If there was a village in the way it would be moved, and 50ft masonry towers were built at the end of the baseline if there wasn't a convenient hill available. Then a huge brass theodolite would be hoisted to the top of the tower, and the exact angle between the baseline and the sightline to a third point would be measured. Sightings were made using mirrors to flash sunshine at far-distant colleagues, and blue lights were used at night if the heat of the day caused refraction.

A triangle was thus formed and, as every schoolchild knows, if the length of the baseline and the two angles are known, the length of the other two sides can be worked out. This meant that surveyors didn't have to measure them on the ground.

The height of a mountain was calculated by measuring its angle of elevation from several different places, drawing vertical imaginary triangles this time. This was important, as it meant that the surveyors could now work out the height of distant unclimbed mountains in an inaccessible country.

A typical expedition employed four elephants for the surveyors and 30 horses for the military officers – both groups wishing to avoid encounters with tigers – and more than 40 camels for the equipment. The 700 accompanying labourers travelled on foot and clearly had to take their chance with the tigers.

The survey was begun in the southernmost point of the subcontinent, at Cape Cormorin, very close to where Somervell's hospital at Neyyoor would later be built.

Begun by Major William Lambton, the survey was supervised for most of its extent by Colonel George Everest, a man noted for his exacting accuracy. When he took over the job the survey equipment used by Lambton was worn out. There was the great brass 36-inch theodolite made in London by Cary, weighing 1,000lb (which had been accidentally dropped a couple of times), a Ramsden 100ft chain that hadn't been calibrated in 25 years, a zenith sector also by Jesse Ramsden, now with a worn micrometer screw, and a chronometer. These were all repaired by an instrument maker brought in from London, and Everest pressed on with his life's work.

Ill-health, the bane of many a Briton in India, eventually caught up with Everest, and so Andrew Waugh had to finish off the job. Interestingly, he re-measured the Bidar baseline with the special Colby compensating bars. The error after 425 miles and 85 triangles was only 4 inches in a line length of 41,578ft.

What is not generally acknowledged is that the surveyors often became rich. Knowledge of the terrain was clearly useful. The Chamrette dynasty of surveyors – grandfather, father and son – owned over 1,800 acres, and George Everest bought 600 acres of land near Dehra Dun. The British Empire became wealthy, too, with the possession of this fabulous land. If I were an Indian citizen reading this now I would be feeling fairly angry. The only (poor) defence is that other nations were also playing the Great Game in the region, and partly what drove the British Empire to survey its borders was fear of invasion from the Russian Empire.

Eventually this great endeavour reached the border with Nepal, a land that was forbidden to the British. The surveyors focused their instruments on the far Himalayas, drew their triangles and measured 79 of the highest mountains, including K2 and Kangchenjunga. Eventually they computed in 1854 that the most lofty was a mountain on the remote border between Nepal and Tibet. They had to allow for the gravitational pull of the Himalayan range (which will even distort the surface of a puddle), the refraction of the atmosphere and a number of other variables, and it is a wonder to me that they got the height so close: 29,002ft. It took over 150 years to pin down a more accurate result, although still no one agrees on exactly how high the mountain is. All measurements are now made in metric units, and China insists that the measurement should be made up to the topmost rock, at 8,844m (29,015ft), whereas Nepal measures to the top of the overlying snow-cap, at 8,848m (29,028ft). The US National Geographic Society measurement using satellites came to 8,850m (29,035ft) – a difference of 33ft from the original Great Trigonometrical Survey result, or around 0.1 per cent error. Not bad, considering the pioneers were using telescopes and brass theodolites, aimed from across the border.

The first scrawl on the map announcing Mount Everest styled it as 'Peak B', then 'Peak XV', somewhat in the manner of K2 in the Karakorum, which after a brief existence as Mount Godwin-Austen reverted to its surveyor's notation. There has been much debate about the name of Mount Everest. Traditionally, British surveyors always tried to use the local name for geographical features. This was an honourable intention, as otherwise the world's maps would be plastered with the names of British dignitaries. In Mount Everest's case, however, they found that there were several possible local names. The Swedish explorer Sven Hedin claimed that it was called Tchoumou Lancma, and said that the name had been recorded by French Jesuit priests who had been in China in the 18th century. When spelled as Chomolungma, the name has been fancifully translated by imaginative writers as 'Goddess Mother of the World', but this has little connection with the truth. Charles Bell, who knew a thing or two about Tibetan culture, insisted that the local name was Chamalung. David Macdonald, the trade agent who dealt with the early Everest expeditions, claimed the mountain was called Miti Guti Chapu Longnga, which translates rather more convincingly as 'the mountain whose summit no one can see from close-up [true only from the south], but can be seen from the far distance, and which is so high that birds go blind when they fly over the summit'. I rather like this name, except that my companion on the summit in 1993 saw an alpine chough fly right over us. It didn't appear to go blind. This name would also make all the innumerable books about the mountain even longer. In the end, though, the British chose the name of the former Surveyor-General Sir George Everest.

It is unlikely that Everest himself ever laid his eyes on the mountain that bears his name, but Andrew Waugh, Everest's successor as Surveyor-General in India, wrote: '... here is a mountain most probably the highest in the world without any local name that I can discover ...', so he proposed 'to perpetuate the memory of that illustrious master of geographical research ... Everest'.

This went completely against contemporary cartological practice, and it was the start of the long story of the mountain being hijacked for ulterior motives. Everest himself said his name could not be written in either Hindi or Persian, and nor could the local people pronounce it. Nor can we. He pronounced his name Eeev-rest, as in Adam and Eve, while the rest of us happily mispronounce it as Ever-rest, as in double-glazing.

At the beginning of the 19th century the British wanted to know how the Russian Empire might plan to invade India, and they were not going to be deterred by forbidden frontiers. Geographical knowledge was power. Heights of mountains were important, and even more important was the accessibility of the passes between them. In 1800 the Surveyor-General of Bengal permitted British officers to enter and survey any country they chose. Unfortunately, some were caught in Afghanistan and murdered, but not before some spectacular heights were reported among the Himalayan giants. It was clearly unwise to send blue-eyed, fair-haired young men into these parts, and Captain Montgomerie of the Survey (who surveyed and named K2) soon realised it would be better to employ local men from the Indian

Border States as surveyors. They were given two years of training in the use of the instruments and were then sent over the border disguised as holy men or traders. They were known as *pandits*, Hindi for 'learned man'. We derive our word 'pundit' from these remarkable men.

Perhaps the most remarkable was Pandit 001, Nain Singh, a Bhotian school teacher. He left Dehra Dun in 1865 and entered Nepal, travelling through the country into Tibet, where he reached Lhasa and met the Panchen Lama. Using a sextant (I wondered where he hid it) and a boiling-point thermometer he calculated the location and the altitude of the forbidden city.

I used the boiling-point technique to determine altitude at Base Camp on Mount Everest in 2007 while filming a science programme for the BBC. The first thing we did was to get a big pan of water to a good rolling boil, as Mrs Beeton would call it (she was writing her cookbook just as the pundits were setting off in the 1860s). I then stuck the big glass thermometer into the water and got a reading of only 85°C. Water boils at 100°C at sea level. This meant the altitude was around 4,600m (15,000ft). The reason that water boils at a lower temperature at higher altitude is that water is trying to turn into a gas (steam) when it boils, and it is easier for the steam to push against the air molecules when there are fewer of them (lower pressure). Bubbles – or boiling – are the result. When I got frostbitten fingers on the summit in 1993 I was able to dangle them in a pan of boiling water at Camp II. It only felt hot, rather than painfully hot.

If someone were to boil up a kettle for tea on the summit of Mount Everest – and I'm sure they will sooner or later – it would start boiling at only 68°C. And it wouldn't make very good tea. Incidentally, it was hard to keep the long glass thermometer unbroken on our journey into Base Camp in 2007. Pundit Nain Singh concealed his in a walking-staff, but how he didn't break it is beyond me.

The map-makers of British India now had a mystery on their hands. As well as locating the city of Lhasa, Nain Singh had also mapped a large section of a huge river in Tibet, the Tsangpo, which plunged into a gorge and disappeared. Hundreds of miles away the sacred river Brahmaputra issued from the Himalayas, but there were thousands of feet of height between them. Were they the same river? Nain Singh thought they were. So was there an undiscovered giant waterfall, many times higher than the Victoria Falls? That was the riddle of the Tsangpo.

It was partly solved by another pundit, Kinthup, in a truly amazing journey. In 1880 he was sent into Tibet in the company of a Chinese lama, to whom he would act a servant. They were to throw marked logs into the Tsangpo and surveyors on the Brahmaputra would wait to see if any logs came through. Unfortunately, the lama was a less than ideal master. He womanised and drank, then sold Kinthup into slavery. The pundit eventually escaped, but was captured and resold to another lama.

It took Kinthup four years to get to the point on the Tsangpo from which he had to send his timber signal. He prepared five hundred logs and threw fifty into the river per day. Eventually he got back to India, where he asked if anyone had seen the logs. But all of those who had sent him on his mission had either left India or died. 'Which logs?' the men of the Survey said, and poor, disillusioned Kinthup left to become a tailor. One can only imagine his chagrin after so many years of work, and what a modern employment tribunal might make of it all. In the end the surveyors Morshead and Bailey explored the river from the south, and at last, in 1913, Kinthup's reports were believed. The Tsangpo and the Brahmaputra were accepted as the same river, and this great explorer was at last recognised with a pension, grants of land and a medal.

I have a personal theory about the pundits: I think they were partly the inspiration for James Bond, Agent 007. Consider this: they were numbered 001, 002, 003, etc., and were spies in enemy territory. They carried maps hidden in prayer wheels, and counted their carefully practised 2,000 paces a mile on special Buddhist rosaries on which every tenth bead was slightly larger ...

At about the time Mount Everest was being measured, thousands of miles away in Europe the leisure sport of alpinism was being invented by the sons of English gentlemen who had been enriched by the Industrial Revolution. Before then, most sensible mountain-travellers regarded the high peaks as dangerous wastelands inhabited by demons. All this started to change in the early 19th century, when Samuel Taylor Coleridge, the Romantic poet, wrote about his climb on Broad Stand, in England's Lake District.

In June 2010 three friends and I retraced Coleridge's route to try to experience exactly what he felt. He was on the summit of Scafell, England's second highest mountain (Scafell Pike is the highest), having scrambled up a safe route. He then decided to experiment with the then fashionable sublime feelings of terror by picking a descent route that looked possible – but only just – down through a series of tumbling rock terraces. Later, boasting to his girlfriend (as we all do), he wrote:

> I began to suspect that I ought not to go on, but then unfortunately tho' I could with ease drop down a smooth Rock 7 feet high, I could not climb it, so go on I must and on I went. The next 3 drops were not half a Foot, at least not a foot more than my own height, but every Drop increased the Palsy of my Limbs – I shook all over, Heaven knows without the

least influence of Fear, and now I had only two more to drop down, to return was impossible – but of these two the first was tremendous, it was twice my own height, and the Ledge at the bottom was so exceedingly narrow, that if I dropt down upon it I must of necessity have fallen backwards and of course killed myself.

I was impressed by Coleridge's boldness. The route descends over downward-sloping ledges that are separated by higher and higher rock walls, with a deadly drop-off onto the jagged scree below. It all feels rather intimidating. Halfway down an irreversible descent he got himself completely stuck above a big drop, unable to return upwards or progress downwards. This same predicament has since led to the deaths of climbers. He then experienced those feelings of terror that are only too familiar to us:

> My Limbs were all in a tremble – I lay upon my Back to rest myself, and was beginning according to my Custom to laugh at myself for a Madman, when the sight of the Crags above me on each side, and the impetuous Clouds just over them, posting so luridly and so rapidly northward, overawed me. I lay in a state of almost prophetic Trance and Delight – and blessed God aloud, for the powers of Reason and the Will, which remaining no Danger can overpower us![1]

I lay in exactly the same spot and thought about Coleridge's power of Reason. He was clearly not just an excitable Romantic. He had calmed himself down and thought about how to get out of his predicament. Just below and to the left of this final ledge there is a narrow chimney that is not immediately obvious. In the event he was able to explore sideways and slither down this chimney, which is now known as Fat Man's Peril. If there had been no exit we may have lost one of our most interesting literary figures. This just goes to show the importance of careful reading. If only British climbers had stuck to Coleridge's idea of rock-climbing *downwards*, modern mountaineering would be very different.

His wasn't the first rock climb in Britain, though. There are modern routes that were first climbed long before the sport evolved, some by shepherds rescuing crag-fast sheep, some by birds-nesters, and some just by young dare-devils. In 1695 men were described using ropes for rock climbing on traditional fowling expeditions in the St Kilda archipelago. Slowly, rock climbing evolved into an activity in its own right, and as with many cultural movements it is hard to pin down a moment when rock climbing as a sport began. It started in at least three areas: the sandstone crags of the Elbsandsteingebirge, near Dresden; the Dolomites in Italy; and the Lake District in England, where a small group of climbers started rock climbing above the valley of Wasdale, beneath Scafell Pike.

Many were serious-minded, middle-class Victorian gentlemen who sought an escape from the industrial northern towns of Liverpool and Manchester. The father of English rock climbing was Walter Parry Haskett Smith, who, 84 years after Coleridge's climb, made a solo first ascent (upwards instead of downwards) of Napes Needle, an obelisk-like pillar just across the Wasdale valley from Broad Stand. An early climb that is in touch with modern standards was O. G. Jones's 1897 climb of Kern Knotts Crack, graded Very Severe, and significantly Jones was attracted by a photograph of Napes Needle that he saw in a shop on the Strand in London. Similarly, the television films that we make on Mount Everest draw new recruits to mountaineering. And if they learn about the fun of climbing, then why not?

The British are usually credited with inventing the sport of alpinism, and it was largely because of leisure. Britain was 'an island of coal surrounded by a sea of fish', and happened for many reasons to be the first nation to industrialise (it could so easily have been the Romans, who were close to steam power, or the Indians, who had even more resources). The Industrial Revolution provided many a wealthy man's son with ample time and money while the average Swiss peasant was far too busy scraping a living off the mountainsides to waste time raising his eyes to the summits.

Sir Alfred Wills, who was Edward Norton's grandfather, kicked off the Golden Age of Alpinism with his 1854 ascent of the Wetterhorn (although it wasn't actually the first ascent, which had been made ten years earlier by Stanhope T. Speer with his Swiss guides). There then followed an explosion of climbing, with most of the major peaks being bagged within ten years. There was a similar period in the Himalayas a century later, when all the 14 peaks over 8,000m (26,247ft) were climbed within 11 years of each other.

The Alpine Club was founded in London in 1857. Simon Schama in his *Landscape and Memory* notes that the members of the Club were predominantly upper-middle-class rather than aristocratic, and that they thought of themselves as a caste apart, a Spartan phalanx, tough with muscular virtue, spare with speech, seeking the chill clarity of the mountains just because, as Leslie Stephen, who became the club's president in 1865, put it, 'There we can breathe air that has not passed through a million pairs of lungs.'[2]

It is curious that so many writers had brothers who became Himalayan climbers: Greene, Spender, Auden. It is interesting, too, that it seemed to be the left-wing intellectuals who wanted to place themselves above the masses. John Carey writes:

The cult of mountaineering and alpine holidays among English intellectuals ... seems to have been encouraged by

Nietzschean images of supremacy. Climbing a mountain gave, as it were, objective expression to the intellectual's sense of superiority and high endeavour, which otherwise remained rather notional.[3]

There is a danger in this search for purity that surfaced later in the Nazi fascination with mountain climbing.

The pace of Alpine climbing accelerated, with Edward Whymper knocking off the Col de Triolet, the Aiguille de Tré-la-Tête and the Aiguille d'Argentière in one week in 1864 with guide Michel Croz. His 1865 book *Scrambles in the Alps* was a sensation, describing the first ascent of the Matterhorn and the ensuing accident that killed four of his companions. Suddenly, the new sport assumed a dangerous new edge in the public mind, and the short but golden age of Alpine climbing was over.

Back in England there was a disaster high on Scafell Pinnacle in 1903 that Somervell and Mallory would have been very well aware of, as it was much discussed at the time. The tradition then was that 'the leader must not fall', because the hemp ropes climbers used were not strong enough to take much of a shock, and modern protection devices such as Friends – camming devices that expand into cracks in the rock and to which a climbing rope can be attached – were as yet undreamt of. All that the climbers could do was to loop the rope over a spike of rock, if available, or jam a rock into a crack and pass the rope behind it. In the 1903 accident, there was no belay point available, and four men fell 200ft to their deaths.

As we shall see, George Mallory would have had the need for a belay very much in mind on 8 June 1924 as he scanned the cliffs above him for a route to the top of Mount Everest.

3

Renaissance Men

I was a bookish child, and rather shy. I didn't quiz Uncle Hunch about his story, but when we got home from Aunt Dolly's memorial service I found out more about him, Mount Everest and his friend Mallory in the memoir that he wrote titled *After Everest*. I have the book next to me, still wrapped in my grandmother's sewn cover. His climbing life, including Mount Everest, takes up less than a third of the pages, and he makes it clear that his medical missionary work was far more important to him. So many Everesters keep going back and back to the mountain of their obsession, and it is entirely typical of him that he was able to develop himself away from it.

One of the problems of assessing multi-talented individuals is that most of us can only appreciate one aspect of them at a time. If anyone has heard of T. H. Somervell nowadays they might think of him as one of Mallory's fellow-climbers on Everest, or maybe as a painter of mountain landscapes. Some readers in India might still remember his medical work in their country, but he excelled in several fields and was one of the most interesting characters on those early Everest expeditions.

He was born in 1890 to a well-to-do evangelical family in Kendal who owned K Shoes, a prosperous boot-making company. At Cambridge he at first derided modern art, then adopted it. Similarly, he toyed with atheism, joining a society named the Heretics, and 'for two years I strenuously refused to believe in God, especially in a revealed God'.[1] Afterwards he felt there was something missing from his life, and felt that his atheist fellow students were 'wallowing in an intellectual nowhere'. After a chance prayer-meeting he rediscovered his faith and became for a while a passionate evangelical. This mellowed into a steady religious faith that remained with him and informed all the major decisions of his life. It is almost as if the young Somervell had to experiment with opposites, push hard in contrary directions, before he could find his place in both art and religion. Perhaps the extreme horror of his war-time experiences swung him towards extreme faith.

I wanted to know how he began climbing. The 18-year-old Somervell had taken to solitary walking in his native Lake District, and one day saw a party of rock climbers. He followed them up their route on his own, and when he reached the top he was ticked off for climbing without either a companion or a rope. On buying one of the Abraham brothers' guidebooks he was delighted to realise he'd done a climb described as 'Difficult'. He continued going rock climbing, and this eventually led to the Alps, where one of his early climbs had an ecclesiastical flavour: he teamed up with a parson and the Bishop of Sierra Leone. Unfortunately, the bishop slipped off an overhang and dangled in mid-air, swinging like a pendulum. Somervell started to lower him but the noose around his waist was loose, the unfortunate cleric raised his arms and the rope slid off. He hung by his hands alone, and 'certain death was beneath him if he could not hold on.'[2] Somervell redoubled his lowering, and got the bishop to the safety of a snow-slope before his strength gave out. This calm rescue of another climber foreshadowed his rescue of porters on Everest in 1924.

Next came his experience of the army. After Gonville & Caius College, Cambridge, and qualification as a surgeon at University College Hospital, London, he joined up in early 1915 and went to the Front. This experience had a profound effect on him, as it did on other members of the Everest expeditions. His casualty-clearing station, the 34th, was on the Somme Front, at Vecquemont, between Amiens and Albert. Another Cambridge man, Second Lieutenant George Mallory of the 40th Siege Battery, was not far away at Pioneer Road, Albert. Mallory's job as an artillery officer was to pound the enemy lines with high-explosive shells in preparation for the greatest British offensive of the war, when 300,000 men attacked the Germans on 1 July 1916.

It was a disaster. Somervell's clearing station, with its two surgeons per six-hour shift, was expected to deal with a thousand casualties; instead, streams of motor-ambulances a mile long brought nearly 10,000 terribly wounded young men after the attack. The camp, in a field of five or six acres, was completely covered with stretchers. The surgery was a hut with only four tables, and Somervell had to walk among the victims and choose which they could try to save.

> Occasionally, we made a brief look around to select from the thousands of patients those few fortunate ones whose life or limbs we had time to save. It was a terrible business. Even now I am haunted by the touching look of the young, bright, anxious eyes, as we passed along the rows of sufferers.
>
> Hardly ever did any of them say a word, except to ask for water or relief from pain. I don't remember any single man in all those thousands who even suggested that we should save him and not the fellow next to him ... There, all around us, lying maimed and battered and dying, was the flower of Britain's youth – a terrible sight if ever there was one, yet full of courage and unselfishness and beauty.[3]

Beauty seems an odd word to use about this most grotesque of wars, and it is worth being alert to it, as it is relevant to our subject. Somervell goes on to explain:

> I know that, again and again, when, sick of casualties and the wilfulness of man that maims these poor bodies, I did see an unselfishness, a fine spirit, and a comradeship, that I have

never seen in peace-time. But in spite of all that, the very glori-
ousness of the spirit of man is a call to the nations to renounce
war and give love a chance to bring forth the best that is in
mankind.[4]

Note the reference to the spirit of man. The Poet Laureate
Robert Bridges chose *The Spirit of Man* as the title for an antho-
logy of prose and poetry, published in 1915. It is a curious book,
written during the war under the auspices of the War Propaganda
Bureau, and full of exhortations to self-sacrifice. 'We can therefore be happy in our sorrows,' writes Bridges, 'happy even in the
death of our beloved who fall in the fight; for they die nobly, as
heroes and saints die; with heart and hands unstained by hatred
or wrong.'[5] Mallory and Somervell were to read selections from
the book as they lay in their shared tent on Everest in 1922.

It was not noble to die chopped up by a machine-gun or
gassed. *The Spirit of Man* was an encouragement towards self-
sacrifice. Like the older members of my family, these men had a
culture of public-spiritedness and Christian unselfishness that
would be inconceivable to most of today's Everest climbers. I
think it might have influenced the climbing choices that Mallory
and Somervell made, and partly explains the extreme guilt they
felt when seven Sherpas died in the accident that ended that
expedition of 1922, a guilt I have rarely seen in the carnage of
a modern Everest season.

The casualty work was exhausting, and on one occasion
Somervell had to operate for two and a half days on end, without sleep. One day during the Somme campaign he went for a
short walk on the battlefield and sat down on a sandbag. He
saw a young lad asleep in front of him, looking very ill. After a
while, with horror, he realised what he was looking at:

My God, he's not breathing! He's dead! I got a real shock. I sat
there for half an hour gazing at that dead boy. About eighteen
… For a moment he personified this madness called War …

Who killed him? The politicians, the High Command, the merchants and financiers, or who? Christian nations had killed him by being un-Christian. That seemed to be the answer.

Somervell's view was that the two world wars were simply one prolonged war, with the failure of the Versailles Treaty to curtail German aggression meaning that it reasserted itself during the 1930s. Somervell felt that if Germany had been occupied and stabilised, the horror and madness of the Third Reich could have been contained.

A few miles away, Mallory's experience as an artillery officer was somewhat different, as he would not have seen as much of the bloody consequence of shelling as would a surgeon. Although the two men's roles were different, the common experience of the Great War formed a similar outlook and cemented their later friendship.

It is difficult to exaggerate the effect the conflict would have had on those survivors of the Great War. Gas was used on the Somme on 18 July:

> *Gas! Gas! Quick, boys! – An ecstasy of fumbling,*
> *Fitting the clumsy helmets just in time;*
> *But someone still was yelling out and stumbling,*
> *And flound'ring like a man in fire or lime ...*
> *Dim, through the misty panes and thick green light,*
> *As under a green sea, I saw him drowning.*
> *In all my dreams, before my helpless sight,*
> *He plunges at me, guttering, choking, drowning.*
> *If in some smothering dreams you too could pace*
> *Behind the wagon that we flung him in,*
> *And watch the white eyes writhing in his face,*
> *His hanging face, like a devil's sick of sin;*
> *If you could hear, at every jolt, the blood*
> *Come gargling from the froth-corrupted lungs,*
> *Obscene as cancer, bitter as the cud*

Of vile, incurable sores on innocent tongues,
My friend, you would not tell with such high zest
To children ardent for some desperate glory,
The old Lie; Dulce et Decorum est
Pro patria mori.[6]

Wilfred Owen, the author of this poem, was losing his Christian faith by the time he was killed, just a week before the end of the war. Arthur Wakefield, another Lake District surgeon at the Somme who experienced the same horrors as Somervell, and who also went to Everest, completely lost his faith. So did another Everester, Odell, who was also at the Somme. Many others lost their confidence in the solidity of things, and perhaps those first attempts to climb Mount Everest tried to put things right for an empire that had taken such a grievous battering.

For Howard Somervell, however, the horrific work somehow made his faith stronger, not weaker. His sons both said to me that it was the most important thing about him; it was the key to his character.

After the war Somervell resumed climbing. He went to Skye in June 1920 and made the first solo traverse of the Cuillin Ridge, from Sligachan to Gars Bheinn at the south end. I have done this route – but not all in one day – and it is a tough proposition. Like others of Somervell (and Mallory's) climbs that I have repeated, it is surprisingly extended and sometimes poorly protected – that is to say, the rope running out behind the leader goes a long way back to an attachment to the rock, and those attachments are not very secure.

We modern climbers like to think we are better than our predecessors because we do harder climbs, but when we strip out the technology we realise they were probably tougher and braver. They lived harder lives in unheated houses, and maybe just walked more than we do.

After Skye, Somervell returned to the Alps in 1921, where he climbed nearly 30 Alpine peaks in one holiday. Here he was accompanied by Bentley Beetham, who went to Everest in 1924. He climbed in the Alps with Noel Odell and Frank Smythe a couple of years later, and these trips were a way of testing climbers for an Everest expedition. Some modern pundits tell us that these men formed an exclusive upper-class clique devoted to keeping colonials and the lower classes out of their club, but I think they just chose to climb with congenial people they knew, just as the rest of us do. Later on, Irvine was selected, because he also knew Odell. Then Somervell thought his big chance had come:

> Everyone who is keen on mountains ... must have been thrilled at the thought – which only materialised late in 1920 – that at last the world's highest summit was going to be attempted. And by no means the least thrilled was myself ... I had at least a chance of being selected to go on an expedition which was then being planned for 1921.[7]

Somervell applied to join the 1921 reconnaissance expedition to Mount Everest, but was not chosen. However George Mallory *was* taken, as he was considered the foremost alpinist of the day. They did not know each other well at that stage since Somervell had gone up to Cambridge after the older man. So, for the moment Howard Somervell had to stand on the sidelines and watch.

4
Galahad of Everest

Brothers till death, and a wind-swept grave,
Joy of the journey's ending:
Ye who have climbed to the great white veil,
Hear ye the chant? Saw ye the Grail?

Geoffrey Winthrop Young, 1909

How to approach an understanding of George Mallory? On the face of it he was a somewhat unfulfilled teacher who died trying to climb a mountain. However, if we go by the sheer number of words written about him he is one of the most studied characters in British history, about whom there are at least a dozen biographies. Other, more conventionally successful members of his Everest expeditions, such as Norton or Somervell, do not even rate one published biography. How can this be?

After all these books that have been written about Mallory, it is hard to say much about him that is unclouded by them. There is a strong whiff of hero-worship about much of what has been written, and so an objective view of the man is elusive. Most of the books avoid any mention of his sexuality, some misunderstand it, and some misrepresent the circumstances of the finding of his body. That said, a book of this sort depends heavily on its predecessors, and it was far easier to learn about Mallory than Somervell.

I have met Mallory's son John (now deceased), and I know his grandson George (who has climbed Mount Everest himself) and his granddaughter Virginia. I have followed his climbs in Wales,

Scotland, the Alps and on Mount Everest itself, and I have read a fair few of his writings. Yet I still do not feel that I know the man. All I can do is struggle towards an understanding.

His first biographer was David Pye, whose *George Mallory* was published in 1927. Pye was his constant friend and fellow-climber, and knew his subject almost better than anyone. Like many of Mallory's friends he became eminent in his own field, the development of aircraft engines, a science that led to the need for oxygen sets for the pilots who were being propelled to higher and higher altitudes. Then in 1969 David Robertson, who was married to Mallory's daughter Beridge, wrote a biography – or rather a hagiography – in which our hero disappears like Sir Galahad. Mallory's heroic status has hardly faltered since. An early death does wonders for your career; and this might be one clue to his appeal.

In 1981 Walt Unsworth's magisterial *Everest* was published, which was rather less complimentary about Mallory, followed by Dudley Green's 1990 illustrated biography, and *Because It's There* in 2000, prompted by the finding of Mallory's body. Audrey Salkeld, the foremost Mount Everest researcher, wrote a series of books on the subject, including the larger part of *The Mystery of Mallory and Irvine* and *Last Climb*. Then Peter and Leni Gillman's book *The Wildest Dream* (2000) mined the vast number of letters between George and his wife Ruth, and turned up innumerable documents from other sources. They depicted Mallory's life in painstaking detail. Even more detail on the expeditions and their participants appeared in Wade Davis's *Into the Silence* (2011), which among other things examined the experience of the First World War and how it might have shaped the characters of the climbers. There will be more books about Mallory, I am sure, as his life seems to hold endless fascination for all kinds of writers. There are also a number of films that have been made about him, one or two of which I have had a hand in making. But who was he, and why does he have such a hold on our imaginations?

I found answers to these questions by looking at him through the eyes of those who have been influenced by him. These include his student contemporaries, his climbing companions, his pupils, and the theorists who try to work out what might have happened to him on his last climb. On the way we may also find answers to the question 'Why climb Everest?'

The bare bones of George Mallory's life are well known. He was born the eldest son of a rector in 1886 in the village of Mobberley on the Cheshire plain, which, ironically, is one of the flattest parts of England. He roamed the countryside as children do, and climbed walls and the family house roof, as well as his father's church. His sister Avie recalled that he was completely fearless:

> He climbed everything that it was at all possible to climb. I learned very early that it was fatal to tell him that any tree was impossible for him to get up. 'Impossible' was a word which acted as a challenge to him. When he once told me that it would be quite easy to lie between the railway lines and let a train go over him, I kept very quiet, as if I thought it would be a very ordinary thing to do; otherwise I was afraid he would do it. He used to climb up the downspouts of the house, and climb about on the roof with cat-like surefootedness.

He started to show his abilities at Winchester College, where he excelled at shooting, soccer and gymnastics. But he was more than just a sportsman; he was good at maths and chemistry, and was becoming a gifted writer.

The English public schools of Mallory's time were nurseries for the military leaders and administrators of the empire, who possessed an aggressive attitude to the acquisition of new lands, and even cast covetous eyes on our nearer neighbours. We, with our post-colonial guilt, might have difficulty imagining a world in which an Englishman could legitimately make his name by conquering territory, but the young George would certainly have imbibed some of this empire spirit.

While he was at Winchester something happened that changed his life. His college tutor, Graham Irving, an Alpine Club member, took George under his wing when he heard about his talent for climbing on roofs, and in 1904 took him for his first visit to the Alps with another boy, Harry Gibson. In his obituary in the *Alpine Journal*, Irving wrote of Mallory:

> He had a strikingly beautiful face. Its shape, its delicately cut features, especially the rather large, heavily lashed, thoughtful eyes, were extraordinarily suggestive of a Botticelli Madonna, even when he ceased to be a boy – though any suspicion of effeminacy was completely banished by obvious proofs of physical energy and strength.[1]

Mallory's physical beauty impressed many of those who first met him, and this advantage gave him many opportunities. It might even have led indirectly to this offer of a climbing holiday. I do not suggest any impropriety, just that his attractiveness might have given him chances in life that were not open to others.

Harry Gibson had to return home after a week, and Irving and Mallory roamed the Mont Blanc region for a further 18 days. In our suspicious times eyebrows might be raised at this teacher–pupil pairing, but in their classically educated days such adult–child jaunts were seen as healthy and mutually beneficial.

That first Alpine season was a turning point in the young Mallory's life; he had found something he was good at and something he loved. On his second season with Irving they tackled the Dent Blanche, a formidable peak with a bad reputation.

The young George wrote to his mother in a good descriptive style, introducing some of the themes that would later become familiar: the importance of an early start, the beauty of the mountain scene and the way he would set his heart on climbing a particular mountain:

> At 3:15 yesterday morning we started by moonlight across the huge snow field, on the most delightful hard crisp snow; and after the most enjoyable walk and a short scramble over easy rocks, we found ourselves on the arête of the Dent Blanche at 7:15. The sun had of course risen as we nearer the Dent Blanche; and, as we had already gone up quite a lot, the view was splendid right over the Mont Blanc range. It was altogether too inexpressibly glorious to see peak after peak touched with the pink glow of the first sun which slowly spread until the whole top was a flaming fire – and that against a sky with varied tints of leaden blue.
>
> We had a halt and breakfast for nearly an hour on the arête and then climbed straight to the top in a little over three hours, arriving there at 10:25 ... We had no difficulty coming down, but a most laborious walk across the snow field. The rest of the party were waiting tea for us at the Bertol hut as prearranged, and rejoiced with our rejoicing – the Dent Blanche was the one peak we had set our hearts upon doing.[2]

Going up to Cambridge in 1905, he found new male admirers: his college tutor A. C. Benson was a celibate homosexual who collected beautiful young men and who fell earnestly in love with Mallory at first sight. The son of the Archbishop of Canterbury, Benson had written the Coronation Ode, including *Land of Hope and Glory*, which boys of my generation belted out to Elgar's music in the school chapel. Poor Benson was a tortured individual who was not able to express the love he felt. The intense attention he lavished on Mallory helped the young student gain access to a privileged inner circle, who went on to form the Bloomsbury set. This select group of artists and writers contained talents such as the poet Rupert Brooke and the economist John Maynard Keynes. They were at the forefront of liberal thought, the Suffragette movement and socialism, and later included the writer Virginia Woolf and the painter Clive Bell. George Mallory never quite seemed to make his mark, though – until much later.

Cambridge was a hotbed of homosexual intrigue – the love that dared not speak its name – and the Gillmans' biography uncovers an affair between George Mallory and James Strachey, the younger brother of the writer and wit Lytton Strachey. It is not clear just how serious this was, but one gains the impression that the naive but beautiful Mallory was inveigled into the relationship by a scheming John Maynard Keynes. It was around this time that Mallory took to dressing in black shirts and garish ties, and grew his hair long.

I have a copy of *The Yellow Book*, with drawings by Aubrey Beardsley, the fin-de-siècle publication from the 1890s that so influenced this group. A glance inside at Beardsley's arch, pen-and-ink gothic figures conveys something of the look of these young men. The kind of impression Mallory made is conveyed in this passage from Lytton Strachey. His high-camp squawk gives a hint of the febrile atmosphere of Cambridge at the time:

Mon Dieu! George Mallory! When that's been written, what more need to be said? My hand trembles, my heart palpitates, my whole being swoons away at the words – oh heavens, heavens! I found of course that he had been absurdly maligned – he's six foot high, with a body of an athlete by Praxiteles, and a face – oh incredible – the mystery of Botticelli, the refinement and delicacy of a Chinese print, the youth and piquancy of an imaginable English boy. I rave, but when you see him, as you must, you will admit all – all! ... He's going to be a schoolmaster, and his intelligence is not remarkable. What's the need?[3]

Notions of sexuality change over the ages, and that Cambridge concept of male friendship was not the same as what we now call 'gay'. It was more along the lines of Platonic love, and perhaps we have lost something by our assumptions about same-sex friendships. The comradeship forged in mountaineering can be closer than a romantic relationship, but among the hundreds of climbers I have met I cannot remember one who has come out as gay. They must be there, but it is a robustly macho pursuit. Mallory's later relationship with his wife Ruth certainly seems to have been a straightforwardly conventional one, and many of his contemporaries married after experimenting with same-sex friendships.

His climbing career certainly benefited from his attractiveness to men. Charles Sayle was a founder member of the Climbers' Club and took him climbing in North Wales, introducing him to an older mentor, Geoffrey Winthrop Young. This was a significant meeting. Winthrop Young was a colourful character, an educationalist and a brilliant writer. It was he who conferred the name 'Galahad' upon Mallory. He was vigorously homosexual, and visited clubs that catered to his tastes in Berlin and Paris. He was attracted to the young Mallory at once. Winthrop Young was the leading climber of his day and organised the legendary Pen-y-Pass meets in Snowdonia. Every year he gathered around him a coterie of bright young things, and tackled increasingly difficult routes on the Welsh crags. George was soon part of the scene, impressing Winthrop Young with his lithe climbing style and inventive approach to routes. Here is Winthrop Young's assessment of him as a climber:

> He was the greatest in fulfilled achievement; so original in his climbing that it never occurred to us to compare him with others or to judge his performance by ordinary mountaineering standards. Chivalrous, indomitable, the splendid personification of youthful adventure; deer-like in grace and power of movement, self-reliant and yet self-effacing and radiantly

independent. On a day he might be with us; on the next gone like a bird on the wing over the summits, to explore some precipice between Snowdon and the sea; whence he would return after nightfall to discuss climbing or metaphysics in a laughing contralto, or practise gymnastics after his hot bath, on the roof beam of the old shack, like the youngest of the company.[4]

After several more seasons in the Alps, Mallory was considered as one of the best British climbers of his day. His writing style was developing, too, and he made a serious stab at explaining why we climb in a long article in the *Climbers' Club Journal* entitled 'The mountaineer as artist'. He compares a long alpine climb to a symphony, with separate movements for each section of the climb. This might today be considered pretentious, but he makes the point that mountaineering has a spiritual dimension that other sports perhaps lack. It certainly attracts poets and writers. In another piece, written in the trenches, he remembers the joy of reaching the summit of Mont Maudit, and this quotation for me sums up the modest delight of the man:

We're not exultant; but delighted, joyful; soberly astonished … Have we vanquished an enemy? None but ourselves.[5]

Just before the outbreak of the First World War he met and married the love of his life, Ruth Turner, the daughter of Hugh Thackeray Turner, a wealthy architect who had worked closely with William Morris, the founder of the Arts and Crafts movement. Their letters reveal that Ruth, although not the clearest of writers, was a wonderful soul-mate, with an unerring ability to get to the nub of things.

In 1910 George had taken a position as a teacher at Charterhouse School in Godalming, Surrey, and attempted to settle down into married life with Ruth. With the outbreak of war, however, he became restless and guilty, feeling that he ought to join up, and obtained a commission as an artillery officer. He was off to war. This was the beginning of many absences from his beloved Ruth, but they wrote to each other nearly every day for the rest of his life.

Mallory survived the war, unlike so many of his climbing peers. Artillery officers had a better chance of survival than 'the poor bloody infantry' as they spent less time on the front line, although they were hardly safe. On Mallory's very first day with his battery, a bullet passed between him and a man walking a yard ahead. On another occasion two men walking with him were killed feet away from him as they laid out a telephone wire.

Of course, if that bullet had swerved a fraction of a degree, the history of Mount Everest would have been different. My father had a torpedo pass right under his ship during the liberation of the Netherlands in the Second World War, and he and his future family were thus inches away from oblivion. Such is the contingency of life, and during dangerous climbing one is well aware that possibilities such as this are multiplying before your eyes. That stone melting out of the ice a thousand feet above you might have your name on it.

Geoffrey Winthrop Young also survived the First World War, although he lost a leg. When he and Mallory organised another of the Pen-y-Pass parties, it was noted that out of 60 climbers mentioned in the diaries from before the war, 23 had died and 14 had been injured.

The more I studied that little band of men in the black and white photographs of the 1921 expedition to Mount Everest, the more I saw the ghosts of the First World War.

Today it is hard to imagine the degree of disconnection between the general public and the soldiers engaged in the slaughter. Now we have live television feeds from journalists embedded on the battlefields, and the death of even one soldier in Afghanistan is headline news. On the first day of the Battle of the Somme in July 1916, however, when Somervell was operating at his field hospital, 19,000 of the British forces were killed: 20 per cent of their total fighting strength. That is over six times the number killed during the 9/11 attacks on the US in 2001, and yet General Sir Douglas Haig, the British commander, felt able to write in his diary the next day: 'This cannot be considered severe in view of the numbers engaged, and the length of front attacked.'

During the First World War heavy guns were heard in Kent, but successful propaganda duped the British public into believing that all was going well, with the press reporting only light casualties. And the fact that the conflict was so localised and so immovable meant that life could go on in Berlin or London without non-combatants realising what horrors were being perpetrated in their name. One result was that the participants felt disconnected from life at home, even when they returned, and in some cases effectively became walking ghosts.

One such was Mallory's pupil Robert Graves, who was badly injured by shellfire at the Somme on 20 July while leading his men through the churchyard cemetery of Bazentin-le-Petit. His injuries were so severe that it was reported to his family that he was dead. On his return to London he suffered from hallucinations, seeing the streets filled with corpses. Like many of these veterans he seemed to be slightly lost for the remainder of his life.

What effect might such feelings have on the 26 men in the photographs at Everest Base Camp taken a few years later? And in particular, what consequences might there be on a man making climbing decisions at high altitude?

Most of the members of the 1921 expedition had served in the war and they were being led by a colonel. They saw their attempt to climb the mountain as similar in many respects to warfare, and the whole bandobast of Gurkha soldiers, pack animals and baggage resembled a military expedition. Norton described it as 'our mimic campaign', and Mallory wrote in his last *Times* despatch: 'We have counted our wounded and know, roughly, how much to strike off the strength of our little army as we plan the next act of battle ...'

For Mallory, any notion of warfare as a chivalric enterprise must have swiftly evaporated in 1914 as his former pupils at Charterhouse were shipped off to the trenches: 686 of them would perish in the mechanised slaughter. As we have seen, the reproach of his fireside became intolerable, and he sought some way of joining up, but the headmaster of Charterhouse refused to release him. His university friend the poet Rupert Brooke died in April 1915 in the Aegean on his way to Gallipoli, provoking Mallory to write to Benson: 'I've been too lucky; there's something indecent, when so many friends have been enduring such horrors, in just going on with one's job, quite happy and prosperous.'

Eventually the headmaster relented and Mallory joined the Royal Garrison Artillery, a relatively safe billet behind the lines compared with living in the trenches. His ankle injury, suffered in a climbing accident in 1909, was ignored by the medics, but it would become a recurrent problem.

The horrors of the Somme were too terrible to write about to his wife, but in a curious forerunner to Wilfred Owen's 'My subject is war, and the pity of war', Mallory wrote to Ruth: 'Oh the pity of it, I very often exclaim when I see the dead lying about.'

We have already seen his narrow escapes from bullets and shells. He had a curiously lucky war with his postings, too, and it now appears that he had a guardian angel. Eddie Marsh, Winston Churchill's private secretary, had interceded to make sure Mallory had ten days' leave at Christmas 1916, and it is possible that he kept a lookout for him throughout the conflict. Marsh was another of those who had become enamoured of

George Mallory – and Rupert Brooke – when, ten years before, he had seen the pair on stage at Cambridge.

One senses an invisible hand guiding events. After his leave Mallory was sent well behind the lines to act as an orderly officer. Then, when he had successfully applied to return to his battery at the front, he was invalided out by the ankle injury the day before the attack at the Battle of Arras. A 'Blighty wound' was one that enabled you to be sent back home to Blighty, and one that many soldiers devoutly wished for. After convalescence, Mallory managed to crush his right foot in a motorcycle accident, and missed the Battle of Passchendaele. Then, just before the Spring Offensive of 1918, he was assigned to another training course. In all, he managed to miss nearly a year and a half of the most murderous fighting at the front, even though he had actively sought to put himself in the way of danger by joining up in the first place.

I suspect that Mallory felt a sneaking sense of guilt at surviving the war unscathed while all around him were being killed or maimed. And all because of a slightly embarrassing ankle injury caused by falling off a minor crag, with perhaps a little help with his postings from a well-placed admirer. Could this have fed into a relative lack of concern for his own physical safety high up on the mountain?

A more tangible effect of the war on the first Everest expeditions was that it forced the selection of older men who had done little recent climbing. Sandy Irvine, for instance, was ten years younger than the average age of the other members in 1924. This would have reduced the overall strength of the team, and on his last climb Mallory simply didn't have a powerful back-up of climbers forcing stores and Sherpas up the mountain behind him.

Mallory's experiences in the war may have led him to go too carelessly, too impatiently against the greatest enemy he ever faced. His Blighty wound may also have helped his demise, as it was his right ankle that broke once again in his last fall (having saved him in the war, it may have contributed to his death after it). No one can have been very surprised at Mallory and Irvine not returning from their battle with Mount Everest, and in the official history of the 1924 expedition it seemed that Norton had seen it all before:

> We were a sad little party; from the first we accepted the loss of our comrades in that rational spirit which all of our generation had learnt in the Great War, and there was never any tendency to a morbid harping on the irrevocable. But the tragedy was very near; our friends' vacant tents and vacant places at table were a constant reminder to us of what the atmosphere of the camp would have been had things gone differently. To several of us, particularly to those who, on previous expeditions to Mount Everest or Spitzbergen, had been close friends with the missing climbers, the sense of loss was acute and personal, and until the day of our departure a cloud hung over the Base Camp. As so constantly in the war, so here in our mimic campaign Death had taken his toll from the best, for they were indeed a splendid couple.[6]

5
The Reconnaissance
of 1921

The British Empire was driven by bloody-minded individuals with a sense of mission, such as Livingstone, Napier and Burton, and one such was Francis Younghusband, the man largely responsible for the first attempts to climb Mount Everest.

He was a small, heavily moustached man, who was almost the personification of Empire. He had become the youngest member of the Royal Geographical Society, and in 1890 received the RGS Patron's Medal for his great journey through Manchuria, undertaken when he was only 23. While on leave from his regiment, he pioneered a route between India and Kashgar, prime Great Game territory. Later, as a captain, he was ordered to survey part of the Hunza valley, where he bumped into his Russian counterpart, Captain Grombchevsky, who was surveying possible invasion routes. After dinner they swilled brandy and vodka, and compared their soldiers. They also discussed the possible outcome of a Russian invasion. After this friendly sparring, straight out of a buddy movie, they rode off in opposite directions.

The threat from Russia was therefore very real, and there was an obvious psychological advantage in gaining the high ground between the two great empires. Lord Curzon, the Viceroy of India, clearly wanted the highest point of the Himalayas climbed, writing that:

> As I sat daily in my room, and saw that range of snowy battlements uplifted against the sky, that huge palisade shutting off

India from the rest of the world, I felt it should be the business of Englishmen, if of anybody, to reach the summit.

In this context it can be seen that the climbing of Mount Everest was more of a political decision than a 'wild dream'. In its way it was the British Empire's moon-shot, with similar political motivation to the United States' moon-shot of the 1960s. Crucially, it would plant the British flag on the northern bounds of India. The problem was that the Tibetans didn't want to talk to the British and pursued a policy of splendid isolation, keeping foreigners at an arm's length. Myths arose about this forbidden land, and the desire to explore it grew.

Then in 1893 Captain Charles Bruce of the Gurkhas, who had climbed with Martin Conway in the Karakorum the previous year, met Younghusband at a polo match. He put the idea of climbing Mount Everest to him and between them they started a train of events that was to prove unstoppable. Younghusband was then Political Officer in Chitral, and the idea fermented within him, particularly as he knew that he could count on the support of the establishment. In the meanwhile Curzon became more anxious about Russian influence in Tibet and decided to do something about it. His chance came when a small group of Tibetans crossed the border and stole some Nepali yaks. This incursion was the excuse for the infamous Diplomatic Mission to Lhasa of 1904, led by Younghusband, who, on his way to Lhasa, saw the mountain at last:

> Mount Everest for its size is a singularly shy and retiring mountain. It hides itself away behind other mountains. On the north side, in Tibet … it does indeed stand up proudly and lone, a true monarch among mountains. But it stands in a very sparsely inhabited part of Tibet, and very few people ever go to Tibet.

Younghusband certainly did go to Tibet, and in some style. He was leading a force of British soldiers carrying Maxim machine-guns and cannon. A force of 2,000 Tibetans attempted to resist at Gyantse with matchlock muskets, spears and swords. Their lamas assured them the British bullets would not harm them, but when the smoke cleared over 600 of their number had died. By the time the British reached Lhasa the casualties were nearly 3,000 Tibetans killed, compared with only 40 British soldiers. This was a lesson on the effectiveness of machine-guns as devices for cutting up men, a lesson that was initially ignored by the First World War generals.

Britain gained privileged access to the closed country, and eventually set up telegraph poles all the way to Lhasa. Trading could begin, although some in Europe were sad that one of the last veiled mysteries of geography had been ripped aside so brutally. Curiously enough, the belligerent Younghusband had a mystical experience on his way back from Lhasa and later became a spiritual writer. He saw Mount Everest from one of his camps 'poised high in heaven as the spotless pinnacle of the world'. In later life he said he regretted his invasion of Tibet.

By Mallory and Somervell's time the new breed of alpinist was thinking about even higher mountains than those in the Alps and the Caucasus, and were organising the first Himalayan expeditions. However, because both Nepal and Tibet were closed to foreigners Mount Everest seemed an impossible dream. This opinion changed subtly after the geographical poles were reached, and particularly after the tragedy of Scott's expedition to the South Pole in 1912.

Scott's endeavour was an example of serious exploration in the old style; that is, exploration with a strong scientific purpose. When his last camp was found it was only 11 miles from the next food dump that might have saved his party. And yet they had man-hauled 30lb of rock samples behind them all the way from the Pole.

There was another example of this serious scientific interest. The palaeobotanist Marie Stopes had applied to join Scott's second expedition. She had been turned down on the grounds of her sex, but following her advice Scott had looked for a specimen of a coal-forming, fossilised fern named *Glossopteris*. The discovery of this specimen in the dead explorer's collection established that Antarctica had once formed part of the first super-continent of Gondwanaland.

In his diary entry for 8 February relating to this discovery near the Beardmore Glacier, Scott writes that they spent 'the rest of the day geologising ... under cliffs of Beacon sandstone, weathering rapidly and carrying veritable coal seams. From the last, Wilson, with his sharp eyes, has picked several plant impressions, the last a piece of coal with beautifully traced leaves in layers, also some excellently preserved impressions of thick stems, showing cellular structure.'

Scott's last words, written as he lay dying in his own lonely tent, made a powerful impression on me as a schoolboy:

> For my own sake I do not regret this journey, which has shown that Englishmen can endure hardships, help one another, and meet death with as great a fortitude as ever in the past. We took risks, we knew we took them; things have come out against us, and therefore we have no cause for complaint, but bow to the will of providence, determined still to do our best to the last ... Had we lived, I should have had a tale to tell of the hardihood, endurance, and courage of my companions which would have stirred the heart of every Englishman.

There seems to be something in the English psyche that celebrates the concept of heroic failure. One doesn't see it in Scottish culture, nor do the Americans have any truck with losers. It is hard to disentangle, but both Scott and Mallory are examples of this phenomenon. Franklin of the North-West Passage is another. I'd suggest it might have to do with the English public schools' paradoxical injunction to try your very hardest, but not to boast of any success. Bragging is considered one of the cardinal sins. The top winning strategy in this contradictory game is therefore to die heroically trying to reach some impossible goal. I believe heroic failure may have played a small part in Mallory's psychology, as well as in the minds of his predecessors.

Scott and his party had been beaten by the Norwegian polar explorer Amundsen, who pipped them to the post by employing more effective dog-teams, keeping his attempt secret and treating his expedition as a race. Scott thought it was unsporting to use dogs and insisted on man-hauling the sledges, rather as later explorers thought it would be unsporting to use supplementary oxygen to climb Mount Everest. British moral indignation rose in step with Scott's elevation to heroic status. 'Amundsen even ate his dogs!' they cried. Edward Whymper had referred to Everest as the Third Pole, and this term now gained currency. British pride had to be assuaged, and the ascent of Everest would do as well as anything else.

So, after more years of negotiations and the intervention of the First World War, the Dalai Lama reluctantly gave permission for Mount Everest to be reconnoitred in 1921, with a climbing party to be led by General Bruce the following year. This turn of events was largely thanks to the persistence of Younghusband. By then president of the Royal Geographical Society, he was determined to get an expedition out to the mountain. His 1920 presidential address hints at why people still want to climb Mount Everest:

> The accomplishment of such a feat will elevate the human spirit and will give man, especially us geographers, a feeling that we really are getting the upper hand on the earth, and

that we are acquiring a true mastery of our surroundings ...
if man stands on earth's highest summit, he will have an
increased pride and confidence in himself in the ascendancy
over matter. This is the incalculable good which the ascent of
Mount Everest will confer.[1]

Before Younghusband's address the Royal Geographical Society
had staged a talk in March 1919 from a truly remarkable
Everester. John Baptist Lucius Noel was another one of those
privileged soldiers, his father being the second son of the Earl of
Gainsborough. Noel was a handsome man and something of an
entrepreneur, as later events revealed. I have an interest in Noel
because he was the first man to film on Mount Everest, predat-
ing my own filming there by some 70 years.

He stood up to read a paper entitled 'A Journey to Tashirak
in Southern Tibet, and the Eastern Approaches to Mount
Everest'. Noel described how, when stationed in Calcutta as a
lieutenant, he would take his leave in the baking summer months
up in the hills to the north, searching for a way to the highest
mountain on earth. As with so many of us he became captivated
by Everest. Eventually he crossed the Choten Nyi-ma La, a high
pass in Sikkim to the north of Kangchenjunga (I saw this pass
in 2009, which is now heavily guarded on both sides by soldiers
from China and India). Unseen, Noel slipped across, disguised
as an Indian Muslim trader:

> To defeat observation I intended to avoid the villages and
> settled parts generally, to carry our food, and to keep to those
> more desolate stretches where only an occasional shepherd
> was to be seen. My men were not startlingly different from
> the Tibetans, and if I darkened my skin and my hair I could
> pass, not as a native – my colour and shape of my eyes would
> prevent that – but as a Mohammedan from India.[2]

His plan was to find the passes that led to Mount Everest and, if possible, to come to close quarters with the mountain. Unfortunately, as I too saw in 2009, there is a difficult tangle of high country between that north-west corner of Sikkim and Everest, and Noel could not get closer than forty miles before he was intercepted and turned back. But it was the closest any Westerner had been, and Noel would play a key part in the 1922 and 1924 expeditions.

His lecture stirred up public debate about the possibility of climbing the mountain, which of course it was intended to do. After many years of wheeling and dealing, of encouragement from Lord Curzon and obstruction by Lord Morley, the Secretary of State for India, an expedition was mounted.

As a result, the 1921 Everest reconnaissance was highly political. The leader was the posh Lt Col Charles Howard-Bury, wealthy and well connected. He was just the man for the job. He moved easily in high diplomatic circles, and proved his worth in helping to secure permission for a reconnaissance in 1921 and a climbing attempt in 1922. He had a most colourful life, growing up in a haunted gothic castle at Charleville in County Offaly, Ireland, travelling into Tibet without permission in 1905, and being taken prisoner during the First World War. He was a keen naturalist and plant hunter (*Primula buryana* is named after him), and he was the first European to report the existence of the yeti. He never married and during the Second World War he met Rex Beaumont, a young actor with whom he shared the rest of his life. Mallory didn't care for his high Tory views, nor for the way he treated his subordinates, but Howard-Bury got a difficult political job done, then led the expedition off the map.

The Mount Everest Committee, a joint committee of the Royal Geographical Society and the Alpine Club whose purpose was to fund and organise the reconnaissance, chose the team members on the basis that they had to be able to provide a thorough survey of the massif and give a good assessment of the climbing possibilities. The committee was run by Arthur Robert Hinks.

Hinks is an excellent example of why bureaucrats should not run expeditions. He was a mathematician specialising in map projections and the weight of the moon, but he had no field experience whatsoever. He was contemptuous of those he regarded as intellectually inferior to him, and he was a snob. He failed to be open-minded about climbing talents such as Finch, and his ability to rub people up the wrong way annoyed everyone. Even though the press and film-makers paid for all the Everest expeditions, he was full of loathing for journalists. They were a 'rotten lot ... all sharks and pirates'. Hinks's pernicious influence as secretary of the Mount Everest Committee probably helped to put back the climbing of the mountain by thirty years.

As with Scott's Antarctic expedition, there was strong emphasis on the scientific value of the expedition, with the geographers keen to travel around the mountain and draw maps. The surveyors were Henry Morshead, Oliver Wheeler and Alexander Heron. The climbers were drawn from the ranks of the Alpine Club, which was desperate to get a man to the top. Harold Raeburn, a 56-year-old Scottish climber with an impressive record of guideless climbing, was appointed mountaineering leader, but proved to be prematurely aged and, struck down by illness, didn't perform well. Then there was Alexander Kellas, who had huge Himalayan experience gained during his studies of high altitude, and Mallory. George Finch, another talented alpinist, was dislodged at the last minute by skulduggery within the committee, and so Mallory proposed his school-friend from Winchester, Guy Bullock, who had limited climbing experience. The team doctor was Sandy Wollaston.

Of all the climbers, Alexander Kellas brought most experience to the expedition. Even contemporary climbers owe him a huge debt, as he discovered the techniques necessary to climb the mountain. In 2009 I filmed and climbed in an area of Sikkim north of Kanchenjunga that was his high-altitude testing ground. This politically sensitive mountainous region had not been visited by Westerners since Frank Smythe's climbs there in the 1930s, and it was hard to reach. I had gone there to learn about Kellas's work on human physiology at high altitudes.

The ancient Greeks knew that the body would deteriorate at high altitude but it wasn't understood why until the late 19th century, when it was realised that low levels of oxygen led to a condition known as hypoxia. Kellas spent the war at the Air Ministry, working with Professor J. B. S. Haldane on the high-altitude oxygen deprivation suffered by pilots who were flying higher and higher. Before that, he taught chemistry to medical students at Middlesex Hospital, combining laboratory experiments with tests on his own body while climbing high Himalayan peaks during the holidays.

He made many first ascents, culminating in an ascent of Pauhunri at 7,128m (23,386ft), and by 1921 he had spent more time at 7,000m than anyone else on earth. He realised that hypoxia led first to loss of appetite, then to loss of weight, reduced brain function and ultimately death. Above a certain altitude the body deteriorates faster than its natural ability to restore itself. Journalists like to call this the 'Death Zone', and fix it at 8,000m (26,247ft), but really it is any height above which people cannot sustain permanent habitation, which is around 5,100m (16,728ft). Climbers deteriorate steadily above this height, but it becomes marked on their summit days above the 8,000m contour, when their lungs are drowning in fluid and their brains are swelling with cerebral oedema.

Kellas's achievements as a scientist and mountaineer were remarkable enough, but it was his discovery in this remote Sikkim valley that revolutionised the sport of Himalayan climbing, and it is one without which no modern Everest expedition would even be able to leave Base Camp. After being disappointed by a pair of hired Swiss guides in Sikkim in 1907 he came across an ethnic group called the Sherpas. He recognised their natural aptitude for mountaineering and noted: 'They seemed more at home in diminished pressure.'

I worked with Sherpas in the very same area that Kellas first employed them, and their ability is immediately apparent; not only are they sure-footed on steep ground, they are remarkably strong and almost always good-humoured individuals – all vital characteristics on long mountain trips. I noticed a few years ago during blood oxygen-level testing on Everest that the Sherpas on the expedition had much the same or lower O_2 levels than the rest of us, and yet they were able to climb much faster. How could this be? Recent research into why Sherpas do so well at altitude suggests that instead of having more haemoglobin in their blood stream than lowlanders, they have more capillaries to distribute the blood. As this ethnic group has only moved to high altitudes within the last 10,000 years, this research suggests that human evolution is still taking place.

The Sherpas might wonder why we lowlanders bother to come and join them at altitudes that are difficult for us. I asked Thendup Sherpa, our cook on the Sikkim expedition, why he thought Westerners came to the Himalayas: 'To get famous,' he instantly replied.

There is a danger in lumping together a disparate group of individuals as 'Sherpas'. It is rather like the wider imperial designation of 'natives'. In a recent obituary in the *Guardian*, there was a reference to two European women killed in 1959 in a Himalayan avalanche with 'their Sherpa'. Imagine obituaries of two Nepalese men climbing in the Lake District with 'their Englishman'. As with any group that seems homogeneous, a little time spent in their company reveals their differing characters.

Traditional Sherpa culture consisted of a few wealthy individuals employing a poor majority in work such as porterage or agriculture. In return they expected their chief to remain loyal and protect them, rather in the manner of the Scottish clan system. The switch to European employers was acceptable to them when they saw the money and equipment being offered. What they gave in addition was a degree of loyalty, even unto death, that surprised the foreign climbers. On the other side of the deal there was also ready acceptance of the Sherpas by British climbers. In the Alps British climbers were used to employing local guides and porters, and the historian Simon Schama suggests that mountain conquests were 'a victory of imperial confidence over timorous native superstition'.[3] The rulers were demonstrating to the ruled the virtues deriving from their muscular modernity, and by such demonstration they were legitimising their power. The whole imperial structure of the British Raj rested upon the sepoys of the Indian Army – the Indian soldiers themselves – and when they revolted in the Indian Mutiny, or Great Sepoy Rebellion, of 1857, all the vicious insecurities of the imperialists, and the resentment of the ruled, came boiling to the surface.

So Kellas dispensed with the usual mountain porters, and employed Sherpas instead. This collaboration was not, however, appreciated by everyone. When Kellas was being considered as a possible expedition leader in 1919, John Percy Farrar, the President of the Alpine Club, sneered:

> Now Kellas, besides being fifty, so far has never climbed a mountain, but has only walked about on steep snow with a lot of coolies, and the only time they got on a very steep place they all tumbled down and ought to have been killed!

This is an absolute travesty, and shows that the elders of this particular tribe were considerably less tolerant of outsiders than the young bloods. In fact, Kellas was doing the kind of climbing that is currently much admired by members of the Alpine Club.

In a paper published in the *Geographic Journal* in 1917 Kellas wrote that in his opinion 'a man in first-rate training, acclimatised to maximum possible altitude, could make the ascent of Mount Everest without adventitious aids, provided that the physical difficulties above 25,000 feet are not prohibitive'. By adventitious aids he means bottled oxygen. The advances made during the First World War in aircraft-engine design meant that pilots struggled to stay conscious at the higher altitudes being achieved, and there were greater losses of pilots as a result of hypoxia than enemy action. This led to the design of lightweight oxygen sets, which Kellas soon realised could be carried up high mountains. There soon followed a vigorous debate about this.

History has shown that Kellas was right, in that the very strongest climbers can just reach the summit of Mount Everest without supplementary oxygen, providing the air pressure is not too low on that particular day. Reinhold Messner and Peter Habeler did exactly that in May 1978, Habeler racing down from the summit to the South Col in just one hour, terrified by his fear of brain damage. Creationists might ponder the fact that the highest summit on earth is just achievable with the strongest pair of human lungs. However, I was very glad to sleep on oxygen just before my attempt, despite the fact that the actual climb was dogged by an intermittent supply. On the summit I found that it was perfectly possible to take off my mask and move about, although climbing would have been much harder without it.

In 2007 I filmed a medical research expedition to Mount Everest that was trying to identify the genes that enable certain people to survive at high altitude while others deteriorate and suffer from hypoxia. We conducted the most comprehensive medical-expedition tests ever attempted at altitude, using over 200 subjects and taking arterial-blood samples near the summit. It was remarkable that the partial pressures measured in live climbers were so low that they had only previously been seen in corpses. In other words, you are not only dying on the summit – you are very nearly dead.

Kellas had to suspend his mountain research during the First World War while he worked for the Air Ministry, and his letters reveal that he suffered a breakdown, possibly brought on by overwork. He experienced hallucinations and wrote that he heard malicious voices threatening death, speculating that a sensitive microphone could make these voices audible to others. This suggests that he believed they were real, and today he would be diagnosed as suffering from schizophrenia.

This condition is difficult to live with, and it may be that he felt more comfortable with Sherpas than with his colleagues. He had to resign from his post at the Middlesex, possibly because he was behaving oddly. In Sikkim he would remonstrate with the voices in his tent at night, but the Sherpas assumed that he was talking to the spirits of the dead and accorded him respect. After travelling in the area I am staggered that a man labouring under such a disability could have achieved so much with such slender means.

His Himalayan record won him a place on the 1921 expedition. He was 53, with more high-altitude experience than anyone alive and he knew the effects of altitude on the body. Furthermore, he had good relations with the Sherpas. He was given the job of designing and testing oxygen equipment for the expedition. He had carried out oxygen trials at altitude during the previous climbing season but had concluded that the cylinders were 'too heavy for use above 18,000 feet, and below that altitude were not required'. In the end the equipment was simply too heavy to use that year.

Sandy Wollaston was another interesting character. He had led two expeditions to New Guinea, very nearly getting to the top of Carstensz Pyramid – now considered one of the Seven Summits – in 1913. He was only 500ft from the top, which must have been infuriating, particularly after his lengthy disputes with the Dutch authorities, followed by the difficulties of penetrating dense forest. He, too, was a keen botaniser, and like Howard-Bury he discovered a new primula on the 1921 trip. It was subsequently named after him as Wollaston's Primrose, *Primula wollastonii*. Like several others on that expedition he was to meet a violent end. After Everest he was invited to be a tutor at Cambridge by John Maynard Keynes, but he was murdered in his rooms in 1930 by Douglas Potts, a deranged student who first shot Wollaston and then a police officer, before turning the gun on himself.

The individual members of the 1921 Everest reconnaissance expedition made their own separate ways to India, and over a period of a few weeks in April and May they assembled in Darjeeling. By the time they were ready to leave, there was already discord in the party. Howard-Bury, the Tory, and Raeburn, who was rather insecure in his role as climbing leader, clearly didn't get on. Mallory, who could be a charming man, tried to smooth things between them.

To avoid difficulties with accommodation on the long march, the 1921 Everest reconnaissance expedition set off in two groups on 18 and 19 May through Sikkim, heading for Mount Everest. However, Kellas was weakened by his recent expedition around Kangchenjunga, where he was trying to get further pictures of the approaches to Mount Everest, and soon contracted dysentery. On 5 June he insisted that his countrymen went on ahead, possibly as he did not want them to witness his misery. He died as he was carried over the pass by his Sherpas into Khampa Dzong.

The official cause of death was heart failure, as it often is in the last stages of dysentery, but this was possibly to avoid embarrassment to his family. The other members of the expedition were appalled at this disaster. Mallory was mortified: 'He died without one of us anywhere near him.'

They buried him in a place looking south over the border into Sikkim at the great mountains he had climbed. Mallory described the scene:

It was an extraordinarily affecting little ceremony burying Kellas on a stony hillside ... I shan't easily forget the four boys, his own trained mountain men, children of nature, seated in wonder on a great stone near the grave while Bury read out the passage from Corinthians.[4]

We now commit his mortal body to the ground, earth to earth, ashes to ashes, dust to dust.

The very next day the expedition caught the first sight of the summit of Mount Everest, although it was still over 100 miles and many days march away. George Mallory's description of that first view enchanted me as a schoolboy:

> It may seem an irony of fate that actually on the day after the distressing event of Dr. Kellas's death we experienced the strange elation of seeing Everest for the first time ... It was a prodigious white fang excrescent from the jaw of the world. We saw Mount Everest not quite sharply defined on account of a slight haze in that direction; this circumstance added a touch of mystery and grandeur; we were satisfied that the highest of mountains would not disappoint us.[5]

Now Raeburn was not feeling too well either, after contracting dysentery, and then twice being rolled on by his mule, and then twice kicked in the head. The doctor Wollaston, no doubt made anxious by Kellas's death, advised that he should return to Sikkim. I suspect Howard-Bury was privately relieved, but now the expedition had lost the only two climbers who knew anything about Himalayan mountaineering. After a long, gruelling trek across the Tibetan plateau the men of the 1921 reconnaissance were at last rewarded with their first view of the Rongbuk valley.

I have spent many long months there and to me it now feels like a home from home, although at first the air seems thin and the sun painfully bright. The sky is electric blue and the surrounding hills are rusty brown. At the head of the valley stands the great three-sided pyramid of their quest. Now they were closer and the whole mountain was going to be revealed. Mallory's description reads like a monstrous strip-tease:

> We caught a gleam of snow behind the grey mists. A whole group of mountains began to appear in gigantic fragments. Mountain shapes are often fantastic seen through a mist; these were like the wildest creation of a dream. A preposterous triangular lump rose out of the depths; its edge came leaping up at an angle of about 70 degrees and ended nowhere. To the left a black serrated crest was hanging in the sky incredibly. Gradually, very gradually, we saw the great mountain sides and glaciers and arêtes, now one fragment and now another through the floating rifts, until far higher in the sky than imagination had dared to suggest the white summit of Everest appeared. And in this series of partial glimpses we had seen a whole; we were able to piece together the fragments, to interpret the dream.[6]

Wheeler, a tenacious and highly skilled surveyor, was using a new photographic survey technique and he did a remarkable job. He would eventually become Surveyor-General of India and be knighted for his cartographical work in the Second World War. Along with Morshead he filled in a huge blank on the map around the mountain. Meanwhile, Mallory and Bullock undertook a close-up reconnaissance of the peak. They covered hundreds of miles and took scores of photographs from minor peaks around Everest. However, Mallory had put the glass plates in the camera the wrong way around and had to repeat many of his shots. He clearly had little mechanical aptitude.

Mallory and Bullock climbed up to the watershed between Tibet and Nepal, and peered down on to a vast icefall tumbling down a great, silent, icy valley. Mallory named it the 'Western Cwm', an echo of the Pen-y-Pass days in Snowdonia. This would be the way that the successful British expedition of 1953 would eventually go, but to him Nepal was still a forbidden country.

It must have been so exciting, with the feeling of elation one has when going well in the mountains. Bullock, however, was beginning to feel unhappy about Mallory's attitude to safety. His widow, writing many years later, reported:

> My husband considered Mallory ready to take unwarranted risks with still untrained porters in traversing dangerous ice. At least on one occasion he refused to take his rope of porters over the route proposed by Mallory. Mallory was not pleased. He did not support a critical difference of opinion readily.[7]

This is a foretaste of the dreadful accident of 1922, when seven inexperienced porters were killed, and of the accident in 1924, when the novice Irvine was involved. As a climber I would suggest that Mallory perhaps did not know how good he was, and it should be noted that as a schoolmaster his manner of teaching was to assume equality with his pupils. This might have led to a climbing style that did not take the ability of the novices into consideration, an important point that bears on the solution to our mystery.

On the plus side theirs was a good effort, considering the climbing party had lost Raeburn and Kellas. It might have gone down in climbing history as the most effective mountain reconnaissance ever undertaken, but Mallory and Bullock have been criticised by historians for their failure to spot that the outlet of the East Rongbuk glacier would provide a direct route up to the foot of the North Col. This is a swooping saddle that connects the North Ridge to Changtse, Everest's neighbour to the north, and seemed to be the key to their attempts to climb the mountain from the north.

In *Into the Silence* Wade Davis levels a serious accusation at George Mallory. He points out that the surveyor Wheeler had already found the crucial East Rongbuk glacier, and had sent a rough map to Howard-Bury. But Mallory suggests in the official account that it was he who found the key to the mountain by his approach from the Kharta valley, and even 'spun the story' to his wife Ruth in his letters home. At the very least Mallory did not give a fair acknowledgement of Wheeler's contribution, and if Davis is right it certainly is a black mark against his name.

From personal experience I know that people are very quick to claim all the credit on Everest expeditions. The stakes are high, and one's better instincts are sometimes overcome by competition and bitterness. However, the historians are wrong if they think the East Rongbuk route is obvious. I was with a young climber in 2004 who had read the literature and attended the briefing at Base Camp given by the leader, who carefully explained the route the team should follow the next day. The next day I hiked up the Rongbuk valley and turned left as usual up the small glacial outflow of the East Rongbuk valley, which is a small breach in the great east wall of the main valley. I rested that evening at an interim camp. There was no sign of our youngster and we all became worried. As night fell we mounted a search party, and retraced our steps. Then came the radio call from a group of Russian climbers camped below the North Face: 'Have you lost a climber? We have him here.'

He appeared the next day, shamefaced. Determined to get up the mountain first he had marched straight up the Rongbuk valley, just as Mallory had done, bypassing the small river that seems too small to drain the North Col basin. He had eventually come up against Everest's huge North Face. These things are only too easy to do.

Incidentally, this route up to Advanced Base Camp is a gruelling start to the expedition. After the turn, one walks past the dry-stone walls that still remain from the British 1920s expeditions' Camp I. There is a hurried traverse under the dangerously crumbling orange rocks of the cliffs above, then on to the glacier itself through the extraordinary ice sharks'-fins that alpinists call *penitentes*. These were up to 100ft high in 1990 when I first saw them, but now they have melted to around 60ft. The classically educated Norton called the next section the 'Via Dolorosa', after Christ's route through Old Jerusalem, which is somewhat less steep and icy – and where you find another kind of penitent. After this comes a view of Kellas Peak, which the members of that 1921 reconnaissance named in honour of the extraordinary man who holds the unenviable record of being the first to die on an Everest expedition.

The 1921 reconnaissance expedition found that the North Col was indeed the key to climbing the mountain, providing both some shelter from the westerly winds and a ridge route attractive to that early generation of climbers. It is still used by the vast majority of climbers who approach from the north side of the mountain. Although the expedition was now well into the monsoon, and therefore too late for a realistic attempt on the summit because of heavy snowfall, they pushed a team of climbers and porters over a high pass and got Mallory and Bullock up to the top of the North Col at 23,000ft (7,010 m).

It is wonderful place, a giant hammock of snow and ice, with the vast wall of Everest's North Face rising up behind. The route to the top looks deceptively easy, but in fact foreshortening disguises the fact that the summit is a terribly long way off.

As regards personal relations it was an unhappy little expedition, with almost a curse laid upon it in the same way that Tutankhamun's tomb, opened two years later, was supposed to be cursed. Each one of the members seemed to dislike someone else. Kellas was the first to die, then Raeburn had a mental collapse on his return home and died shortly afterwards, thinking he had somehow murdered Kellas. Morshead was murdered in Burma in strange circumstances in 1931, and, as we have seen, Wollaston was murdered by a student in his rooms in Cambridge in 1930. And then Mallory was to die violently on the mountain in 1924.

6

The Expedition of 1922

The 1921 expedition established that there was a route to the top, and Mallory had not only performed his reconnaissance with Bullock, he had also taken the first steps on the mountain proper. Moreover, thousands of square miles of uncharted territory around Everest had been mapped by the surveyors. It was a hugely impressive achievement, and preparations raced ahead so that a serious attempt could be made the very next spring. This time they planned to arrive on the mountain well before the monsoon.

To his delight Somervell was informed that he had been chosen by General Bruce for the next expedition, probably because of his recent tally of Alpine routes. It was also a cunning ruse on Bruce's part to increase the number of strong climbers, while appearing to recruit a doctor. I am sure they felt an extra doctor wouldn't go amiss, considering Kellas's fate the previous year. Somervell would have to pay his way to Darjeeling, but from there all costs would be met by the organisers. He replied that as his salary from University College Hospital, London, was £150 a year he would indeed be able to pay his way. He would even contribute something to the expedition by the sale of paintings of the mountain.

Somervell's father William had himself been a painter, and he encouraged his son from early on. Howard had only exhibited nine works to date, but he was already showing great talent – and great self-confidence and he wasn't too impressed by rank. His son David, who was doctor to Prince Charles and Diana,

Princess of Wales, remembered his father having a meal with Prince Philip, who enquired after dessert, 'Do you fancy coming back to my place for a drink?' He meant Buckingham Palace, the residence of the British monarch. Somervell thought for a moment, and then shook his head. 'Sorry, no. I promised my wife I'd be back early tonight.'

(I had my own Royal encounter when I did a lecture at Ludgrove, the prep school attended by Princes William and Harry. My cousin Philip was their English teacher, and when he greeted me at the door I heard some rustling noises in the shrubbery. 'What's that?' I asked. 'Oh, the bodyguards, I suppose.' At the end of my talk I gestured to the pile of oxygen equipment and climbing gear in front of me: 'and if any boy would like to come and try on any of this ...' There was a stampede of small boys to the front, led by Prince Harry, who started wielding an ice axe. I noticed that William, the future King, remained sitting soberly in the dark.)

Somervell was fairly comfortable in any social situation, which was normal for an upper-middle-class Englishman of his time. He also had a good eye for a practical joke. At Cambridge in 1911 he and two other undergraduates organised a spoof Futurist exhibition and then secretly painted suitably modernist art works. They then booked a hall and invited the London critics. The bait was taken, and the critics swooned. But, having satirised modern art, Somervell later took it up. His painting style was a sort of muscular cubism, with very well-drawn mountains, although he wasn't as abstract as Picasso or Braque, the pioneers of the movement. Historian David Seddon considers that 'probably no other artist applied cubism to the high mountains in such a consistent and authoritative way as Somervell'. And Somervell himself said:

> Too many amateurs fail to do good mountain pictures because they don't draw their mountains. They do capable pine trees and lush green valleys, and behind it they put a mountain

without proper dignity, or solidity, or beauty ... don't try to make them steeper than they are in order to be more effective ... Simplify the general outlines, almost one might say 'cubify' them; let not details however delightful or however significant to the climber, take your eye or your pencil from the right proportions.[1]

To me he has something of John Sell Cotman's luminous, almost abstract watercolour style, but without his limpid English light. Before one goes to Tibet, Somervell's hard-blue skies and orange hills might look harsh, but once one travels through the country it is clear that he painted what he saw. Mallory wrote of him:

His most important activity when we were not on the mountain was sketching. His vast supply of energy, the number of sketches he produced and oil paintings besides, was only less remarkable than the rapidity with which he worked. On May 14th he again walked over the uncrevassed snowfield by himself to the Rapiu La. Later on I joined him, and as far as I could judge, his talent and energy were no less at 21,000 feet than on the wind-swept plains of Tibet.[2]

That first trip out to India had been a revelation to Howard Somervell, as it is to most of us. In contrast to the 1921 expedition, the members of the 1922 expedition all travelled together, first crossing to France and then taking the train to Marseilles to join the P&O liner SS *Caledonia*, which departed for Bombay on 3 March. Included in the baggage was a set of steel cylinders.

If there was one helpful word from the future we could whisper to those pioneers it would be 'oxygen'. The vast majority of successful climbs on Mount Everest today are made using the gas, and now we now know that the attempts made without it faced a nearly impossible task. Next to the Sherpas, it was the second innovation introduced by Kellas that eventually made the mountain climbable. The technology was there; the high-altitude war in the skies above the trenches had led to nearly every aeroplane by 1918 being fitted with a set of cylinders and a mask.

The problem was that although it was viewed as a logical tool by the Enlightenment scientists – and how did it differ, they asked, from polar clothing or Thermos flasks? – its use was regarded as unethical by the Romantic alpinists. There was a similar debate around Scott's use of dogs to haul sledges, with the conclusion always being drawn that it was more 'sporting' to man-haul the sledges.

But a further, more subtle reason existed, I would suggest, to the flinching away from the use of supplementary oxygen. Poison gas during the war had been regarded with particular abhorrence as a cowardly form of warfare. Gas masks were dehumanising in appearance and were a horrific reminder to this group of men who had been so scarred by the war. This could explain the strength of the language used. At the time, Mallory described using oxygen as a 'damnable heresy'.

Somervell could see both sides of the argument, and was eventually convinced by Professor J. B. S. Haldane, the world authority on the gas, that although the mountain could in theory be climbed without oxygen, its use would ensure success. Somervell wrote to Hinks on 23 January 1922: 'The only way of being sure of the summit is to take oxygen up.' He himself resisted using the sets as he went well at altitude without oxygen, and disliked wearing the apparatus. In the end he would set a long-standing record with Norton for the highest point reached without it.

The Mount Everest Committee had decided, far too late in the day, to take oxygen. Finch, who had been rejected in 1921, was the obvious man to choose to look after the apparatus, as he was one of the scientists who had worked with Kellas and Haldane. He also possessed formidable climbing skills on snow and ice. For most of the voyage out to India the expedition members were drilled by him in the use of the oxygen set. 'I'm amused by Finch and rather enjoy him,' confided Mallory to Ruth. 'He's a fanatical character and doesn't laugh easily. He greatly enjoys his oxygen classes.' Mallory would in the end be convinced by the use of oxygen, but not until two years later.

The problem was that the oxygen sets were too heavy and fragile, each bottle weighing 5¾lb and the backpack, regulators, pipes, etc. coming in at 9lb. The all-up weight with four cylinders was 32lb, far too heavy a load to carry to the summit in addition to personal kit, drink and food.

The party disembarked on 17 March at Bombay, which Somervell thought was one of the eyesores of the world, the ugliness of West and East conspiring to spoil a lovely harbour. Here the dustiest train in India took them across the sub-continent to Siliguri, where the narrow-gauge steam train still puffs its way 6,000ft up to Darjeeling. (I filmed on this train in 2009 and it is a wonderful real-life Thomas the Tank engine.) In Darjeeling they met General C. G. Bruce, the leader of the expedition and the very same man who had suggested the idea of climbing Everest to Younghusband in 1893, nearly 30 years earlier. He was a jovial character, always ready with a joke and a laugh. As a Gurkha officer he had mastered the language, and with this and his bawdy humour he was popular with the local men. With him was his band of hand-picked Sherpa and Bhotia porters, seven of whom were destined to die that year.

John Noel, who had made the exploratory trip to Sikkim in 1913 and whose lecture had done much to inspire interest in Everest expeditions, was able to accompany them this year in the official role of expedition photographer and cinematographer, and eventually produced a short film, *Climbing Mount Everest*, released later that year.

Noel had been to school in Switzerland, where he found the teachers unconcerned about his actual presence, so he used to bunk off. 'I used to go skating in the winter and mountaineering in the summer ... I also started becoming dippy on photography.'

By 1922 Noel had combined these interests and decided to pursue expedition photography. He went no fewer than 16 times to London's Philharmonic Hall to see Herbert Ponting's exhibition of his photographs of Scott's South Pole expedition. Ponting had immortalised Scott in the film *90 Degrees South*, just as Noel and those of us coming after him have immortalised Mallory. Noel modelled his film equipment on Ponting's, in the same way that the 1924 high-altitude clothing was modelled on that of the Scott expedition.

He had £1,000 to spend – a large amount of money then – as the average house in Britain cost £500. As well as a stills camera he took a Newman Sinclair 35mm cine camera with a couple of special modifications:

> It was handmade in duralumin, which is as strong as steel and as light as aluminium; it weighed just 25 pounds. It also had jewel bearings, so like a watch it needed no oil – because Ponting had discovered in intense cold, oil congealed.

The back of the camera was faced with rubber because of the painful discovery by Ponting when he accidentally licked the back of the camera: 'the tongue had immediately frozen on to the camera and he had to tear the top layer of skin off, freeing it.' (In 1993 I had a similar experience when my face froze to my oxygen mask on my summit day, and I had to rip it off, taking a large patch of skin with it.)

Noel found that working with cameras on Everest introduced all kinds of unexpected problems. The dry air produced static discharges in the black bag he used for loading the magazines with unexposed film, which led to sparkles appearing on the film. He said the static inside his camel-haired sleeping bag was so powerful he could read his watch by the light if he rubbed hard enough. Drying the film was another problem. He brought a special light-proof tent and had to heat it with dried yak-dung ferried up to the camp by teams of men.

In the event the 1922 film was not a commercial success, but even so, before he returned in 1924 the enterprising Noel bought the rights of all photographic work on the expedition for the huge sum of £8,000. This paid for the entire trip.

Edward Norton was one of the great finds of that expedition. He had fought throughout the First World War as an artillery officer, like Mallory. 'Norton is one of the best,' Mallory wrote to Ruth, 'extraordinarily keen and active and full of interest and gentle and charming withal.' He was a natural and inclusive leader of men, and Mallory readily deferred to him when Norton took the expedition leadership over from General Bruce in 1924. Like Odell he had lost a brother in the war; like some of the others he was a naturalist; and like Somervell he was a fine painter.

Morshead had proved so popular on the first expedition and such 'a stout fellow' that he had been invited back by General Bruce as a climber on the 1922 trip. As we saw earlier, in 1913 he had explored the Tsangpo Gorge, demonstrating beyond doubt that the Tsangpo and Brahmaputra rivers were one and the same, and thus confirming the work of the pundits Kinthup and Nain Singh. In 1920 he went with Kellas to Kamet, and then performed well on the Everest expeditions. However, this accomplished life came to a bizarre end. He was out riding in Burma one May evening in 1931 when he was murdered: shot dead by his sister's Pakistani lover. He was only 49.

Somervell loved the forest country of Sikkim, and in *After Everest* he describes how their cavalcade set off in 1922 with 400 animal-loads and high hopes. This is often the very best part of an expedition, swinging along chatting to your new friends through beautiful country.

Soon, though, they crossed the border into Tibet. Here is Mallory, writing in the periodical *Asia*:

The sensation of coming up to Tibet from the Chumbi valley, from the country of flowers and butterflies, of streams and meadows, of rich greens on the hillsides and deep blue atmospheres, the regret of leaving all that has delighted the senses and exchanging it in one short march for everything that is dreary is one of the most poignant experiences that I remember.[3]

Some of the loads were carried by hill-women, whose strength is legendary. They heard of one woman who carried an upright piano from the Tista Valley to Kalimpong – a height difference of 5,000ft – and arrived fresh at the top (I imagine she then sat down and performed 'Yes, we have no bananas'). Soon they crossed the Jelep La into Tibet and passed Chomolhari, one of the most beautiful peaks in the Himalaya, on their way to Phari, where Somervell was called to treat a rich young Tibetan lady who had broken her arm.

The house was a strange mixture of sumptuousness and neglect; priceless objects of Chinese and Tibetan art jostled with dirty hessian and cracked plaster ... Her ladyship was clad in silk brocade, her broken arm wrapped in a brown, treacly mess. I was informed that this was bear's bile, a cast-iron proof against devils. On removing it, I found beneath, beautifully applied by the local medicine-man, a splint on the principle invented by Gooch a few decades ago in Europe, but used probably for many centuries in Tibet. This curious mixture of periods set aside, the fracture was dealt with in accordance with modern surgical practice, and efficiently splinted – but hardly more efficiently than it had been before. A generous presentation of two carpets and a fine fox-skin ensued, after which the elite of Phari saw me courteously through their magnificent gateway into the filthy street.[4]

Somervell the musician was also fascinated by the country. Where his companions just heard a discordant cacophony, Somervell would be busy transcribing the music played by Buddhist monks into Western notation. He became excited when he developed the notion that jazz, just then popular in London, appeared to have its roots in Tibetan music.

After a month's gruelling journey through Tibet the expedition arrived at Rongbuk monastery, where the head lama blessed the Nepalese and Tibetan porters. John Noel saw the subject of his film properly for the first time. I found the following descriptions of his on an obscure BBC recording:

> Our arrival at the Rongbuk monastery was a great landmark in our adventure, because it was the end of nearly 300 miles of slogging on foot. Then we were exhilarated by this magnificent sight of the great mountain filling the end of the valley. You could see every rock in the mountain.

Like any filmmaker on Everest he was desperate for some local colour to shoot, and the delight in his voice still cuts through in the old, crackly recording:

> The chief lama, to placate the evil spirits and as an act of friendship to us, he put on this ceremony which lasted a whole day. They performed these ritualistic dances which symbolised the spirit of good and evil of their religion and the dance would placate them.[5]

On 1 May they found a lovely spot for Base Camp at 16,500ft (5,000m), although it was some way short of where General Bruce wanted it – a porters' strike prevented it being established further up the Rongbuk glacier. We camped at the same spot in 1990. It was a little grassy meadow in the shelter of the moraine, and was to become the site of Mallory's memorial in 1924. Next to it ran a tiny stream of water that froze every night. I felt very lucky to look out at the same view down the valley as Somervell and Mallory in the morning. In 2006 it was sadly changed. Under the shadow of a Chinese concrete blockhouse the site was covered with litter and excrement from the prostitutes' tents pitched along the approach road.

It must have been so exciting for the pioneers, though. Somervell was impressed by the view up the valley:

> The thing which struck most of us who were strangers to those parts was the extreme clarity of the atmosphere. Mountains thirty miles distant were just as clear as those not more than a mile or so away. Everest from the Base Camp – a continual delight to the eye by reason of its changing shadow and cloud effects – though sixteen miles off, seemed to be almost impending. Some of us felt it was not a beautiful mountain. Its outline is stately rather than fantastic, and its dignity is the solid dignity of Egyptian buildings rather than the dome-like grandeur of some of the Kangchenjunga's satellites. Everest is, on its northern aspect, rather a cubist mountain, and to one who, like myself, is of a modern tendency in artistic appreciation, it offered constant satisfaction as a subject for numerous sketches. I did some six oil-paintings and over ten water-colour drawings of this view of Everest.[6]

I once heard someone questioning the value of visual art. 'Why not just take a photo?' he said. 'It's a more objective record of the scene.' But surely that's just the point. Somervell said a picture should communicate something the artist wishes to say. To me his geometrical style expresses the harsh clarity and remoteness of Tibet.

There were no fewer than three doctors on this expedition: Howard Somervell, Arthur Wakefield and Tom Longstaff. Tom Longstaff was nominally doctor-in-charge, although as he said to General Bruce:

I want to make one thing clear. I am the expedition's official medical officer. I am, as a matter of fact, a qualified doctor, but I feel that it is my duty now to remind you that I have never practised in my life. I beg you in no circumstances to seek my professional advice, since it would almost certainly turn out to be wrong. I am however willing to sign a certificate of death.

Longstaff had more experience of Himalayan mountaineering than the rest of that 1922 expedition, with an ascent of Trisul (23,359ft/7,120m) with Bruce in 1907, which was recognised as the highest summit attained by man until 1930 (they were also the first to try oxygen on a major climb). However, he had no wish to be part of the climbing team, and he did admit in his autobiography that he didn't much care for the expedition but was there for the trip through Tibet.

Deputy expedition leader Bill Strutt, Longstaff, Norton and Morshead went on up the mountain to prospect sites for the higher camps while the others sorted out loads and basked in the warm sun. Somervell usually shared a tent with Mallory, in whom he had found a kindred spirit. Not only were they both Cambridge men, with Mallory preceding Somervell by a couple of years, they also shared a similar outlook on life.

I wanted to know more about Mallory and how he was viewed by his expedition team-mates, and in the course of making a Radio 4 archive programme I gained access to rarely heard BBC archive recordings of the pioneers. Through the surface crackles their clipped, patrician accents cut through. Here are Noel Odell's first impressions of his team-mates in 1924:

Norton was a delightful person to travel with, not merely a first-class soldier ... and a very good painter. And then Somervell was another, not only a first-class mountaineer but a first-class musician, composer, painter, one of the outstanding surgeons of the day, and he was a very likeable person to travel with. And then of course George Mallory himself, a very interesting person because he was so critical and a very contentious person in many ways. He was critical of certain aspects of the British Indian Government. He offered some criticism to the Governor-General during a dinner party up at Simla after the first expedition which rather shook the rest of the party when George Mallory was giving advice to the Governor-General, the Viceroy [*laughs*].[7]

Mallory was clearly opinionated. Listening to this I felt Odell was slightly over-emphasising his liking of Norton and Somervell to make plain his antipathy towards Mallory. Could this be one of the reasons why Mallory didn't choose him for his last climb in 1924, and took instead the far less experienced Irvine? This could help to explain the small mystery that has puzzled many Everest historians. Audrey Salkeld points out that Mallory had also pinched Odell's young protégé, Irvine, then took him on his final climb instead of the vastly more experienced Odell, who was after all in charge of the oxygen apparatus.

As we have seen, Mallory was clearly a talented climber, but was not necessarily considered the man with the best chance on that expedition. As already established, there weren't many climbers left in Britain after the First World War. Possibly the best of them all, Geoffrey Winthrop Young, had lost a leg. He could have provided a great deal of experience and been a great foil to Mallory's energy. Of the three climbers Winthrop Young rated most highly from the Pen-y-Pass days, Hugh Pope had been killed in the Pyrenees in 1912, Siegfried Herford had died fighting at Ypres in 1915 and Mallory's best seasons in the Alps were before the war.

If only the class-bound committee members had cast their net more widely they could have had a stronger climbing party. Alpine experience was demanded, though, and the British working classes simply could not have afforded it. Later, Hugh

Ruttledge sneered at an application from a steeplejack to join the 1933 expedition (this was Alfred Bridge, a talented climber and friend of John Hoyland).

Mallory did indeed have an excellent physique. I have worn replicas of his climbing clothes on the mountain and found he was slim, and slightly shorter than me. He stood five feet, eleven inches, a height Norton considered 'the best all-round build for a man: 5 foot 11 inches in height and 11 stone 7 lb. in clothes. Mallory, Somervell, Geoffrey Bruce and Hazard fulfilled these conditions so nearly that they might have all exchanged clothes very respectably ...'[8]

He was ambitious, like most climbers. Having become disillusioned with school-mastering he had given up his teaching post at Charterhouse. Many of the other members of the expedition were heading upwards in their professions, and he might be excused for wanting to make his name. Norton was on his way to an eventual governorship of Hong Kong. Somervell was already eminent in his profession. Also, Mallory's younger brother Trafford was doing rather well in the Royal Air Force, having ended the war as a squadron commander and being well on his way to heading Fighter Command during the Second World War. Everest must have seemed a tremendous opportunity.

I have never seen this suggested as an element in his motivation, but Mallory surely must have felt time slipping by, with his peers getting ahead of him. At Cambridge he had been surrounded by the best and brightest of the day: the poet Rupert Brooke was dead but lionised, John Maynard Keynes was by now a world-class economic theorist, having worked out how to pay for the war, and Lytton Strachey had published his much-applauded *Eminent Victorians*. Of his Pen-y-Pass climbing friends, four earned the Nobel Prize, five became cabinet ministers and fifteen were knighted. What had George Mallory achieved?

Walt Unsworth resists the temptation to deify Mallory, and in his definitive book *Everest* he describes him as 'a drifter, uncommitted and indecisive'.[9] Unsworth doesn't think Mallory was particularly talented, and certainly considered him forgetful and lacking in any practical ability, citing his failure to operate the survey camera properly in 1921. He thinks he became obsessed with the mountain, even to the point of being frightened of the power it held over him. As evidence he quotes Mallory in a letter to Winthrop Young:

Geoffrey, at what point am I going to stop? ... I almost hope I shall be the first to give out![10]

I think Unsworth's judgement is harsh, possibly in reaction to too much Mallory-worship by other writers, and ignores his many good qualities. He was hardly untalented, as he managed to win scholarships to both Winchester and Cambridge, the second after switching from maths to history at a late stage. He was a committed and decisive climber, as anyone who has attempted one of his routes can testify. Added to these qualities, he was a sensitive and evocative writer.

Audrey Salkeld, who has studied him more than most, has this to say:

Yes, GM could be absent-minded and sometimes clumsy. But, despite the camera plates, I don't believe he could be described as impractical after serving in WWI in charge of one of the big guns; and I don't think you could describe him as uncommitted.[11]

His whole life was one of commitment to building a fairer future – even if that didn't always stretch to domestic commitment coming high on the priority list.

Here is another voice from a man who actually knew him at that time. Robert Graves was taught by Mallory at Charterhouse in its most philistine period, and in *Goodbye to All That* he describes him thus:

The most important thing that happened in my last two years ... was that I got to know George Mallory: a twenty-six or twenty-seven-year-old master, not long up from Cambridge and so very youthful-looking as to be often mistaken for a member of school. From the first, he treated me as an equal ...[12]

Mallory was notably young-looking all of his short life, and it was one of his attractive qualities. Rather surprisingly, for anyone who has seen photographs of him looking like a matinee idol, he smoked a pipe and occasionally wore spectacles. He was a kindly and egalitarian master who spotted Graves's literary talent and nurtured it. Graves's family was not wealthy and he wrote poetry, and as a result of both of these he was ostracised and bullied. Graves wrote that Mallory made a point of looking after boys who were having a hard time:

> He always managed to find four or five boys who were, like him, out of their element, befriending and making life tolerable for them.

Although he generally took the liberal view in debate, he was not pious. In many of the team photographs on Everest he is clowning about. In one shot he is clearly head-wrestling with Somervell just as the camera-shutter clicks. General Bruce is turning round to see what all the commotion is about, and the other members are looking rather bemused.

In 1990 David Breashears and I found the exact spot where in 1922 Morshead, Mallory, Norton and Somervell posed after the first-ever attempt to climb the mountain. David matched up the boulders in the foreground and we studied the original. Morshead is clearly suffering from his frostbite injuries and Somervell looks fairly dour but Mallory looks as though he is puffing himself out in comical grandiosity. In other stills he has his foot on someone's shoulder and in the moving footage he seems to be cracking jokes and making the others laugh. One gets the impression that he didn't want to be taken too seriously.

Somervell described what they talked about:

> Sometimes we played card games for two, such as piquet, but more often we read selections from the *Spirit of Man*, by Robert Bridges, or bits of modern poetry, each reading aloud to the other passages of which we were particularly fond. We discussed climbs in the Alps and planned expeditions for the future. We made, among other things, a detailed plan for the first complete ascent of the Peuterey ridge of Mont Blanc.[13]

This is very much what we do nowadays on the mountain: poetry reading and planning expeditions for the future (the first ascent of the entire Peuterey Ridge, including the Aiguille Noire de Peuterey – the *Intégrale* – had to wait until July 1934).

Mallory knew many of the artists in the Bloomsbury set. He had stayed in France with Simon Bussy and his wife, and knew the English artist Duncan Grant even better – he sat nude for him, telling Grant 'I am profoundly interested in the nude me'. He enjoyed the iconoclasm of modern art and the way it challenged established views, and Somervell's brand of muscular cubism was to his taste.

What is striking is the amount of love he engendered in his friends. He was a 'great dear'. Somervell went on to say:

> During this and subsequent Everest expeditions, George Mallory was the man who I always felt that I knew the best, and I have seldom had a better or more intimate friend. When one shares a tent for days on end throughout the better part of six months with such a man, one gets an insight into his character such is vouchsafed to few other men. These many days of companionship with a man whose outlook on life was lofty and choice, human and loving, and in a measure divine,

still remains for me a priceless memory … in general he took always the big and liberal view. He was really concerned with social evils, and recognised that they could only be satisfactorily solved by the changing and ennobling of individual character. He hated anything that savoured of hypocrisy or humbug, but cherished all that is really good and sound. His was a great soul, and I pray that some of its greatness may live on in the souls of his friends.[14]

I have always admired men like Somervell and Mallory, but I try to see them with clear eyes. As boyhood heroes they gave me something to live up to, and as an adult I still find them inspirational. They were much more than just mountain climbers; they were Renaissance men and polymaths. Mallory had a genuine belief in the improving power of education, and had he survived he could well have helped Kurt Hahn and Geoffrey Winthrop Young in setting up Gordonstoun, a school that embodied some of his beliefs. Somervell told of his schemes to bring the classes together. Equally, he might have become a socialist politician within the League of Nations.

However, it is important to note that in 1915 Ruth and George had four servants: a nursemaid for the children, a cook, a maid and a gardener. This was quite normal for a middle-class family at the time; even a bank clerk such as T. S. Eliot would be expected to have a house-maid. In 1921 George suggested to Ruth in a letter from the Kharta valley that they might employ another servant. He was one of the expedition porters, Nima, an eighteen-year-old boy:

… he would fetch and carry – he is a coolie whose job is to carry; and if you want a box weighing 70 pounds brought from the station, you would simply send him … He would save many a taxi drive by carrying luggage to the station … His present diet is chiefly flour and water, rice, occasionally meat, and as luxuries a little tea and butter … He might inhabit part of the cellar … Would the other servants like him? Well, he is a clean animal and though he would look a bit queer to them at first they couldn't help liking him. He is not very dark skinned like a plainsman.

This might read to us today as the most breathtaking, patronising racism, but remember that Mallory was considered a liberal. Most of his British companions would have had similar attitudes. It did not mean that they despised their local employees; the attitude was more like that of benevolent pet-owners. They loved their men, and when they died in their service the Europeans were genuinely grieved.

Mallory had a curious aversion to Canadians, for no apparent reason. 'Wheeler I have hardly spoken to,' he wrote to Ruth in 1921, 'but you know my complex about Canadians. I shall have to swallow before I like him, I expect. God send me the saliva.' However, Mallory did not just restrict his prejudices to Canadians; he had it in for the Tibetans, too. He described their land as 'a hateful country inhabited by hateful people'. As for progress towards a fairer world, the war threw all classes and races together, and helped to do more for social equality than any amount of talking. Servants were hard to find after 1918.

My feeling is that Mallory had ambitions as a writer and wanted to make writing his career, as is made clear in a letter to Graves. His chapters in *Everest Reconnaissance 1921* far out-shine Howard-Bury's account. His writing is full of the excitement of exploring new country, and the details of puzzling out the landscape. The reader is drawn into the quest for a route up the great mountain. Had he climbed Everest and returned I could see him having the same kind of success that T. E. Lawrence ('Lawrence of Arabia') had with *Seven Pillars of Wisdom*. Like him, he would have had a story of great adventure to tell, and like Lawrence – with his good looks and whiff of homo-eroticism – he would probably have become the public's darling.

Mallory clearly had plans for the future and I believe he was well aware of the cachet he would obtain if he climbed the mountain. This fame would help to further these plans. When he hesitated in 1921, considering the fact that he was married with three children, Winthrop Young went down to see him and Ruth, and urged him to go to Everest for this very reason – to get 'ticketed':

> I saw them both together, and in twenty minutes talk, Ruth saw what I meant: how much the label of Everest would mean for his career and educational plans.

And this is when I think the rot set in. People often try to climb Everest 'to get famous', in the words of Thendup Sherpa. The mountain has been seen as a ticket to success since the very beginning.

7

1922, and the First Attempt to Climb Mount Everest

After establishing a set of intermediate camps, Camp IV was established on the North Col, at a height of 23,000ft (7,010m). Mallory, Morshead, Norton and Somervell were chosen to make the first attempt on the peak.

The first climb on Mount Everest was to be an oxygen-less attempt, and on 20 May they set up Camp V at around 25,000ft (7,620m) at the top of the long snow-slope leading from the North Col. I filmed there in 1990 with David Breashears and Brian Blessed, and it is an awful camp, stony and sloping at an angle of 30°. Worse, it lies in the funnelling wind-blast between Changtse and the North Ridge. The next day they climbed to about 27,000ft (8,230m). Norton said, 'Our tempers were getting a bit edgy, and though no actual quarrels broke out we were each feeling definitely quarrelsome.' After climbing higher than anyone had ever climbed before, they decided to call it a day.

On the way back, with Morshead suffering from extreme dehydration and clearly very unwell, there was a slip that nearly killed them all. This seems to me a strange portent of an accident that was to happen not far from this spot two years later. The incident is worth examining, as I think it might help us understand how the fall that killed Mallory in 1924 might have begun. Somervell tells the story:

I was going last and Mallory first, at a place where we had to cross the steep head of a long, wide couloir which swept down to the foot of the mountain, 3,000 feet below us. The man in front of me slipped at a time when I was just moving myself, and I, too, was jerked out of my steps. Both of us began sliding at increasing speed down the icy couloir. The second man checked our progress for a moment, but could not hold us. He, too, was dragged off his feet.[1]

Having been involved in a couple of accidents myself this all seems terribly familiar. Most start with a tiny mistake, which leads to a small problem, which leads to a full-blown disaster, as happened with Whymper's party on the first ascent of the Matterhorn. It often begins with carelessness, such as not bothering to fasten a loose crampon strap, or fatigue, when you can't be bothered to check where your feet are going. Somervell was nursing Morshead in front of him, although he decently refrains from naming him. Morshead was clearly at his last extremity and this is when slips happen. So here, as described by Somervell, are three men sliding down the mountain on their way to a fatal end to the first attempt to climb Mount Everest:

But Mallory had had just enough time to prepare for a pull on the rope, digging his axe firmly into the hard snow. It held, and so did the rope, and the party was saved. I remember having no thought of danger or impending disaster, but experimenting, as I slipped down, as to whether I could control my pace with the pick of my axe in the snow and the ice of the couloirs, and whether the rest of us could, too. I had just decided that my pace was constant, and was not accelerating, and was feeling rather pleased with myself when the rope pulled us up with a jerk. My experiment was stopped, for Mallory had saved my life and the lives of us all.

Very often during an accident one observes it dispassionately as Somervell does here, which means that one can try to retrieve the situation. Mallory in this case had time during the development of the accident to dig his axe in and brace himself. One wonders if there had been just two climbers, as in 1924, whether he would have had the time.

Morshead proved to have been badly frost-bitten, and was 'obviously not far from death'. Today we might guess that he had become severely dehydrated by the dry air of high altitudes, which, exacerbated by the high respiration rate, sucks the fluid out of you faster than you can believe. Modern-day climbers at great altitude try to drink at least three litres of fluid a day.

To our pioneers' horror Camp IV on the North Col below them had been abandoned and the stoves taken down, so they were left with no means to melt water. They suffered appalling thirst and when they eventually got back Somervell drank 17 large cups of tea without stirring from his seat. Morshead's frostbite had been exacerbated by his lack of fluid intake, as the more viscous blood would not circulate properly to his extremities. Poor Morshead. He tried to remain cheerful in company, but used to go off on his own and cry like a child with the pain of his frostbite injuries. He was to lose the tops of three fingers on his right hand.

The first attempt to climb Mount Everest had been made, they had come very close to death, but important lessons had been learned about dehydration, the value of Sherpas and the need for parties to be supported by manned camps below. Finch was about to prove the effectiveness of oxygen. We benefit by those lessons even today.

Next up the mountain were the oxygen party of George Finch, determined to prove the benefits of his derided gas, with his inexperienced companion Geoffrey Bruce, here on his first-ever mountain climb, and on the way setting an altitude world record. Can there be any other sport in which this would be possible? Everest has often been kind to amateurs. It is worth remembering that they really didn't know what they were letting themselves in for. I found a recording of Geoffrey Bruce in the BBC archive, and realised that they must have been concerned about the altitudes they were going to:

> We were warned it would probably be extremely dangerous to attempt to spend the night at 23,000 feet above sea-level, and that it might even be fatal to attempt to penetrate without oxygen to a height of 26,000 feet. We were able on that very first attempt to show that the human frame was able to stand up to very considerably greater exertions than the scientists had told us.[2]

Finch had proved his point with the oxygen apparatus, getting to around 27,300ft (8,320m), but they had only added a few hundred feet to the record. They went the same way as the others, indeed by the same route taken by all the pre-war British attempts: a traverse under the Second Step into the Norton Couloir (also known as the Great Couloir).

After a retreat to Base Camp, there was an ill-considered last attempt at the beginning of June, the party consisting of Somervell, Mallory, Noel, Colin Crawford and 14 porters. Pressure was being applied from London, and General Bruce was aware that with a worsening political atmosphere in Lhasa this might be the last chance.

Finch was supposed to go, too, but retired with exhaustion and an enlarged heart. Is it possible that with his superior snow-craft he was uneasy about this last, desperate attempt? Was there a disagreement? Could this partly explain his non-selection for the next expedition, considering what was about to happen? We know he was more experienced in snow mountaineering than Mallory, good with the oxygen and strong, but he was also didactic and opinionated. The Everest pundits tell us that this was a class antipathy, with the horrid colonial being shunned by the English upper-class gentlemen, but I suspect there might be more of I-told-you-so in the reason.

The 1922 expedition closed with a dreadful accident on 7 June, which horrified those caught up in it. Somervell explains what happened:

> When we began the initial walk to the foot of the North Col – normally an easy business – we found that we had to plough our way through snow of a most unpleasant texture, and took two hours for this first half-mile.[3]

Nowadays this would have rung alarm bells for experienced climbers. In good climbing conditions the snow covering on the glacier is dry and crunchy, rather like walking on polystyrene foam. But the monsoon had just set in and the snow was lying deep. Mallory had noted that there had been wind driving fine particles through the tent walls two or three days previously. As climbing leader he really should have recognised the danger.

The wind had probably whisked the fresh snow over the crest of the North Col, pulverising it into a fine ice-dust and laying it down in the form of wind-slab. This is a hard crust which is deadly dangerous because it is poorly attached to the underlying snow. When disturbed by climbers it detaches, and thousands of tons of heavy snow slide with astonishing speed: an avalanche. It is bad enough being inside one of these maelstroms, as limbs can be torn off and bodies crushed. But worse still, when the whole mass stops it quickly freezes, setting like concrete. You have only minutes to get to the surface before being trapped forever. We only know these things by learning from the pioneers.

They obviously sensed something was wrong:

> At 10.15 we started the ascent of the snowy slopes of the North Col, which are steepest near their lowest part. Here we considered it most likely that an avalanche would occur. We

tried to start one by stamping and jerking and treading out long trenches across the slope. But the snow would not budge, and we put all thoughts of such a possibility from our minds.

Somervell led up the slope, Mallory was next, then a porter, followed by Crawford, and behind him thirteen more porters, all heavily laden. This was quite a load for the slope. Noel had retreated, finding the weight of his cameras too exhausting. Somervell had un-roped and was moving ahead, kicking steps to save time while Mallory and Crawford waited for the toiling porters below.

> I had reached a point only 600 feet below our objective, the camp on the Col, when, with a subdued report ominous in the softness of its violence, a crack suddenly appeared about 20 feet above me. The snow on which I was standing began to move, slowly at first then faster.
>
> I was rolled over, and slid down under the snow on a swift journey which I was convinced was my last. So utterly certain of this was I that I felt no conscious fear. To my intense relief, however, the sliding mass began to slow up and, after a short time, stopped.

To his horror, though, he could only see some of the porters. The avalanche had swept over an ice-cliff and some had been killed by the fall and others by suffocation in the rapidly hardening avalanche debris. The survivors dug frantically, trying to get to their companions before they died.

> The first to be dug out was my servant, Narbu. He was dead, poor fellow; with four cylinders of oxygen still tied to his back ... I remember well the thought gnawing at my brain. 'Only Sherpas and Bhotia killed – why, oh why could not one of us Britishers have shared their fate?' I would gladly at that moment have been lying there dead in the snow, if only to give

those fine chaps who had survived the feeling that we had shared their loss, as we had indeed shared the risk.

Somervell was clearly distraught by this accident and it probably contributed to a decision about his future in India that he was soon to make. Today we recognise a condition known as survivor guilt, which is sometimes experienced by those left alive after wars or accidents. It has recently been reclassified as one of the indicators of post-traumatic stress disorder. Somervell had survived both war and accident, but he was not blameless. Longstaff clearly considered him as one of those responsible:

Mallory is a very good stout hearted baby, but quite unfit to be put in charge of anything, including himself. Somervell is quite the most urbanely conceited youth I have ever struck – and quite the toughest. He was very politely scornful of our refusing to countenance the German-alpine, forlorn-hope, success at any-cost, death-doesn't matter, stunt. He was honestly prepared to chuck his life away on the most remote chance of success.[4]

However, it seems Mallory was largely responsible for this accident, and ultimately he would be responsible for at least nine deaths, including his own. It is significant that in his account of the climb in *Asia* magazine, he skates over the incident. Salkeld points out:

The 1922 avalanche – I mean it *was* Mallory's fault, and he was right to feel so guilty. And it reinforces that caution of Geoffrey Winthrop Young's about sweeping along weaker brethren, 'carried away by their belief in you, to take risks or exertions that they were not fit for.'[5]

The matter of Somervell's big-headedness was noticed by others, and any dispassionate assessment of him has to acknowledge it. He clearly knew he was tough and talented, which goes some way towards explaining it. He was also comfortable and confident in his Christian faith, which perhaps led to a superior attitude. Perhaps the aftermath of the 1922 accident and a lifetime of service in India knocked some of that out of him. Wade Davis describes him thus: 'Immensely strong, with a stout body and a head so large the men teased him about his hat size, Somervell was in fact the gentlest of souls, decent and compassionate, a devout Christian of unfailing good humour.[6]

It is unclear whether in this assessment of the team, published on his return to England, Bruce thought Somervell was big-headed, or just had a big head:

SOMERVELL – Stands by himself from the point of the Himalaya in his capacity as an absolute glutton for hard work, not so much that he is better on any particular day as for his extraordinary capacity for going day after day. He is a wonderful goer and climber. He takes a size 22 hat, that is his only drawback.

MALLORY – Second to Somervell in going capacity. Genuinely anxious to look after all his men. Everything else you know about him. He is a great dear but forgets his boots on all occasions.

NORTON – the great success of the expedition. Is a first rate all round mountaineer, and full of every sort of interest. Is recovering now but was very overdone.

MORSHEAD – A first rate goer, absolutely unselfish. Just the man for this sort of expedition, irrespective of his professional qualifications.

FINCH – Probably the best snow and ice man on the expedition, but has a curious constitution. On his day can probably last as well as any man, but apparently very soon shoots his bolt. I should say not a robust man for a long strain and has delicate insides. Is extraordinarily handy in all sorts of ways outside his scientific accomplishments. A convincing raconteur of quite impossible experiences. Cleans his teeth on February 1st and has a bath the same day if the water is very hot, otherwise puts it off until next year. Six month's course as a lama novice in a monastery would enable one to occupy a Whymper tent with him.

And in case one makes the mistake of taking Bruce's opinions as altogether serious and unprejudiced, here is his assessment of the expedition's Catholic, John Noel:

NOEL – Stupor mundi St. Noel of the Cameras. He is an R.C. Please approach the mountaineering Pope for his beatification during lifetime.[7]

After the disaster of the avalanche, it was obvious that there could be no more climbing that year and the expedition started for home. Crawford and Somervell decided to leave early and do a bit of climbing around Kangchenjunga. They climbed several virgin peaks of around 18,000ft (5,500m) and attempted Jonsong Peak (23,344ft/7,095m) from the Lhonak side, making a crude map as they went. If they had succeeded this would have been the highest mountain climbed to the summit up to that time, even though they had been a couple of thousands of feet higher a few weeks before. It shows that they still had a healthy desire to break records.

This is where I travelled in pursuit of the shade of Kellas, and it is great country still virtually unvisited by Westerners since Frank Smythe climbed Jonsong Peak on the Dyhrenfurth Kangchenchunga Expedition in 1930. They exited over the

Lhonak Pass and returned to Kalimpong. Once at Darjeeling Somervell decided to take a look at India, and with £60 set off on his travels.

This part of his life is an interesting reflection on his character. He saw something that changed the whole course of his life, something far more compelling than the high mountains: the unrelieved suffering of India.

He had taken up an invitation from a Dr Pugh to visit Neyyoor Hospital, which was probably at that time the largest medical mission in the world in terms of patients dealt with annually. Medical missionaries taught religion, as well as dispensing more corporeal relief. Somervell found patients awaiting operations, some of them having been waiting for weeks. He rolled up his sleeves and dived in to help, and after ten days he felt an urgent need to make this his life's work:

> I have often told my friends that if I had not then gone to India at the call of suffering I should never have dared to look God in the face, nor to say prayers to him again. Nobody who saw such need and neglected to relieve it could call himself either a Christian or a sportsman. I take no credit for taking this decision, and deserve none. I simply felt that my job lay in Neyyoor, and that there was no getting out of it.[8]

That word 'sportsman' is interesting. It refers to a code of ethics that was followed by that generation, instilled in them at school and similar to the codes of the European knights or the Japanese samurai in that all of them encouraged self-denial for the benefit of the community. Almost as a test of his mettle, on his return to London he found that University College Hospital had given him a position on the surgical staff, which meant that the front door to his chosen profession had been opened. The temptation was placed squarely before him. He would also miss his home and his family and Europe, with the Alps and the Dolomites and 'a thousand other delights'. But he was adamant, and when he told his professor of his decision he felt he had done the right thing.

> When I had thus burned my boats a great peace of mind, and a contented feeling that things were all right, came over me.
>
> I felt that I had at last obtained an object in life. I had had an unsettled existence, both during the War and after it had finished, sleeping very often in a tent, sometimes in an hotel; now cooking my own food in a dugout, now eating a good dinner with well-chosen wine in London; at one time shivering among the snows of the Alps or the Himalaya, at another scorching under a tropical sun. Now that was all ended, and it was to be the tropical sun for the rest of my life. So be it. It was a grand thing to have got it settled and off my chest. 'The peace of God which passeth all understanding ...'⁹

Somervell wasn't finished with climbing, though, nor with music. He had to write the score for the Everest film that Noel had been making and arrange it for a small orchestra of nine players. He had preserved the atmosphere of the Tibetan folk-tunes he had been collecting and recorded them in Western notation. Then followed an unrelenting six months of lectures with the film when he had to give two, sometimes three talks a day, at first in London, then in all the big cities. There was clearly much public fascination with Mount Everest, one which remains today. Meanwhile Mallory was doing a similar lecture tour in the US.

In 1923 Somervell met the girl who was to become his wife: Margaret Simpson, the daughter of Sir James Hope Simpson, a Liverpool banker. She stayed with the family at Kendal, and it was at this time that he thought about marriage. But he knew by now that he was to be selected for the next year's expedition, and he thought it unfair to ask her to marry him before he took this serious risk. This suggests that these pioneers thought that death was a real possibility. (I have to say that before every one of my expeditions I too would visit family members and put my financial affairs in order in case I didn't return.) He hoped that no one would snap her up while he was away. I have noticed that many climbers marry immediately after an Everest expedition – in fact I did, too, in 1999. Howard married Margaret in 1925.

After Somervell's lecture circuit there followed a glorious mountain holiday, perhaps with a bittersweet taste, as it may have felt like the last one he was to have for a while. At first he climbed in the Dolomites with his brother Billy and Frank Smythe, whom he had helped to introduce to rock-climbing in Yorkshire three years earlier. Smythe was being evaluated for the next Everest expedition. After a visit to Venice they met Beetham, Rusk and Brown to test the oxygen system for the next Everest expedition. Beetham, too, was being assessed. In the end they made the wrong decision: they took Beetham, who performed badly, whereas Smythe went on to be the foremost climber of his generation.

The oxygen set had been modified and slightly lightened. They chose a traverse of the Eiger from Scheidegg to maximise the cutting and kicking of steps, so as to test the balance of the apparatus and to see how much it hampered them. Somervell wasn't impressed:

> We got up all right in spite of its awkward size and thirty pounds weight, but we were glad when the tests were finished and we could climb again unhindered.

One might question the value of testing oxygen at such relatively low altitudes. We now know it doesn't come into its own until 10,000ft (3,050m) higher. Somervell was more interested in how it felt to carry. It does not surprise me that he did not use the apparatus in the following year. He clearly went well at altitude and didn't consider that the advantages outweighed the disadvantages of the cumbersome device.

I have tried one of these 1924 sets and it was an unpleasant experience. The metal frame jabbed me in the kidneys, the weight was more than you would comfortably want to carry at that altitude and I found it tended to swing me off balance. All the pipes felt fragile and I had to be careful not to bang them on a rock. The mask was unpleasant to wear and obscured the view of my feet.

The Russian Poisk set I used to the summit in 1993 was lighter, and the cylinder slid inside my rucksack, so there was no uncomfortable carrying frame. The leather mask was horrible, though, restricting visibility, and with a valve that kept on freezing up. When it worked, however, I could feel a distinct improvement and was able to make upwards progress without a feeling of suffocation. Undoubtedly oxygen would make climbing faster and the summit a possibility for the pioneers.

Before his passage out to India in October 1923 Somervell had to make preparations for six years' residence there, as well as collecting equipment for another Everest expedition. On his way out he found the usual mixed bag of fellow-passengers:

> I cannot help recording that the missionaries among them were not the most pleasant people on board. I was reprimanded by them for dancing and playing bridge ... I cannot help thinking that these people do more harm than good to the Kingdom of God, and when I hear objections to missions and missionaries, I am inclined to agree with them heartily – so far as that variety is concerned.

He was himself no holy Joe, and clearly preferred practical imitation of Jesus Christ to pontificating about a set of rules. In 2009 I interviewed his son David and asked at the end, 'Just sum up. I haven't got to grips with him yet: what was your father *like*?' He considered for a minute, and then said, 'He was just a good bloke.'

8

'No trace can be found, given up hope ...'

The first Winter Olympics opened at Chamonix on 25 January 1924. Medals were awarded for the 1922 Mount Everest expedition. Colonel Strutt accepted them on behalf of Charles Bruce, Geoffrey Bruce, Finch, Mallory, Norton, Somervell, Tejir Bura, Narbu Sherpa, Lhakpa Sherpa, Pasang Sherpa, Pemba Sherpa, Dorje Sherpa, Temba Sherpa and Sange Sherpa. The Sherpas' medals were awarded posthumously, as they had been killed in the avalanche. It is somewhat unusual to award Olympic medals posthumously, even for 'the greatest feat of alpinism in the preceding four years'. And that brings us to a nice point.

As Doug Scott has pointed out, there have been many attempts to bring climbing into the Olympic fold.[1] He argues that while indoor events can be judged competitively, outdoor mountaineering is a completely different kettle of fish. Most of the participants seem to agree that there should be no competition in the high mountains, and how would one judge it, anyway? Scott goes on to say that imposing external organisation on to a small group of individuals compromises their decisions and may even threaten their lives. I would add that it was precisely that kind of external pressure from Hinks and the Mount Everest Committee that helped to bring about the 1922 disaster. Alpinism is not a game.

The whereabouts of the medals awarded to Bruce, Mallory, Somervell, Wakefield and Finch are known, but not those awarded to the Sherpas. Baron de Coubertin, the father of the modern Olympic games, suggested that one of the medals should be placed on the summit of Everest and, in May 2012, the year of the London Olympics, the British climber Kenton Cool took a medal loaned by Wakefield's family to the top. He said, 'This promise needed keeping, and after ninety years the pledge has been honoured for Britain.'

Norton, Mallory, Geoffrey Bruce and Somervell were chosen for the 1924 attempt from the 1922 team. General Charles Bruce would again be leader, having demonstrated his excellent relationship with the porters. With success expected, Hinks, secretary of the Mount Everest Committee, wrote to congratulate Somervell and asked him for a pastel sketch from the summit. Quite what he thought the conditions would be like on the top is hard to imagine.

A Quaker climber, Richard Graham, was selected for the 1924 team, but someone objected anonymously to a pacifist being chosen. With the First World War still recent history, conscientious objectors were loathed by many of the military men that made up the expedition. But Mallory wrote to General Bruce immediately:

> precious few men are so valuable that I would want to keep them in if they are determined to kick out Graham at this stage; and can't see why anyone outside the party should have a word to say on the matter.[2]

Somervell cabled his resignation to the Alpine Club and wrote this:

> I cannot conceive how the propriety of the Alpine Club could stomach such a low down trick after they had elected him in the full knowledge of his convictions ... it is a dirty piece of work.[3]

As usual Hinks was involved, and it wasn't to be the only dirty work done by Everest committees. Years later Shipton was sacked from the leadership of the 1953 expedition in a similarly underhand way.

It turns out that it was Bentley Beetham who had impugned Graham's reputation, presumably because he wanted a place on the expedition. This is ironic, as he himself had avoided war service by hiding under the umbrella of a protected profession: that of schoolmaster. Mallory, it will be remembered, had voluntarily left his position as a schoolmaster to go to war. In the end Graham withdrew, feeling that his position was impossible. He was replaced by Jack Hazard, a bad decision that cannot have helped Hazard's popularity. He had served in the war with Morshead, had been a strong climber keen on going to Everest, but his war wounds had never healed properly and his strength was diminished on the mountain, and he ended up ignominiously as a scapegoat.

Mallory and Somervell come out of the episode with honour, demonstrating a shared sense of fair play. However, Beetham's shameful behaviour did not benefit him; he failed to achieve anything meaningful on the expedition. Finch was dropped from the 1924 team on dubious grounds after a 'fixed' medical. His rather dogmatic character had not endeared him to his colleagues in 1922. Odell would join them, plus the 'experiment', as Mallory called the 22-year-old Sandy Irvine.

Thurston Irvine was only ten years old when he saw his brother off at Liverpool Docks with the rest of the 1924 Everest Expedition. 'Well,' he proclaimed, 'that's the last we'll see of him.' This was horribly prescient. It was indeed the last his family saw of him, but not the last we will hear of him. His great-niece Julie Summers wrote an excellent biography of him, *Fearless on Everest*, after finding a cache of family letters, and in it he emerges at last as an interesting young man in his own right.[4] He had impressed Odell on an Oxford University sledging expedition to Spitzbergen, and, like Mallory, he was an enormously powerful rower, another activity like climbing that needs strength and endurance. He was part of the winning eight in the 1923 Boat Race. The 1921 expedition had shown the committee the dangers of selecting men who were too old, in the shape of Kellas and Raeburn. Irvine was their experiment with a man perhaps a little too young.

There has been much speculation about the reasons why Mallory chose Irvine and not Odell on his last climb. Some Everest historians have even suggested a predatory homosexual interest, but there is no evidence for this. It suggests a misunderstanding of that part of Mallory's nature. His experiments at Cambridge bear little relation to modern notions of homosexuality and were more like a crush. As for Irvine, he was known to be robustly heterosexual; he had had an affair with his best friend's step-mother, which caused a divorce.

There were more likely reasons for Mallory's choice. Odell was slow to get going in the morning, and he and Mallory clearly irritated each other. Irvine, however, was an expert at the oxygen apparatus, and keen to work hard. Here's a letter from Somervell to his brother, Billy:

Mallory, although a schoolmaster, is able to lay aside the didactic manner of that profession, and is a very real friend of mine with much the same interests and outlook upon life. Odell is very nice, slow, tidy, particular, though a stout fellow, and when he is put to it, he'll make good, I'm sure … Irvine, our blue-eyed boy from Oxford, is much younger than any of us, and is really a very good sort; neither bumptious by virtue of his 'blue' nor squashed by the age of the rest of us. Mild, but strong, full of common sense, good at gadgets (none of the oxygen apparatus would have worked had it not been for him, all the tubes being of porous brass which he has rendered non-porous with solder etc.). If ever a primus-stove goes wrong, it goes straight to Irvine, whose tent is like a tinker's shop. He's thoroughly a man (or boy) of the world, yet with high ideals, and very decent with the porters.

I was once in the position of being the youngest climbing member on an Everest expedition, and I remember exerting myself to become a valued member of the team. I enjoyed tinkering with stoves and generators, and putting myself out to help. I think Irvine was eager to please in this way. He was good at fixing the oxygen sets whereas Mallory was not mechanically minded. It is possible that as a schoolmaster Mallory simply enjoyed the company of young people. Odell, however, would be less biddable (he is described here as 'particular', and I have learned to be alert to Somervell's exact choice of words).

Mallory's choice of an oxygen 'believer' at this early stage indicates that he had already decided that using it gave him the best chance of the top. By the way, it is interesting to see that Irvine was 'decent with the porters'. It is perhaps one of the reasons he was well liked.

They set off once more from Darjeeling on 24 March in two parties. Somervell describes how their last expedition began:

Started off in a car, then Mallory and I then walked together down the steep hill to Tista Bridge, taking short cuts where we could ...

It must have felt like old times, and seems to have been when they had most fun:

March 31st ... Down to a quaint and primitive Tibetan bungalow, where we left a whisky bottle filled with cold tea, with a note saying we had too much and this was left over. The second party completely fell, having not realised what it was.

April 1st – They dished it out all around before they discovered its true nature!

Here is Howard Somervell up to his practical jokes again. This sort of humour can sometimes contain a tiny grain of malice, so perhaps he was not quite as saintly as he might first appear. At least they all had a good laugh over it.

Problems soon intruded, however. General Bruce suffered from a recurrence of malaria and had to return to Darjeeling on 13 April. Losing his avuncular presence must have been a blow to climbers and porters alike. Norton was appointed overall leader, and Mallory, with his unequalled knowledge of the mountain, the climbing leader.

The Tibetan coinage had been changed from silver to copper as a result of the practice of 'clipping' (removing small shavings of the precious metal), and so ten mules had to be taken, laden with 75,000 copper coins, the money for the expenses of the expedition. In 1922 they had only needed three silver-carrying mules.

It is interesting to see how they lived. Each expedition member had a servant who would make their bed. Champagne (Montebello, 1915), the general's 120-year-old rum, and quails in aspic were served. In fact, most of the champagne froze in the terrible weather, burst the bottles and was lost. Things are rather different now. We generally eat local food, and there are no personal servants. Champagne is taken, though, to celebrate success, and there is a unique way of serving it. I have found that because of the reduced atmospheric pressure the bottle erupts like a fire extinguisher when opened. The trick is to stand across the mess tent some feet away, and catch the jet of foam in a bucket.

Somervell was busy as usual, removing a decayed tooth from the mouth of a Tibetan porter with home-made pliers, and discussing modern art with Mallory on one six-mile section of the march. At Base Camp he would be conducting blood tests and overseeing the meteorological readings. He was also getting to know the others, and he describes another member in a letter to his brother. Hazard was something of a loner, and this proved to be a problem later on.

Hazard has built a psychological wall around himself, inside which he lives. Occasionally he bursts out with a 'Gad, this is fine!' – for he enjoys (inside the wall) every minute of the Tibetan travel, and even hardship. Then the shell closes, to let nothing in.

One sees all kinds of ways of coping with the crucible of expedition life. The way one man clears his throat might irritate you beyond belief after three months. Some climbers joke, some become tetchy and some retreat into a shell – and these last are the ones that get scapegoated. In the course of many expeditions and film trips I have seen this unpleasant phenomenon more than once. After the poor goat has been excluded from the group, the air clears and the members get on with the business in hand. There is a historical precedent for this. Among sailors, another group of men thrown into battle with the elements, there was the similar phenomenon of the Jonah, a man who was singled out as the cause of all the ills on board the ship. They were occasionally tipped over the side on a dark night. Scapegoat or not, Hazard had the misfortune to be responsible for the mistake that directly affected their chances of a successful ascent that year.

The weather was abominable in May. Camp III below the North Col had been established with great difficulty. It is a tough hike from Base Camp at the best of times, and Mallory had an awful time with exhausted porters and freezing winds in the unseasonable weather. Shebbeare, the transport officer, was shocked to find out that Mallory had taken oxygen equipment up to Camp III in preference to warm bedding for the porters. A Gurkha lance corporal, Shamsherpun, suffered a blood clot on his brain, and the cobbler Manbahadur had both his feet frozen to the ankles. Both died later, victims, Wade Davis suggests, of Mallory's growing obsession with climbing the mountain.

Further below, Norton and Somervell were encouraging another party of porters up the glacier. Geoffrey Bruce wrote:

'Somervell ... was always a great favourite with the men, and ... had a happy way of getting the best out of them ...'[5] This relationship was about to become vital. Seven days at Camp III 'reduced our strength and made us thin and weak and almost invalided, instead of being fit and strong as we had been during the 1922 ascent,' reported Somervell. On 21 May he, Irvine and Hazard escorted a party of 12 porters on a new, safer route up to the North Col that Mallory, Norton and Odell had prepared, well to the right of the scene of the 1922 accident. They made it to the top safely, and left Hazard and the porters in Camp IV.

On 22 May it snowed hard, and everyone's minds must have turned to the avalanche-prone slopes above Camp III. Then on 23 May:

> Hazard seems to be coming down from the Col with his coolies – the best thing to do, as a bit more snow would have marooned them and it would have been a proper mess-up. Later – Hazard arrived with only eight coolies – that means four of them are still up there – we all felt it a great mistake to leave anyone behind; either all or none should have come down.

It *was* a proper mess-up. Hazard has been rightly castigated for leaving the men behind. One can only imagine what Norton must have thought, with the disaster of 1922 still in his mind and the realisation that a rescue must inevitably deplete his forces. But it was clear that something had to be done.

Somervell is modest in his description of the ensuing rescue, but it was a fine piece of work, reminiscent of the rescue he undertook on his second Alpine climb. The frightened men had to be persuaded to cross a steep slope of ice above a gaping crevasse. Norton described it thus:

Somervell slowly and laboriously made his way diagonally upwards and across: he punched big safe steps and continually stopped to cough and choke in the most pitiful manner. After one or two of these fits of coughing he leant his head on his forearm in an attitude of exhaustion, and so steep was the slope that the mental picture I have of him as he did this shows him standing almost upright in his steps with his elbow resting on the snow level with his shoulder.

Something was happening inside Somervell's larynx that was to have repercussions on his summit attempt. The lining was becoming frostbitten with the great gasps of super-cooled air passing through to his lungs.

He climbed obliquely across the slope, roped from below by Norton and Mallory. 20 feet from the men the rope gave out. Somervell untied, continued unprotected, and grabbed each man in turn, passing them back to the others. But then there was a slip:

The first two reached him safely. One of them was across with us and the second just starting when, with my heart in my mouth, I saw the remaining two, who had stupidly started from the big shelf together, suddenly flying down the slope. A big patch of the fresh snow surface had given way and the men were going down on their backs, feet first, in an almost upright position. For one paralysing second I foresaw the apparently inevitable tragedy, with the two figures shooting into space over the edge of the blue ice cliff, 200 feet below; the next they pulled up after not more than 10 yards, and we breathed again … Somervell, as cool as a cucumber, shouted to me, 'Tell them to sit still', and still as mice they sat, shivering at the horrid prospect immediately beneath their eyes, while quite calmly Somervell passed the second man to us, chaffing the wretched pair the while – so that one of them actually gave an involuntary bark of laughter.

He grabbed them one by one and passed them back to Norton and Mallory.

> Finally Somervell followed, after again tying the rope round his waist; and it was a fine object lesson in mountain craft to see him, balanced and erect, crossed the ruined track without a slip or a mistake.

The porters were all saved, and a repeat of the 1922 disaster averted. It was the right thing to do, but it had serious repercussions for the summit attempts over the following weeks, and in later years, Francis Younghusband suggested that Norton and Somervell might have climbed higher if it had not been for the efforts of the rescue. It exhausted all three climbers and now the inside of Somervell's throat was badly frost-bitten by gasping in the freezing air.

They had a council of war at Camp I on 26 May. The weather had been awful, and the disaster of 1922 was still at the forefront of their minds. They decided that they dare not risk armies of porters on the treacherous slopes of the North Col, so three non-oxygen attempts were to be made by Mallory and Bruce, then Norton and Somervell, then Odell and Irvine. They would be staggered a day apart so that each party would be supported by the one below. Mallory was dismayed by the decision to dispense with the oxygen.

Nowadays their arrangements would look rather thin. We know a little more about avalanche conditions on the Col, and after studying the old photographs and actually climbing the route several times I think it is safer in modern times, possibly because of glacial recession due to climate change. Certainly the icefall on the south side of the mountain seems to be shrinking and retreating, too. Now on good-weather days huge lines of porters and climbers are to be seen hauling supplies up the mountain. High camps are lavishly equipped compared with those in the 1920s. Ropes are fixed by Sherpas all the way from the foot of the North Col to the summit to safeguard climbers. Communications are far better now on the commercial expeditions, with hand-held radios keeping expedition leaders aware of everyone's location.

Things were far tougher then. Setting off a day ahead of Norton and Somervell, Mallory and Bruce had to turn back on 2 June from the first attempt when a porter fell sick at Camp V at 25,000ft (7,620m) and they failed to persuade the other porters to carry any further. Mallory was clearly saving his energy for an oxygen-assisted attempt with Irvine. They retreated to Advanced Base Camp, where Mallory asked Irvine to inspect the oxygen apparatus and select the most reliable sets. Then it was Norton and Somervell's turn. Their climb is worth studying in detail as it would have been very similar to Mallory and Irvine's last day, on 8 June.

The weather had certainly improved. May had ended with a hot day for them to climb up the Via Dolorosa to Camp III, and 1 June was a glorious day for them to climb to the North Col, with the snow settling down into good condition at last. It was cold, though, and when they met Mallory and Bruce the next day coming down the long slope from Camp V there wasn't time to talk.

Somervell was using his Kodak vest-pocket camera with which he was soon to take the highest photographs taken to date:

> I well remember the intensely cold wind, of which we got the full force soon after leaving No. 4 Camp (the North Col). I tried several times to take a photograph of the wonderful early-morning view, but I could only expose my bare hand to the wind for a second or two at a time. The first time the gloves were off I got the camera opened but could not press the shutter-release. Gloves on again; hands warmed up, and another shot at it – no good; hands won't work. The third attempt was successful and produced a photograph of the

north-west shoulder of Everest, with the shadow of the North Peak [Changtse] on the glacier below.[6]

I have one of these VPK cameras, and I had to scout around to find suitable black-and-white film for it. Somervell would have used the Kodak A127 stock, but I had to make do with film manufactured in Slovenia. I took some photographs on the mountain in 2001 to see how the camera performed. Answer: very well, but it is difficult to operate. You have to squint downwards through a prism to see the image, and then click a tiny metal lever. The results were pleasing, and they looked just like the 1924 shots.

On the summit in October 1993 I was wearing three pairs of gloves and removed one pair to take pictures with my Olympus OM1. It took five minutes to knock off some shots of Steve Bell and the view, but in that time the index finger on my right hand was so badly frostbitten that I nearly had to have it amputated. It is cold up there.

Norton and Somervell got going at 9:00am after a night at Camp V, four hours after they woke up, and struggled to persuade the porters to continue. One imagines that these men had spoken to their descending compatriots the day before and were not encouraged. But Lhakpa Chedi, the stoutest of the four porters, persuaded the others:

One did hold back; but the others were at last persuaded to come on, although Semchumbi had had his knee cut by a falling stone and it looked a bit sore. I take off my hat to him, and to Narbu Ishay, the other starter; but I make a more profound obeisance to Lhakpa Chedi, a real sportsman with guts. It seemed a sad contrast when I last saw him, a waiter in a Darjeeling cafe, dispensing ices and creamy cakes to painted and 'permed' English ladies.

One wonders whether Lhakpa Chedi's family knows what he achieved. It would be a fine project one day to visit the Khumbu (the Sherpa district of Nepal) armed with the team photos and track down his descendants.

Up they went. Somervell describes this part of the mountain-side as 'easy', which it is, but he didn't know about the technical difficulties further up. At this point he says they were hampered by Semchumbi's knee (Somervell carried part of his load) and their physical condition, but most of all by the 'atmosphere'. This is still true. Everest is not so much a climbing problem as an altitude problem. They were not using oxygen sets. In the thin air you literally take one step, then ten breaths, then another step. It is agonisingly slow.

They levelled a camp site at 26,700ft (8,140m), at a place with good shelter behind a rock. It was 2,200ft below the summit, and a bit too low, Somervell says. Given the time-consuming route finding further on, they were committing themselves – and Mallory and Irvine a few days later – to a very long summit day by placing their last camp so far from the top. Interestingly, the South Col on the south side of the mountain is at 25,940ft (7,906m), and it is where everyone camps nowadays for an attempt on the Hillary route, although the first few successful ascents started from a camp at 27,900ft (8,500m).

> Norton and I settled down to melt snow for to-night's supper and to-morrow's breakfast, looking out from time to time to see the porters bucketing down the mountain-side, and far beyond them at a sunset all over the world, as it seemed – from the rosy fingers of Kangchenjanga in the east, past the far-distant peaks of mid-Tibet, separated from us by several complete ranges of mountains, to Gaurisankar and its satellites in the west, black against a red sky.

And here was a comment on their approach to the limits of human ability:

I remember a curious sensation while up at this camp, as if we were getting near the edge of a field with a wall all round it – a high, insuperable wall. The field was human capacity, the wall human limitations. The field, I remember, was a bright and uniform green, and we were walking towards the edge – very near the edge now, where the whitish-grey wall said: 'Thus far, and no further.' This almost concrete sense of being near the limit of endurance was new to me, and though I have often felt the presence of a Companion on the mountains, I have only on this single occasion had this definite vision of limitation.[7]

The human limitation they were to encounter the next day was a lack of oxygen, and we will meet the phenomenon of the Companion in Chapter 17.

Somervell awoke at 5:00am on 4 June with an extremely sore throat and to the announcement from Norton that the cork in one of the two Thermos flasks had come out, and that they would therefore have to melt more snow. They set off an hour and forty minutes later, taking with them axes, a short rope, a few cardigans, a Thermos flask of coffee and the vest-pocket Kodak.

Somervell had his own ideas on what to wear for this kind of outing:

I used to have a sort of short mackintosh coat with buttons up to the top and I used this as an outer windproof thing and varied the thickness. I had boots to take four pairs of socks inside. I had a woollen vest, a flannel shirt and three cardigans.[8]

Dressed like tramps, Somervell and Norton climbed up into the jet stream, higher than anyone had ever climbed before. In a BBC recording Somervell remembered that day:

We had no rope between us because we felt that if one fell the other couldn't hold him so it was better to risk one life at a time rather than two. I felt absolutely done to the world. Norton was all right in his breathing. I was breathing [*he gasps, gasps and coughs*] like that, and I tried to cough, to cough this thing out but it would not come. I said I can't go on any further so I stayed on a ledge and in spite of my difficulty in breathing I felt a kind of elation about the wonderful view we got. It was a magnificent day. We had no excuse that we could blame on the weather for not getting to the top, simply that we were two ordinary mortals and we couldn't do any better.[9]

His throat was beginning to bother him:

A couple of crocks slowly and breathlessly struggling up, with frequent rests and a lot of puffing, and blowing and coughing. Most of the coughing, and probably most of the delay, came from me.[10]

The apparent weather conditions were the best they could have hoped for, with a warming sun and a less cutting wind. However, there was a hidden aspect of their environment that was invisible: the air pressure. At around 27,500ft (8,360m) they found that the effects of altitude suddenly asserted themselves. From climbing at 300 vertical feet an hour they were cut down to 100. Finally, at around 28,000ft (8,510m), with the summit only half a mile away, Somervell felt he could no longer continue. His throat had become more and more obstructed, and he told Norton to carry on without him.

He watched as Norton picked his way across to the great couloir now named after him. It is worth noting that they did not contemplate trying to climb the Second Step, a sheer cliff above them, now ascended by a fixed aluminium ladder installed by the Chinese in 1975. Norton got about 100 feet in height and

300 yards in distance beyond where they had rested and reached a point later measured by Hazard by theodolite as 28,126ft (8,570m). He was at the end of his endurance, too, and shouted down that he was becoming snow-blind, asking his companion to come up and bring the rope as he could not see where to put his feet. As Norton descended, Somervell went up and joined him. They returned, Somervell being so far from normal that he dropped his ice axe for the first time in his climbing experience.

Stopping at Camp VI they picked up a tent pole to replace the ice axe and un-roped as the going got easier:

> Alas that we did so! Somewhere about 25,000 feet high, when darkness was gathering, I had one of my fits of coughing and dislodged something in my throat which stuck so that I could breathe neither in nor out. I could not, of course, make a sign to Norton, or stop him, for the rope was off now; so I sat in the snow to die whilst he walked on, little knowing that his companion was awaiting the end only a few yards behind him. I made one or two attempts to breathe, but nothing happened. Finally, I pressed my chest with both hands, gave one last almighty push – and the obstruction came up. What a relief! Coughing up a little blood, I once more breathed really freely – more freely than I had done for some days.[11]

He rejoined Norton, who thought Somervell had hung back to make a sketch before the light went, and together they met Mallory and Odell coming out of Camp IV, carrying oxygen (it is interesting to note that by now Mallory was regarding the gas as a panacea). They didn't want any, but were more heartened by the news that Irvine was brewing hot tea and soup in the tent below.

As a footnote, Somervell tells his medical readers that the obstruction in his throat was a slough of the mucus membrane lining the larynx, due to frostbite caused by the inhalation of very cold air. He thought this happened during the rescue

attempt on 24 May. After being warmed and fed they retired to
their sleeping bags. Conditions seemed to be as good as they get
on the mountain. But they had been beaten by their weakness:

> no fresh snow, no blizzards, no intense cold had driven us off
> the peak. We were just two frail mortals, and the biggest task
> Nature has yet set to man was too much for us.

Norton and Somervell had just pulled off one of the most
remarkable climbs in history. Without oxygen, and while not at
all fit, they had climbed together to 28,000ft (8,510m) on a new
route on Everest and had the mountaineering judgement to turn
back before they got into serious trouble. Norton's record of
28,126ft (8,570m) stood for 55 years. Mallory, however, had
become obsessed with the summit and wanted one more chance.
John Noel, in one of the BBC recordings, said this:

> I myself, knowing Mallory's character, that he was obsessed
> by climbing Mount Everest, it dominated his life, so did he
> feel he could do it? Did he feel that if he didn't do it he would
> die anyway? He was late. Did they go on and reach the
> summit and die there or on the way back? They knew they
> were doomed.

As in 1922, this was to be a third, disastrous attempt that would
end in death. Norton and Mallory lay in their tent on the North
Col that night, and Mallory explained that he had been down
to Camp III to get more cylinders for an oxygen-assisted attempt.

Norton surely would have briefed Mallory about where the
top camp was, about the route he had followed that day and
how close the summit seemed to be. Mallory told him of his
decision to take Irvine instead of Odell, as Irvine had 'a peculiar
genius for mechanical expedients'. Norton did not agree with
this decision but did not attempt to interfere with it. Sometime
after 11:00pm Norton was smitten by snow-blindness, a partic-

ularly painful affliction caused by the removal of his goggles at altitude. The next morning he was badly snow-blind and had to stay in a darkened tent on the North Col. Somervell was advised to go down to Base Camp. He could do useful work there, such as continuing the meteorological readings.

From the porters' reports – and from notes sent down – we know that Mallory and Irvine made it safely up the familiar route to Camp V, where they spent the night of 6 June. In a note to Odell, Mallory wrote: 'There is no wind here, and things look hopeful.' The next day they pushed on up to the small tent that Norton and Somervell had established at Camp VI. Here Mallory sent down two additional notes; one to Odell:

> Dear Odell, we're awfully sorry to leave the camp in such a mess – our Unna cooker rolled down the slope at the last moment. Be sure of getting down to IV tomorrow in time to evacuate before dark, as I hope to. In the tent I must have left a compass – for the Lord's sake rescue it: we are here without. To here on 90 atmospheres for the two days – so we'll probably go on two cylinders – but it's a bloody load for climbing. Perfect weather for the job! Yours ever, George Mallory.

Once again, unfortunately, Mallory was losing things. On the approach march he was notorious for leaving a trail of forgotten items behind him, his companions picking them up while he strode on ahead, perfectly unaware. Here they seem to have lost a cooker, which was vital to produce drinking water, a compass, vital for a safe return to camp in blizzard conditions on an unknown route, and later Odell was to find they had left behind an electric torch, vital for a descent in the dark. Luckily, Norton and Somervell had left a stove at Camp VI. Most climbers I know neurotically check and check again the items they need as they prepare for their final climb. The curious collection of impedimenta found later in Mallory's pockets, such as bills and nail scissors, suggests a disorganised mind.

The other note was to Noel:

Dear Noel, We'll probably start early tomorrow (8th) in order
to have clear weather. It won't be too early to start looking
out for us either crossing the rock band under the pyramid or
going up the skyline at 8.o p.m. Yours, G Mallory.

The obvious mistake of '8.o p.m.' instead of '8.o a.m', and the
contraction of the former 'George' to 'G', suggest he was in a
hurry to finish the note off and let the porters get away quickly.
By the 'rock band' he meant the rocks beneath the summit pyramid – the way Norton and Somervell had gone. If he hoped to
get there in a couple of hours he was sadly mistaken. It can take
modern climbers five times as long from a closer top camp, and
using fixed ropes and lighter oxygen. By the 'skyline' he meant
the ridge route, the route he originally favoured, implying that
he was keeping the two route options open.

The next morning Mallory and Irvine left their tiny tent, and
climbed up into oblivion, leaving behind them the greatest
mystery in mountaineering history. There was a brief and
controversial sighting of them by Odell later that day, whose
note to Norton after his long but futile search had a valedictory
cadence: 'No trace can be found, given up hope, awaiting
orders.'

Before he left the North Col Mallory had asked Somervell if he
could borrow the VPK camera, as he had forgotten his own.
Here are Somervell's actual words in a BBC interview:

When Mallory set off on his expedition he borrowed my
camera, and of course it never came back. If ever Mallory's
body was found I wonder if the camera will still be in his

pocket. If so we may find out whether or not he reached the top.[12]

Here we freeze-frame our story and return to the small boy listening to the old man on a lawn in Gloucestershire, 40-odd years later. 'If my camera was ever found,' said Uncle Hunch to me, 'you could prove that Mallory got to the top.'

9

A Pilgrim's Progress

After university I got a job at the BBC, and eventually this allowed me to pursue my climbing in the Himalayas. Running parallel to this was my interest in mountaineering history, and in particular Somervell's story of the 1924 Everest expedition.

The facts have been examined over and over again in the intervening years, and many theories have been put forward. But the question that still hovered over the whole incident was this. Did Mallory and Irvine get to the top? And therefore, was Everest climbed in 1924, nearly thirty years before the New Zealander Edmund Hillary and Sherpa Tenzing reached the summit on the British expedition of 1953? Somervell had a hunch that they had done it, as did other members of that 1924 expedition. So did people who knew Mallory well.

I realised that it is very hard to prove that they *didn't* do it, and I became desperate to prove that they had. Over the years it became an article of faith with me. It seemed that if I could prove that these two men had won against all the odds, then this would inspire the struggle against impossibility. It became a sort of pilgrim's progress.

In 1986 a book was published that reignited the debate. *The Mystery of Mallory and Irvine* put forward the theory that Mallory had climbed the mountain. Tom Holzel had become fascinated by the lack of a conclusive answer to the question. He collaborated with the English mountaineering historian Audrey Salkeld, who knew many of the characters and whose library contained the documentary evidence their book needed. He contributed two chapters and Audrey Salkeld wrote most of the rest. She has become a great friend and support to me over the years, supplying rare letters and evidence to help the search.

The mystery has gripped mountaineers ever since 1924. There have been a few scattered pieces of evidence, some of which can be considered as reliable clues and some as less reliable ones. The first real clue came when an ice axe was found on the 1933 Everest expedition by Percy Wyn-Harris and Lawrence 'Bill' Wager on their summit attempt, probably marking the site of an accident. I would call this axe and the place it was found a reliable clue. I have handled the axe at the Alpine Club, of which I became a member in 1990. How I wished it could tell its story! It was smaller and rather lighter than I expected. Compared with my modern, machine-made, aluminium axe, it felt more like the work of a craftsman, with a dark-stained, wooden haft and a finely forged head. Turning it round in my hands I was struck by the three notches near the neck, supposedly marking it as Irvine's as they matched three similar notches cut into his swagger stick. In the 1933 *Alpine Journal* I found Hugh Ruttledge's account of how it was found:

> Traversing diagonally upwards [from Camp VI] they found after about an hour's climbing, an ice-axe which must have belonged to either Mallory or Irvine. It was lying loose on a slab at an angle of about 30°, about 60 feet below the crest of the N.E. arête.

In his full account of the expedition Ruttledge described where it was found in more detail:

> about 60 feet below the crest of the ridge and 250 yards east of the first step, Wyn Harris, who was leading, found the ice-axe about which there has been so much controversy. It was lying free on smooth, brown, boiler-plate slabs of rock, inclined at an easy angle, but steepening considerably just

below. It was in perfect condition, looking quite new. On the polished steel head was stamped the name of the maker – Willisch, of Täsch, in the Zermatt valley.[1]

My father also used this term 'boiler-plate slabs' as a descriptive feature. The name refers to the vast steel plates manufactured for the old steam ships. On Arran I once climbed a rock route called Sou'wester Slabs, which features these smooth boiler-plates. On a hot, dry day they provide plenty of friction, but with snow or pebbles lying on them they are lethally slippery, even at an easy angle. Ruttledge goes on:

> Firstly, it seems probable that the axe marked the scene of a fatal accident … neither climber would be likely to abandon it deliberately on the slabs, and its presence there would seem to indicate that it was accidentally dropped when a slip occurred or that its owner put it down possibly in order to have both hands free to hold the rope. The slabs at this point are not particularly steep, but they are smooth and in places have a covering of loose pebbles which are an added danger.

Wyn-Harris later wrote of the place:

> The angle of the slab was such that it appeared inconceivable to me that a climber would be unable to prevent a slide if he slipped while ascending. Whereas coming down exhausted it would be just the sort of place where it would be just too easy for a man to slip and fall helpless on his back; with the two oxygen cylinders acting as runners such a fall could all too easily end in a fatal slide down the steepening rocks below.[2]

Then there were more nebulous clues. The most famous sighting in the history of mountaineering must be the one made by poor Noel Odell of his team-members Mallory and Irvine, two days after they parted from Norton and Somervell on the North Col. I say 'poor Odell' because he was quizzed about this for the rest of his life, and whenever he changed the exact details of his account he was quizzed about that, too.

The 'well-known firm' of Odell and Irvine had been providing excellent support to the summit teams, cooking all the meals on the North Col during the previous week, bringing in exhausted porters and climbers, and looking after the sick. They had both been down to Camp III and back up to Camp IV on three consecutive days. Odell was twice to go up to Camp VI at 26,700ft (8,140m) in support of his companions. We now know this is the kind of altitude profile that is best for acclimatising to great altitudes. I call it 'spiking' – climbing high during the day, and then sleeping lower, with a steadily increasing gain in over-all height.

Odell's extraordinary performance over the next few days is even more remarkable when one realises that he had been turned down by Mallory for the final summit push in favour of the far less experienced Irvine. He showed no resentment, though, exerting himself to the utmost. What a man! If only Mallory had chosen him as his climbing companion history could have been very different. His sighting of the pair has been agonised over by countless authorities, so it is worth going back to see exactly what he wrote. I will add an emphasis to certain words to show the changes in what he recounted.

After his crucial sighting of Mallory and Irvine on 8 June he first recorded his observation in a single line in his diary:

At 12.50 saw M & I on ridge *nearing base of final pyramid.*

This was subsequently expanded in the expedition dispatches and later printed in the *Alpine Journal* thus:

The entire summit ridge and final peak of Everest were unveiled. My eyes became fixed on one tiny black spot silhouetted on a small snow-crest beneath a rock-step in the ridge; the black spot moved. Another black spot became apparent and moved up the snow to join the other on the crest. The first then approached the great rock-step and shortly emerged at the top; the second did likewise ... The place on the ridge referred to is the *prominent rock-step at a very short distance from the base of the final pyramid.*[3]

Forty pages on in the same *Alpine Journal*, though, is a subtly different version of the same story, also by Odell:

I saw the whole summit ridge and final peak of Everest unveiled. I noticed far away on a snow slope leading up to the *last step but one from the base of the final pyramid* a tiny object moving and approaching the rock step. A second object followed, and then the first climbed to the top of the step. As I stood intently watching this dramatic appearance, the scene became enveloped in cloud, and I could not actually be certain that I saw the second figure join the first.[4]

Another slightly different version appeared in the official expedition book. I have a first edition of it open in front of me, a grand, green giant of a book, with the title *The Fight for Everest 1924* picked out in gold letters on the front. Odell writes:

At about 26,000 I climbed a little crag which could possibly have been circumvented, but which I decided to tackle direct, more perhaps as a test of my condition than for any other reason. There was scarcely 100 feet of it, and as I reached the top there was sudden clearing of the atmosphere above me and *I saw the whole summit ridge and final peak of Everest unveiled.* I noticed far away on a snow slope leading up to what seemed to me to be *the last step but one from the base of the final pyramid*, a tiny object moving and approaching the rock step. A second object followed, and then the first climbed to the top of the step. As I stood intently watching this dramatic appearance, the scene became enveloped in cloud once more, and I could not actually be certain that I saw the second figure join the first.

Then he contradicts himself on the same page. Having said the whole summit ridge and final peak were unveiled he continues:

> Owing to the *small portion of the summit ridge uncovered* I could not be precisely certain at which of these two 'steps' they were, as in profile and from below they are very similar, but at the time I took it for the upper 'second step'. However I am a little doubtful now whether the latter would not be hidden by the projecting nearer ground from my position below on the face. I could see that they were moving expeditiously as if endeavouring to make up for lost time.[5]

I hate to be nit-picking, but this is important stuff. The answer to the whole mystery could depend on the accuracy of his sighting. Could he see the whole summit ridge and final peak, or could he only see a small portion? Were they 'nearing the final pyramid', or were they on the 'last step but one from the base of the final pyramid'?

Odell was not as familiar with the topography of the summit ridge as we are now, and in particular he didn't know that the Second Step is a formidable climbing proposition that now has a ladder attached to it. Most experts agree that it could not be climbed quickly, in the way Odell describes, by Mallory and Irvine wearing their clumsy boots. He also didn't know that the First Step is easily bypassed from below.

Most intriguingly he doesn't mention another step, nearer to the final pyramid, that Audrey Salkeld calls the 'Third Step'. I have been near Odell's viewpoint on the North Ridge and the First and Second Steps look nothing like what Odell describes.

However, the only feature that approximates to a step near the base of the final pyramid is the Third Step. If Mallory and Irvine were surmounting this at 12:50pm they were almost certainly not going to stop until they reached the summit.

In the 1933 expedition book there is a possible solution to the mystery. Shipton and Smythe were climbing near Camp VI and saw what they thought were Wyn-Harris and Bill Wager climbing the Second Step. They stared hard at the two little dots, which appeared to move. Then they realised that they were rocks. Furthermore there were two more rocks on a snow slope above the Step.

The jury is still out on this sighting. One can argue it either way, and people do. Wade Davis points out in *Into the Silence* one 'curious uncertainty' about Odell: that he went to his death convinced that he had been wounded three times during the war. However, Davis could only find evidence of one wound. The implication is that his memory could not perhaps be totally relied upon. In the end I think you have to file Odell's sighting as an unreliable clue, rather like the shifting mists that did – or did not – obscure his vision.

There is another clue that is even more tantalising. My father had a story that a body had been seen back in the 1930s, below where the axe was found. A telescope had been used to spot it. Then we saw a story in the newspapers. In my edition of *After Everest* is tucked the cutting from *The Times* of 21 February 1980. It is a Reuters report headlined 'Riddle of Everest nears solution – Japanese climbers to seek Briton's body'. It states that a Chinese climber, Wang Hong Bao, had found the body of an Englishman during the Chinese Everest expedition of 1975. This was reported by Wang to Ayoten Hasegawa, a member of a Japanese reconnaissance party, as they stood just below the North Col in October 1979.

According to Mr. Hasagewa, Wang, pointing with his pick axe to the final pyramid area, said he saw the body behind rocks and wrote the figure 8,100 on the snow, indicating the height in metres.

Mr. Hasegawa does not understand Chinese but with the help of Wang's gestures and written Chinese characters he understood what Wang wanted to say.[6]

But did he really? In an extraordinary twist of fate Wang himself was killed in an avalanche on the North Col the very day after he had told his story, so it could never be corroborated. The report announced that the Japanese team would be searching for the camera carried by Mallory or Irvine. This was the first of many such search expeditions.

The question my father and I discussed after seeing this news was this: was Uncle Hunch's camera next to the body? The two climbers certainly might have been expected to have taken a picture of the highest point reached. I contacted Kodak, and they said that a printable image could in theory be obtained should the camera ever be retrieved. The old black-and-white film was less susceptible to cosmic rays than modern colour reels. If found and developed, this photograph could solve the mystery. Imagine one's feelings as the image developed in the bath of solution. Is that Lhotse looking lower in the background? Is that Mallory holding up the British flag?

The prevailing opinion within the international climbing fraternity in those days was that Mallory and Irvine died trying to reach the top, and that Hillary and Tenzing were the first to climb Mount Everest in 1953, on a British expedition that had finally learned how to put men on the summit after years of embarrassing failures. Mallory was clearly on their minds in 1953 – Hillary wrote in *The Ascent of Everest* that the first thing he did on reaching the summit was to look for traces of Mallory and Irvine.

I then discovered another vital clue, one that has not until this moment been revealed in public, and is again closely connected to my family.

10

John Hoyland and
a New Clue

*It is a wonderful morning and the sun is full
on the summit of Mont Blanc, high up above
me as I write ... I do not wonder those poor
boys went all out to climb it. 'The Utmost for
the Highest'. I am gazing up at it now with the
early morning sun on the white-domed
summit. Such a tombstone as he would have
longed for, poor boy.*[1]

These words were written by my grandfather, Jack Hoyland, as
in September 1934 he prepared to set off with Frank Smythe to
search for his 19-year-old son. My uncle John had disappeared
on Mont Blanc in an attempt to climb the Innominata Ridge
with his companion Paul Wand, and had not been seen since.

I have the little leather-bound book that my grandfather
edited and had privately circulated. It is entitled *John Doncaster
Hoyland*. John looks out of the photograph with a dark swipe
of hair across his forehead: handsome, diffident, with intense
brown eyes. There is a coil of hemp climbing rope around his
shoulders. As I carefully turn over the tissue paper protecting
the photograph, I read an inscription from Frank Smythe
suggesting the curious mixture of mountaineering and spiritual-
ity that John embodied:

The philosophy of the hills is a simple one. On them we approach a little nearer to the ends of the Earth and the beginnings of Heaven. Over the hills the spirit of man passes towards his Maker.[2]

John's story is a tragic one. His mother, Helen Doncaster, of the Sheffield steel family, had met John Somervell Hoyland (Jack) before the First World War. She was an Oxford graduate and had been to the Mount, a Quaker school. He, too, was from a Quaker family with a long liberal tradition, including support for female emancipation and the anti-slavery movement (the seal of his aunt's letters featured a black American slave and the words 'Am I not a man and a brother?'). Quakers were pacifists and engaged in non-belligerent businesses, such as the chocolate of the Cadburys.

Jack and Helen married, and she followed him to India. However, she died in 1919 of enteric fever shortly after their baby son, Peter, was born. Peter then died of malaria. John, her eldest child, died on Mont Blanc. And Denys, her second son, was later to die fighting the Germans in the fierce fighting at Coriano Ridge on the east coast of Italy during the Second World War. My grandfather's first family was completely wiped out. It must have tested his faith to the utmost, particularly as his own beloved mother, Rachel Somervell, had died when he was five years old, whispering 'Be a good boy, Jack.'

He took her instruction to heart, becoming a missionary in India like his cousin Howard Somervell, and like him won the Kaisar-i-Hind medal, in his case for relief during the 1918 influenza epidemic.

In the Central Provinces alone the mortality during those terrible few weeks was greater than the casualties of the whole British Empire during the whole war. Bad harvests and near famine conditions made things worse. Some villages were practically wiped out; many lost 50% of their people ... They

(John Somervell Hoyland and some of the Christian boys from his school that he took with him) worked furiously, 14–16 hours a day, week after week, snatching a little food when they could ... local doctors supplied the medicines and the instructions, and magnificent work was done. Jack was proud of his volunteers ...[3]

He was described to me by Robin Hodgkin, the 1930s climber, as 'a Quaker saint'. When the local postman was eaten by a tiger he took on the mail round until a replacement was found.

He was also supportive of the Indian independence movement and knew Gandhi, the most famous recipient of the Kaisar-i-Hind. They shared a voluminous correspondence until Gandhi begged, 'Jack, please don't write such long letters.' He came to stay at Woodbrooke in Birmingham, the college where Jack was principal, in 1931. My father, then a little boy, was touched on the head by Gandhi, and was blessed by him. He remembered 'a little old man wearing a dhoti'. The great Mahatma famously visited Buckingham Palace wearing the same loin cloth, probably the first visitor to do so.

Long after Helen died, Jack met a young woman, Jessie Marais, who had also lost her family. Her father, François Marais, had been a doctor in Johannesburg, and in March 1904 he returned home feeling unwell. He had been treating patients among the Indian mining community, and had caught pneumonic plague. A lawyer named Mohandas Gandhi had been helping to segregate those infected.

Jessie's father died very soon afterwards. The family were called to his bedside and kissed him goodbye, but Jessie, then aged 11, refused to kiss him, even though she adored him. She always believed this saved her life, because one by one, in the order they kissed her father, the rest of the family died. Perhaps Jack and Jessie were drawn together by the shared experience of loss. He proposed to Jessie with 1,000 kisses. Jessie later wrote, 'I don't advise this method, it was something to be endured.'

Soon they had three children: my father Michael, who became an artist and writer; Rachel, a marriage-guidance counsellor; and Francis, an artist of religious conviction.

John Hoyland, the eldest son of the first marriage, had been left with his Doncaster grandparents at the age of four, virtually orphaned, while his father went back to India to save souls. Charity ended at home, it seems. His father taught him not to cry when he fell over, but to laugh: an ironic injunction considering the way he was going to die.

John started climbing on Stanage Edge near Sheffield with his Doncaster cousins, who pioneered such climbs as Doncaster's Route in 1935. I have climbed this and it would have been a tough, dangerous proposition in the 1930s, wearing socks over the boots for grip, and protected by only a hemp rope. John went up to Oxford in 1933 to St Peter's Hall to study medicine and surprised the Oxford University Mountaineering Club with his climbing ability during the Helyg meet in North Wales in March 1934.

Here he performed a spectacular rescue on Longland's Climb on Clogwyn Du'r Arddu. Jack Longland himself, repeating his own climb, had just persuaded a Professor Turnbull, of St Andrew's University, to tie on to the end of the rope. It has only recently come to light that the professor, who was somewhat overweight, had arrived at the bottom of the crag wearing two left plimsolls. John's climbing partner, John Jenkins, described the route:

> The most difficult part of Longland's Climb is a sloping crack at the top of a long 100-foot slab. The left hand edge of this slab is an overhang, so if anyone slips on this difficult part they slip over the overhang and there is nothing to stop them until they reach the grass at the foot of the climb.

The fat professor fell off, unsurprisingly, and was dangling 12 feet away from the crag, 10 feet above the ground. John raced down his own climb and managed to climb above the victim, reach his rope and reel him in. 'It was John's rescue of Turnbull that really brought him to the notice of the "great men",' wrote Jenkins.

In fact, the 'great man' Geoffrey Winthrop Young was privately furious with the 'great man' Jack Longland, and ticked him off for endangering the reputation of their famous Pen-y-Pass Easter climbing parties. John Hoyland had certainly made his mark. A couple of days later he joined Winthrop Young's party, where he met 'all sorts of great men – two Everest men and daughters of Mallory among others'.

Longland had been on the Everest expedition of the previous year, 1933. In a letter of thanks to Winthrop Young, John Hoyland wrote:

> I had a very enjoyable climb with the two Mallory girls the day I left. The way they glided up the rocks made me feel quite ashamed, as you said, they were wonderfully grateful and pleased whatever one did with them – even though they were quite as capable of leading as I was.[4]

It must have been heady stuff, socialising with the great and the good of English climbing. Did John push himself too far as a result? Yes, almost certainly. Was he seeking approval from older men, having lacked his own father when he was growing up? Probably.

John wasn't humourless, though. One warm summer's night at Oxford he climbed onto the roof of the Indian Institute, where he removed the elephant-shaped bronze weathervane. Pursued by a knife-wielding Indian caretaker (a light sleeper), he roped down into the darkness and landed on top of the warden's wife, who was asleep in a hammock. John was fairly shy but he must have charmed her, as she let him off if he promised to return the way he came. (I didn't know this story when I abseiled off my college tower on the flagpole line during a circumnavigation of the roof in 1977. Luckily I didn't end up on top of anybody's wife.)

After that first year at Oxford John taught maths and cricket for a few weeks in 1934 at his old prep school, the Downs at Malvern. He was there with his brother Michael (my father), who was the first child from Jack Hoyland's second marriage to Jessie Marais. The headmaster, his uncle Geoffrey (my Aunt Dolly Cadbury's husband), employed the poet W. H. Auden at the school from 1932 to 1935, so he would have known John well. My father remembered staff and boys sleeping outside in the summer and Auden's famous poem about *agape*, or divine love, 'A Summer Night', evokes the scene. It was dedicated to Geoffrey Hoyland:

> *Out on the lawn I lie in bed,*
> *Vega conspicuous overhead*
> *In the windless nights of June;*
> *Forest of green have done complete*
> *The day's activity; my feet*
> *Point to the rising moon …*

Auden and Isherwood's play *The Ascent of F6*, written in 1936 and containing the famous 'Stop all the clocks' stanzas used in the film *Four Weddings and a Funeral*, features a doomed hero-mountaineer who owes more than a little to John Hoyland. I think it might have been influenced by him, as might Auden's poem about loss, 'Johnny', which is a companion-piece to 'Stop all the clocks':

> *O the valley in the summer where I and my John*
> *Beside the deep river would walk on and on*
> *While the flowers at our feet and the birds up above*
> *Argued so sweetly on reciprocal love,*
> *And I leaned on his shoulder; 'O Johnny, let's play':*
> *But he frowned like thunder and he went away.*[5]

This is how the inevitable accident happened, which led to the clue about Mallory's body. John went to the Alps that year with Paul Wand, the son of the Archbishop of Brisbane. Paul was a sensitive soul, and a protector of the weak. His father reported that when travelling in Germany in 1932 they saw a Jew being led out of Würzburg by the Nazis, 'and I had to hurry him off the train for fear he would attempt a single-handed rescue'.

They started with a hard route on the Grépon in the Mont Blanc massif. John wrote 'a very gleeful note' to Longland, perhaps trying to impress the Everest man, and decided to try something even harder. This was the Innominata Ridge on the savage South Face of Mont Blanc, a route that Mallory had looked at in 1920 with his friends David Pye, Herbert Reade and Claude Elliot, but had turned back due to poor weather. If only John Hoyland and Paul Wand had done the same, as the ridge was far too ambitious for such inexperienced climbers. On 22 August they arrived late at the Gamba Hut from Courmayeur and were extremely tired from carrying huge loads. The following day they left in the morning, telling the guardian that they would be attempting the Innominata route. Bad weather came in, and nothing was ever heard of them again.

Jack Longland, who was an educationalist as well as a climber, clearly felt guilty as he knew that he had encouraged the journey to the Alps that ended in the deaths of two young men. In a letter to Geoffrey Winthrop Young he wrote:

> It's a rotten futile business, and I don't feel wholly clear of blame myself, especially after your letter. I encouraged John to go out to the Alps, and begin fitting himself for the future that seemed to lie obviously open to him ... After that it's just a miserable story – tired boys losing their way to the Gamba hut, the too-heavy packs, the pushing off in poor weather, and all of it.[6]

Winthrop Young would have known about those feelings of guilt as he had encouraged Mallory himself years before, and persuaded Ruth in 1921 that Everest was just the ticket her husband needed.

After hearing no news for a month my grandfather asked Frank Smythe to accompany him out to the Alps to look for his son. One can only imagine his feelings during that month of waiting. They arrived in Courmayeur, where Smythe engaged the famous guide Adolf Rey and climbed up to the Gamba Hut (now replaced by the Monzino Hut). It was the first time Smythe had ever climbed with a guide. The next morning they set off up the Brouillard glacier and reached the Col du Fresnay. Just above the col one of the guides found an ice axe protruding from the snow. In the 1934 *Alpine Journal* Smythe wrote about John's accident, and refers to Mallory and Irvine's disappearance, and the discovery of the ice axe:

> The discovery of the ice axe reminded me immediately of the similar find on Everest last year. What most probably happened was that the leader slipped, and the second man having no firm snow into which to drive his axe put it down in order to seize the rope in both hands and, failing to stop the leader, was himself dragged down, leaving his axe behind him.[7]

Looking down from here on to the other side of the col all the way to the Fresney glacier, they saw 'an object on its surface which did not possess the appearance of a stone'. This is a strange echo of Conrad Anker's description of his first sighting of Mallory's body: 'I saw a patch of white, that was whiter than the rock that was around and whiter than the snow that was there.' They descended, coming across signs of gross over-loading:

Full-sized table forks and spoons, heavy skiing gloves, heavy woollen sweaters, guide-book and underclothing, a condensed milk tin, a bivouac tent weighing at least six pounds.

They reached the surface of the glacier and found the bodies of the two students lying about ten feet apart. Smythe was shocked by the sight:

> The bodies were lying some 50 yards beyond the bergschrund and it was obvious from the nature of their injuries that they had been killed instantly.

They were wearing crampons, which in the soft snow would have balled up between the spikes and become dangerously insecure. Their bivouac gear hadn't been used and the watch on John's body had stopped at 3:52pm, suggesting they had been slow, perhaps as a result of carrying too much.

They brought the news back to my grandfather. The next day he set off with Smythe to watch a rescue party of bearers retrieve the bodies. I have next to me a yellowed letter with a rusty paperclip, a letter he sent at the end of that day. It is a painful document, full of stoical grief:

> This has been a long day. It started at 5.30. Smythe and I got off about 7.00 and climbed up and up through meadows full of autumn crocuses to a Col, and then left to a point (eventually) 8,500 feet up, exactly opposite to Mont Blanc. We had borrowed an extremely inadequate telescope, and watched the bearer party struggling up and down over the frightfully rough Fresney glacier towards where we could see the boys lying.

My grandfather was worried that the Courmayeur guides might be injured in this operation. In the event two of the men were slightly injured by falling stones. The bodies were brought down and loaded into a lorry.

At the villages people came out and bared their heads, and at Courmayeur people, especially poor people, ran out and put wreaths on the coffins and gave the Fascist salute.

This is an odd detail but in 1934 Italy had a Fascist government, Mussolini having been in power for 12 years. The following day an Italian padre came from Aosta for the burial, and the coffins were carried by the guides who had retrieved the boys. Two of them carrying John were bandaged from injuries received in the stone-swept couloirs the previous day. Jack's last words in the letter were:

> Everybody has been extraordinarily kind: lots of people shaking hands, and saying 'Courage!'

I have been to the graveyard in Courmayeur. It is a sad little place, filled with the dead from Mont Blanc. I wish every young climber who takes big risks could read Jack's letter. I wish John could have been an uncle to me. The grief caused by mountaineering accidents is immeasurable and never-ending. Sandy Irvine's mother left a candle burning in the porch for years after his disappearance, just in case her boy found his way back home.

The Hoyland family were devastated, and that year Somervell painted one of his best pictures, an oil painting titled *The Aiguille de Grépon*, to help commemorate his young cousin who had climbed the peak just before his death. It still hangs at the Downs School. Jack Hoyland was consoled to some degree by a letter from Longland received before the search:

> I can't say how grieved I am at what has happened. If things are as you fear, I can only say that I looked on John as potentially the best mountaineer of his generation. There is literally nobody of whom I had hoped such great things, and to whose development I looked forward to so intensely. I doubt if there

has been any young climber since George Mallory of whom it seemed safe to expect so much, and there was certainly no one who would have been so certain to fulfil his Everest or Himalayan ambitions in five or six years time.

For my own part, John attracted me and impressed me personally more than anyone else of his generation and I was proud to have his friendship.[8]

What killed John Hoyland – and his hero George Mallory – was obsession. This word crops up again and again. John Jenkins, his climbing friend, knew this very well:

> Men are born into every generation who, from their early boyhood, are destined to become great in some particular sphere. John Hoyland was one of these. All great men make mistakes. Some mistakes don't matter very much and are soon forgotten – an ill-timed speech, a dauby painting, a shoddy poem. But in mountaineering a mistake can be, and often is, fatal … From the very first John had been possessed of an almost fanatical love of the mountains, which later developed into a sort of obsession. He was never really happy unless he was in the hills, and he used to look up at them with a strange look of understanding in his deep-set eyes …[9]

John Jenkins was himself killed 13 years later on Mont Blanc, on the Old Brenva route, not far from where his friend met his end. John Hoyland was obsessive and over-reached himself, but he might have been killed in the Second World War as his brother was. Is it not better to die in the mountains striving, rather than trying to kill another person?

Privately, Frank Smythe was far less complimentary than Longland and Jenkins had been, having, literally, to pick up the pieces. He saw the accident as symptomatic of the sort of do-or-die climbing that was arising on the Continent. He referred to this incident in a to-date unpublished letter to Norton (the letter was kindly sent to me in 2006 by Tony Smythe, Frank's son, although my father already knew the story). The letter was written in response to Norton's praise for *Camp Six*, Smythe's account of the 1933 expedition, and in it he discusses the discovery of the ice axe mentioned in his book:

> I'm afraid I can't have put the ice axe theory very clearly. To begin with I've always assumed the yellow band to continue right up to the crest of the NE ridge as the rock is similar in colour all the way. The axe was found not more than 60 feet from the crest of the ridge and this rules out your idea that it was Somervell's axe. Also it was made by Willisch of Täsch, who is known to have supplied a number of axes to the expedition, and Somervell, who must have seen it, has never claimed it. Even if you had been on the ridge when S. dropped his axe you would have recovered it. I doubt whether it would be even out of sight of the ridge.

And here was the clue about the location of Mallory's body (the emphases are mine):

> Since my search for the two Oxford fellows I feel convinced that it marks the scene of an accident to Mallory and Irvine. There is something else, which I mention with reserve – it's not to be written about, as the press would make an unpleasant sensation. I was scanning the face from the Base camp through a high-powered telescope last year, when *I saw something queer in a gully below the scree shelf.* Of course it was a long way away and very small even when seen through a high-powered telescope, but I've a 6/6 eyesight and I do not believe it was a rock. I remember when searching for the Oxford men on Mont Blanc we looked down on to a boulder-strewn glacier and saw something which wasn't a rock either – it proved to be 2 bodies. *The object was at precisely the point where Mallory and Irvine would have fallen had they*

rolled on over the scree slopes below the yellow band. I think it is highly probable that we shall find further evidence next year.[10]

It is probable that he is referring to Mallory's body, which still lies just where he describes it (or possibly Irvine's, which surely lies nearby). This letter corroborates the family story that an English climber had seen a body at this place. The Wang Hong Bao report seemed to tie in with this earlier sighting: two independent witnesses, which together made it a more reliable clue.

While on leave in Britain between 1935 and 1936 Somervell had met Frank Smythe to discuss the forthcoming 1936 Everest expedition and mentioned to him that he thought it might be possible to place a camp in the Great Couloir that Norton had reached in 1924. I would guess that it was then that Smythe passed on this story, knowing that Somervell was John Hoyland's cousin.

These facts together made me convinced that I should try to search for Somervell's camera at Smythe's suggested location, and look for further evidence along the route I thought Mallory and Irvine had taken.

11

I First Set Eyes
on Mount Everest

I realised I should now start trying to climb the mountain to search for the body that Wang Hong Bao had seen. His report seemed to back up my father's story of the Smythe sighting. Surely Somervell's camera would be lying next to the body? I was learning how to make films at the BBC by then, as this seemed to be the only way I could obtain leave for the three months needed for big-mountain climbing.

This had the incidental benefit of paying for me to indulge in my hobby; indeed I've worked on all nine of my Everest expeditions. I put in my first programme proposal, titled *Mallory's Camera*, to the BBC in 1986. It was to take 13 years before the idea was realised – and then the whole project would be stolen from under my nose.

Uncle Hunch died at the age of 84 in 1975, never knowing about the Chinese climber's grisly find. But he had passed on the torch as effectively as anyone could. I just had to climb Everest myself, and I had to try to find his camera. It was very hard. I am not a mountaineer of his calibre. After learning the techniques in the Alps I knew I had to get out to the Himalayas and try some high-altitude climbing. On my first two trips to Nepal I trekked around the Annapurna massif and the Langtang range, and then I decided it was time to attempt a high peak. In the early 1980s I bought some cheap tickets to Kathmandu from a bucket-shop in London. The carrier was an airline called Ariane Afghan; I hadn't heard of them but they sounded exotic.

The first intimation that this was going to be the flight from hell was the Aeroflot plane standing at Heathrow ready to take us to Moscow on the first stage of the journey. The vicious-looking, grey brute of a plane reminded me that this particular airline was part of its country's armed forces reserve. It took off with a roar from Armageddon and accelerated like an SS20 missile. The stewards looked terrifying.

We stopped at Prague, then Moscow, and were herded on to an Ariane Afghan DC10 that was leaking fuel from its wings. I wondered what the spare parts contract could be, considering that this was an American aeroplane owned by a country that was under occupation by the Soviets, which was still engaged in the Cold War with the US.

It was early on Monday morning, and a group of Russian hard-men clambered on board, presumably en route for a week's oppression in Kabul. The chap sitting behind me suddenly grasped my seat in both hands and unaccountably launched into a frenzy of head-butting. The seat twanged and thumped against his forehead, whilst I politely leaned forward and gazed out of the window.

Kabul airport was a sea of Soviet helicopter gunships, and all photography was strictly banned. We learned here that the locals used Ariane Afghan flights for missile practice, which explained the unconventional, low, jinking landing approach. In the airport lounge there was the head of a Marco Polo sheep mounted on the wall wearing a startled expression, above a legend stating 'Stuffed by Jones Bros., Seattle'. You wouldn't think they would brag about it.

Eventually I made it to Nepal, and set out to trek into the Khumbu area. My aim was to climb Pokalde, a beautiful little snow and ice peak 19,049ft (5,806m) high, a few miles south of the Everest massif. Four of us walked in from Jiri, the rough little village at the road head. As I plodded up the pine-filled ridge up to Namche Bazaar, the Sherpa capital, I looked up. And I recognised it immediately. Through the treetops the black-rock shark's-fin of Everest's summit stuck out above the ridge between Nuptse and Lhotse. I had seen it in a hundred photographs, I had dreamt of it in a hundred boyhood dreams. It looked impossibly high, clean – and somehow sacred.

We had a great climb on Pokalde, with its lovely little ice ridge and a crampon-scrabbling heave-up on to the summit boulder. Oddly enough, in Wilfrid Noyce's book about the 1953 British expedition, *South Col*, he writes that he viewed Everest from the top of this peak, but I found there was a mountain, Nuptse, in the way. These curious facts emerge when you follow in the footsteps of the pioneers.

Pokalde's vast neighbour stood to the north, but I didn't really think I would ever have a hope of setting foot on Mount Everest. I looked back at the mountain as we trekked down the valley, but somehow at that stage it seemed right out of my league. That was for the big boys.

I left Nepal that year wondering how I could get myself invited on to a proper expedition to a slightly bigger mountain.

In 1986 I joined an expedition to Changtse, Everest's neighbour to the north. It was being run by two friends of mine in Bristol, Steve Bell and Steve Berry, who together had started a company called Himalayan Kingdoms. They had begun by organising treks, and this was to be one of their first climbing expeditions – in fact one of the very first commercial expeditions of all. But when I arrived in Kathmandu I was met by a brusque New Zealander, a guide called Russell Brice. 'Changtse's off,' he announced. 'We're going to switch to another mountain.'

There had been trouble in Tibet with lamas rioting against Chinese rule, and so the border was closed. I was very disappointed, as I had hoped to see Somervell's route up to the North

Col. But the attempt on an unclimbed route on Himal Chuli (25,896ft (7,893m)) in Nepal proved to be excellent training, and I made some good friends, including leader Steve Bell, Mark Vallance, who ran a climbing equipment company, and Brice himself. He was a climber with a big reputation, being the first to complete Pete Boardman and Joe Tasker's traverse of the Pinnacle Ridge on Everest – a route on which both had died in 1982. With Harry Taylor, Russell had traversed the ridge but had not managed to complete the route all the way to the summit, which would have joined the Mallory route somewhere around the old Camp V. It was an impressive feat, and I watched Brice with interest.

At first he clearly regarded me as just another whinging Pom, but I was quietly determined not to let him get the better of me. Mark Vallance and I teamed up, and I did more carries of stores up the mountain to Camp I than anyone else – ten, in fact. Commercial trips in those early days had few porters, and no Sherpas. Until I proved I could be a useful porter he ripped the piss out of me mercilessly.

Brice has a vigorous leadership style, and is fond of aphorisms that encourage his clients, such as, 'If you don't eat, you don't shit, and if you don't shit … you die.' Because most of his climbing clients are alpha males he seems to have to top them in the aggression stakes. He can be autocratic, and this has made him some enemies. But after more than 20 years of knowing him I understand that beneath the rough exterior he has a kind heart that only shows itself to his Sherpa guides and cooks – his 'family'. Woe betide any client who dares to treat Russell's staff with anything less than total respect. He routinely rescues people off Everest every season with very little thanks, and to me this makes up for any amount of hurt feelings.

On Himal Chuli he set a furious pace uphill, and used a technique of forced breathing that I have found very effective at altitude. You breathe faster than feels necessary, and on the exhale you purse your lips and force your breath out. This increases air pressure in the alveoli and improves oxygen uptake. It is supercharging for humans. You can hear the Sherpas doing it as they steam past you up the slopes, and I was reminded that Mallory said he had a secret way of breathing that he would reveal once he had climbed the mountain. In fact, he mentioned it in one of his writings:

> The principles were always the same – to time the breathing regularly to fit the step, and to use not merely the upper part of the lungs, but the full capacity of the breathing apparatus, expanding and contracting not the chest only, but also the diaphragm … Probably no one who has not tried it would guess how difficult it is to acquire an unconscious habit of deep breathing.[1]

Mallory would be breathing deeply as he lifted his leg for the next step, just to cram more thin air into his lungs. This seemed to give an extra lowering of the diaphragm on the step up, breathing in time with your steps, but it is hard to do. It is similar to the costal breathing technique used by opera singers. I find the Sherpa method easier.

My personal trick was hyperventilating (by panting hard) as I approached a rise in the route, so that my blood-oxygen level would also rise before I tackled the difficulty. I use the same technique at the end of a rest period, before hoisting my rucksack back on and resuming the climb. Because of the panting in dry air you lose huge amounts of water, and so you drink more liquid that you would ever imagine necessary.

I clearly remember Steve and Russell staring aghast at the route that opened up before us. We were sitting on top of the 18,000ft (5,500m) high, previously unclimbed mountain that formed the southern end of a long, jagged, unclimbed ridge leading to Himal Chuli. They had realised that we needed about a mile of fixed rope, and so Russell had to return to Kathmandu to buy it. Meanwhile I kept carrying loads, and in the end that mountain was nicknamed 'Graham's Knob', as my friends claimed it was small and rarely visited.

The ridge was an amazing climb, and I learned all kinds of techniques, such as penduluming, where you swing past a rock tower on a rope dangling down the side of the ridge. I also experienced the excitement of being the first person ever to set foot on a piece of unexplored wilderness.

Mark and I were chosen to team up with Brice on the first summit attempt, but the weather clagged in. I got soaked and frozen, and experienced mild hypothermia. It was interesting to see how my movements became slow and uncertain. It would have been easy to have slipped, and I thought of Mallory's last hours.

We lay in a tent for three days in a blizzard. After the first morning we had each told our life stories, and we lay there gazing at the roof of the tent, wondering what to do next. Luckily Mark had brought a copy of Jilly Cooper's *Rivals*, a breathily written romance, and Brice had a penknife. We carefully cut it up into three parts. Mark, as owner, was allowed to read it in sequence: A, B, then C. Brice got B, C, then A, but I – as the youngest – was lumbered with C, A, then B, and struggled to comprehend both the plot and the characters. On our return Mark contacted Jilly Cooper and told her the story. She was delighted to have been able to satisfy three large men at once with only one book.

While we were lying there Russell told us another story. During a similar blizzard on the Pinnacle Ridge on Mount Everest, Harry Taylor confessed that he was desperate to go to the loo. 'Piss in the bottle,' replied Russell. 'No,' said Harry, who is a polite man, 'it's the other sort.' 'Oh, no. You can't do it in here.' 'But it's a blizzard outside,' complained Harry. 'Get out,' said Russell. So Harry crawled out, opened the zipped 'bomb doors' on his suit and strained for a while over the thousands of feet beneath him. Satisfied, he crawled back into the tent.

After a while Russell wrinkled his nose. 'Did you stand in it? There's a terrible smell in here.' 'No, no,' protested Harry. He'd seen it go. After a search they found the offending object resting in Harry's hood. The whirling winds of Everest had whisked it up and deposited it back into his possession.

That's how we spend our time in tents in storms.

On our summit attempt I learned another important lesson. Our team had to turn back because of bad weather, despite all the hard work we had put into the climb. The second party had better luck and topped out. But I realised that it is not shameful to turn back. On the contrary, it is a sign of maturity as a climber. As in sailing, only the cautious survive.

Every now and then you get a lucky break in life. You just have to recognise it and be ready to grab it. My happiest Everest expedition was my first, and it was the people on the trip that made it so good.

In 1990 the director John-Paul Davidson had finally managed to get funding for a BBC film about Mallory: *Galahad of Everest*. The high-altitude cameraman was to be David Breashears, already making his name in the field, and soon to be a famous IMAX film director. The bulk of the filming was to be on the north side of Everest in Tibet. I desperately wanted to go, but my friend Dave Blackham was selected to be the BBC soundman. Unfortunately for him, but fortunately for me, he injured a knee in Bhutan and I was instructed to get myself out to Nepal on the next flight. I also carried a spare circuit board for a malfunctioning Arriflex film camera.

The chief character in the film was Brian Blessed, an actor I knew was fascinated by Mallory and the early Everest expeditions, and who had been pushing hard to get this film made. Brian was well known from his role as PC Fancy Smith in

Z *Cars*, the first tyre-squealing, villain-punching police action series.

After my hire car caught fire on the M4 motorway I only just caught the flight to Kathmandu, where I met David Breashears and Jean-Paul Davidson.

I liked the team immediately. Brian Blessed, our star, was a huge man in every way, with an unlikely physique for a climber. He looked rather like a yeti. David Breashears was an interesting character, slim, dark and intelligent, with an intense manner. He had summited Everest twice in 1985, and was famous for guiding entrepreneur Dick Bass up the mountain that year in Bass's pursuit of the Seven Summits, the highest point of each of the continents. The Seven Summits objective has now become a way for a wealthy – or determined – person without great climbing skills to see some of the most exotic corners of the world.

So David Breashears had really started the whole Everest commercial guiding scene, with all that it implies. Furthermore, he has now become a film director in his own right. Quite an achievement. In 1990, though, he was working as the high-altitude cameraman-director on the film.

John-Paul Davidson, or JP, as he is known, is one of the most successful TV film directors, and he is also a thoroughly nice person. JP and David were there with their partners. Veronique Choa, a young woman with artistic talents, was soon to become David's wife. They had met when she had mountain-biked up to the Everest Base Camp on the Tibetan side in 1986. And JP had his new wife with him, Margaret Magnusson, another young woman who was fun to be with. She was then an assistant producer on BBC's *Newsnight*, and was part of one of the many BBC dynasties, being Magnus Magnusson's daughter. (As an aside, I have to say I have nearly always been impressed by the women I meet on Everest. They usually excel in a very male-dominated world.)

Our expedition had a problem, as one of the team didn't have a visa. We did have a spare passport with a valid visa in it, though, so that night we had to find someone adept at making documents. Kathmandu in those days was full of strange characters left over from the 1960s Khampa rebellion, including a lady CIA operative, and a man I have promised to call Q. It was with some nervousness that we tracked him down in his shady room in the hippie enclave, Freak Street. His matted, long, blond hair and the dense cloud of hashish smoke did not fill us with confidence, but he was clearly a master of his trade. First he cut out the page with the visa on it. He then cut out the corresponding page in the new passport and very carefully inserted the page into it, with tiny dabs of glue. In the morning it looked terrible. The little wavy lines on the new page were of a different colour to all the other pages.

When we arrived at the frontier post in the vast gorge of the Bhote Kosi river I think we were all a bit nervous. At the ill-named Friendship Bridge between Nepal and Tibet there was a stiff reception from the People's Army soldiers in their cheap, green-cotton uniforms. We queued up and handed our passports over. The immigration officer started examining the questionable one closely and our hearts sank – he would be bound to spot the addition. Would we be arrested? (In fact I *was* arrested there 14 years later, but that's another story.)

There was a sudden stir, the guards jerked round and the safety catches clacked off their guns. I spun round. To my horror Brian Blessed had *picked up* one of the guards bodily and was staggering off towards the 100-foot drop into the river. Then Brian started bellowing with laughter, there was a pause, and the immigration officer began chuckling, too. The man's colleagues giggled nervously, and Brian put him down. The spell was broken. The passports were handed back. We were through.

From the border, deep in the gorge of the Bhote Kosi – the river that had been first explored and mapped by Morshead and Wollaston in 1921 – we walked across the Friendship Bridge on to the road that the Chinese have driven south through the Himalayan chain to Nepal: the Friendship Highway. Far from friendly, this is considered by many observers to be a potential invasion route for the People's Army. Here squats Zhangmu, one of the ugliest towns in the world, possessing all the most unpleasant attributes of a Chinese frontier town: rubbish, prostitutes and concrete doss-houses. Its only redeeming feature is the situation – it sprawls up the sides of a gorge so steep that natural erosion will one day send it swirling down the Bhote Kosi. There have already been several disastrous landslips. Here, in 1990, the hotel hadn't quite mastered the needs of the Western tourist. I found my room with difficulty, as it shared its number with all the other rooms directly above it. In my room the previous guest had unaccountably defecated in the shower tray instead of the lavatory bowl. It was absolutely disgusting.

After escaping Zhangmu in a couple of hired Toyota Landcruisers we drove up on to the Tibetan plateau and breathed fresh – if thin – air. At once I recognised the landscape. Here were the orange-brown hills and the intensely blue sky of Somervell's pictures. To the south rose the highest mountains in the world.

The human habitations in Tibet are poverty-stricken and not attractive. If you are struggling with your first altitude headaches the filthy towns do not make you overly keen on the indifferent food on offer, either. Nylam had so many rats in the guest house that they were running up the curtains, and during the night I reached out and put my hand on one. We filmed Brian at Shekar Dzong, where the splendid hill-fort had been visited by the pre-war British expeditions. Tingri possessed a fine example of a caravanserai, a courtyard surrounded by small, stone-built cells used for animal fodder and traders alike. These courtyards were common on the ancient Silk Road, and ours was like the one written about by Omar Khayyam:

> *Think, in this batter'd Caravanserai*
> *Whose Portals are alternate Night and Day,*
> *How Sultan after Sultan with his Pomp*
> *Abode his destined Hour, and went his way.*[2]

In the past the caravans of pack-animals were driven into the walled courtyard to protect them from marauders. These days the four-wheel drive vehicles fill the morning air with clouds of diesel smoke. After a night at Tingri we drove into Base Camp. At last I was going to set foot on Mount Everest.

I realise that it might be hard to visualise the mountain, so I will try to sketch out its topography. Everest is roughly a three-sided pyramid, and we can climb up the ridges or the faces. As we look at it from the north, hovering in an imaginary helicopter, we would see the West Ridge on the right, first climbed in good style by Hornbein and Unsoeld in 1963. If we then fly over that ridge into Nepal and turn left around the mountain, we will fly up the Western Cwm – named by Mallory on the 1921 reconnaissance – up the famous Khumbu Icefall and then up over the South Col, which is a saddle-shaped pass joining Everest to Lhotse, its neighbour to the south. This is the most popular climbing route. On our left is the South-East Ridge, which was first successfully climbed to the top by Hillary and Tenzing in 1953.

Keep going round the mountain, across the Kangshung glacier with the vast Kangshung East Face on our left. We will have to fly over the North-East Ridge to get back into Tibet, where we started. An important complication is a subsidiary ridge spotted by the 1921 reconnaissance expedition. This runs northwards from the middle of the North-East Ridge. This is the North Ridge, which was the first route to be attempted on the mountain in 1922 during the British expedition. It swoops down to a pass, the North Col, which connects it to Everest's neighbour to the north, Changtse. It was a good bit of route-finding on Mallory's part, as the ridge is the only weakness in the mountain's defences on the Tibetan side. He was also the first to attempt it. In all there are around 18 routes up the mountain, and there are at least two routes still to be done. One is a secret ambition of mine. And I'm not telling where it goes.

You can actually fly over the mountain, as the Duke of Hamilton showed in a Westland biplane when he flew right over the summit in 1933. Helicopters? One has landed – just – on the summit. On 14 May 2005 a Eurocopter B3 helicopter piloted by Didier Delsalle landed there, and he held his skids on the snow for over three minutes. His flight broke the record for the highest helicopter landing, previously held by Lt Col Madan Khatri Chhetri of the Nepali Air Force, who in 1996 rescued climbers Beck Weathers and Makalu Gau near Camp I at approximately 20,000ft (6,096m).

Was Delsalle's feat sacrilege? I don't think so. Human ingenuity will always push down the barriers erected by our material world. David Hahn, who was one of the Mallory searchers in 1999 and who has reached Everest's summit 14 times, said: 'I look at it kind of selfishly. It improves the possibility of rescues in the future.'

And what of the future? I can envisage the Chinese excavating a spiral railway inside the mountain all the way to the summit, rather like the one that tunnels through the Eiger up to the Jungfraujoch. They could construct a glassed-in balcony for tourists, who would struggle into pressurised suits and plod up to the summit to take photographs. If this sounds far-fetched, don't forget that flying saucers were seen passing over the summit by an oxygen-deprived Frank Smythe in 1933. They were dubbed 'Frank's bloody teapots' by his team.

The West Ridge is considered to be difficult and produced one of the most extraordinary stories: 'the Man who fell into Tibet'. On 30 December 1983 a Belgian climber, Jean Bourgeois, was descending the ridge in a storm when he disappeared. His team members searched for him for several days and then abandoned the expedition, returning to Kathmandu in mourning. Then to their astonishment he turned up alive with an amazing story.

Instead of falling off the steep Nepali (south) side of the ridge, which would have killed him, he had fallen north into Tibet.

Finding it impossible to re-climb the slope he decided to try to make it to the Rongbuk monastery, which he found ruined and empty. After spending several nights out he eventually reached a village and was detained by the Chinese authorities. They eventually believed his story, gave him 500 rupees and packed him off to Kathmandu.

In 1990 I stepped down out of the truck, and gazed around at the place I had been reading about ever since boyhood. Everest Base Camp North is located in a spectacular setting right at the nose of the Rongbuk glacier, with the vast, three-sided pyramid of Everest rearing up at the head of the valley, usually with a mile-long flag of spindrift flying from the summit at 29,028ft (8,848m). Tethered around the camp, clonking the bells around their necks are the heavy-goods vehicles of the Himalayas: the yaks. These are the most fascinating creatures.

> *As a friend to the children commend me the Yak,*
> *You will find it exactly the thing:*
> *It will carry and fetch, you can ride on its back,*
> *Or lead it about with a string.*
>
> *The Tartar who dwells on the plains of Thibet*
> *(A desolate region of snow)*
> *Has for centuries made it a nursery pet,*
> *And surely the Tartar should know!*[3]

Well, Hilaire Belloc, who wrote that, clearly knew nothing about yaks.

After years spent studying them I now have to say they command my greatest respect. A yak is like a hairy bull with a bad attitude. They carry huge loads up to 21,500ft (6,550m), and seem to live on a mouthful of gravel and a sip of glacier water. They are, however, extremely grumpy, especially when being loaded. They tend to wait until the last rope is being tied and then gallop backwards at high speed. The load comes off and is dragged backward through tents and groups of bystanders. We put Brian Blessed on one and it bucked him off in short order. Once, I foolishly put my hand on a yak's horn as I squeezed past on a narrow path, and the animal nearly disembowelled me with a vicious, hooking lunge.

The yakkies, their human owners, are actually quite proud of them, as they decorate the horns with red ribbons – unless it is to warn of the dangerous end. You'll see them in the morning at Base Camp, lovingly feeding their yaks with balls of tsampa – barley flour mixed with butter. Their owners, who are Buddhists, are not supposed to slaughter them for meat, but it is amazing how many fatal accidents they have, and how tasty they are.

As mentioned earlier, an alpine chough was seen flying over the summit by the leader of my 1993 expedition as we stood up there, and I've often wondered how birds can fly from sea level to much greater altitudes than the summit of Mount Everest in a few hours without getting cracking headaches. The answer seems partly to be the same as the Sherpas: birds have a greater density of capillaries than ground-living creatures.[4] Incidentally, the avian world altitude record was (briefly) held by a Rüppell's vulture that collided with an aircraft at 37,100ft (11,300m).

'Can you have a shower on Everest?' I am often asked. Not always. I have evolved a favourite way of washing self and clothes at Base Camp. I beg a huge aluminium bowl of warm water from the cook-tent, put it in my tent and sit in it. Hair is washed first, using a cup, then I wash the rest of me. After that I stamp on my sweaty clothes in the soapy water like a grape-treading French peasant. The remaining water goes into a heartening soup for visiting trekkers.

'Where do you go to the lavatory?' A favourite question from children, this one. These days we take all solid waste off the mountain, so at Base Camp you sit on a lavatory seat attached to a plastic barrel that is later taken down the valley and emptied into tanks. Local farmers then use this waste as fertiliser. Perched on top of the barrel in full view of the whole Base Camp, but gazing up at the summit, is to experience the sublime and the ridiculous at the same time. Up the mountain I remember performing into a plastic bag on a couple of occasions. I – very carefully – packed these and took them off the mountain.

To help acclimatisation you have to drink far more than you normally would. As a result you have to urinate two or three times at night – but not outside. To prevent frostbite of vital parts we use a pee-bottle inside the tent. Old hands can do this inside their sleeping bag without waking up properly – or knocking over the bottle. The resulting bottleful mustn't be mistaken for your orange juice during the night and must be emptied before it freezes. Women climbers seem to manage all this in a way that seems to involve kneeling. I don't look too closely.

When I woke up at Base Camp on the first day of the expedition I found myself in a bright-orange tent about the same size and shape as a Volkswagen Beetle. I wrote in my diary that I was wearing climbing socks, underpants, a vest, shirt, fleece jacket and a fleece hat. I was lying in a light down bag, inside a thick down expedition sleeping bag, inside a big green Gore-tex bivvi bag. Yet I still woke up cold a couple of times the previous night. Maybe the lack of oxygen caused the internal fires to burn colder. That evening we ate tomato soup, yak steaks and potatoes. And Christmas pudding and brandy sauce.

To reach the summit from Base Camp, you hike up a stony valley for 12 miles past the 80ft-high ice pinnacles shaped like shark's fins, and then labour up Norton's Via Dolorosa. Advanced Base Camp is a motley collection of brightly coloured tents strung along the side of the glacier, directly below the flanks of the mountain. The real climbing begins from here. You have to surmount the 23,000ft (7,010m) saddle of the North

Col, the site of Camp I (this is the same camp as the pre-war Camp IV), then spend a day climbing up Camp II at 25,500ft (7,775m). You spend your last evening before your summit attempt in Camp III at 27,200ft (8,270m) melting snow on your gas stove, desperately trying to get as much liquid on board as possible. On account of the dry air, you ought to drink over a gallon a day. You probably don't have much appetite but you must eat, as a climber burns 15,000 calories on summit day. That's the equivalent of 30 Big Mac hamburgers. The year I climbed Everest I went from twelve stone to ten stone in two months – it is a guaranteed Fat Camp. Because you don't have much appetite at high altitude you tend to over-eat at Base Camp. Where else could you stuff yourself until you're bloated, and still end up losing two stone?

Finally, you get up at midnight and go for the summit, wearing a padded down suit and a rucksack containing a couple of oxygen cylinders and a bottle of water. Using a ratchet device called a jumar, you slide up fixed ropes placed days before by the Sherpas. It is tough, but it is hardly exploration. The whole expedition takes around 12 weeks.

We had joined the 1990 Earth Day 20 International Peace Climb, a combined American–Soviet–Chinese trip led by Jim Whittaker, the first American to climb Everest. It was the first time that the three nations had collaborated to climb a mountain. The plan was to bring together mountaineers from Cold War enemy nations to show what could be accomplished through cooperation. As Whittaker wrote in the 1991 *American Alpine Journal*, 'This was before glasnost, before perestroika, before the Reagan–Gorbachev summit, before Gorbachev went to Beijing. We would hold the summit of all summit meetings, enemies becoming friends.'

The International Peace Climb certainly required diplomatic leadership. We were in Chinese-controlled Tibet, and the Chinese had not allowed Soviets on their soil in 30 years. Whittaker went to both countries to get their leaders' support, and it was a laudable effort on his part.

But it wasn't entirely peaceful. Whittaker had to leave the expedition early on with a medical problem and returned two weeks later to find several disputes brewing. Some of the Soviet climbers – who, frankly, were prima donnas – objected to doing the washing-up, presumably because back home they would have staff to do that sort of thing. Some Chinese climbers were seen hiding food up the hill behind boulders, and some of the Americans complained that they were paying for everything. I witnessed one fist-fight, but the trip was successful in that it got 20 climbers to the top – the highest number on a single expedition thus far. Ed Viesturs, a 30-year-old veterinary surgeon from Seattle, was there on his first Everest summit, and he would go on to climb all the 8,000m peaks without supplementary oxygen. Our filming expedition was a small side-show, although Breashears was clearly respected by the international climbers.

One day we walked up to the main camp with our team to film a satellite phone-call that Whittaker was to make to President George H. W. Bush (the father). As we approached we saw a cluster of worried-looking climbers standing around the vital petrol generator that was supposed to power the presidential call. One by one they would pull on the starter-cord and the engine would run for a minute. Then it would die. Apparently they had tried everything: fresh fuel, fresh oil, new plugs, and so on. But it wouldn't keep running, so the call was off.

As the crowd melted away I decided to take a look, being something of a mechanic. I noticed there was a pair of wires disappearing into a switch mounted on the oil-pan that was designed to turn the engine off if the oil level fell dangerously low. The level was OK on the dip-stick, but what if the switch was faulty? I removed the wires and joined them. Then I pulled the engine into life. It ran – and kept on running. The crowd re-gathered, and our filming was back on. During the satellite call I noticed that Whittaker told the president that 'his team' had fixed the problem. I realised then how easily credit could be appropriated by those in charge – something that I wish I had learned properly, as future events in the same place were going to prove.

In the end, David Breashears, Brian and I, carrying an Arriflex film camera, film magazines and a tape recorder, managed to get to where Somervell sat down to die of asphyxiation on the North Ridge, at approximately 25,500ft (7,750m). I was very conscious that the body that Smythe saw was just a few hundred yards away, but there was nothing I could do. Brian performed heroically in getting himself to that height, and we filmed him there putting on one of his loudest performances. But he was exhausted and could go no higher. As it was, we had to support him back into camp. In the end *Galahad of Everest* was a fine film that still stands up to scrutiny today.

Clearing up our camp on the North Col after our climb I heard a bizarre radio call to a Peace Climb member sitting in the tent next to me. 'Torch all the tents!' This was an odd instruction from someone who must have watched too many Vietnam movies. Presumably it was to save carrying them down the hill. The expedition member dutifully held a cigarette lighter to one of the tents, while the Sherpas watched in horror. The flame didn't catch in the thin air and it resulted only in a small, charred hole. We managed to persuade him that the Soviets might be quite grateful to take something home with them, and later we were treated to the sight of hugely laden haystacks of men wobbling down the slopes.

We sent Brian down ahead of us, and David and I also rolled up all our tents and cooking gear into a huge roll the size of a small car. I tried to get it down the route but it was too heavy to haul on to my back. David sighed with irritation and tried to lift it. No luck, either. So we dragged the great, baggy, orange roll to the edge of the North Col and looked over the edge. We could see Brian Blessed far below, waddling down the snow slopes towards Advanced Base Camp like a hungry bear. Or maybe the Abdominal Snowman. Carefully aiming the roller well away from him, we pushed it off. It started slowly, and then gathered speed, curving unerringly towards the small figure. We watched, silent and appalled, as it accelerated and started bouncing in great leaps. Then together we yelled, 'Brian! Brian! Look behind you!'

Brian, who performs a lot of pantomime, seems to ignore shouts of this kind. The roll took one huge leap and burst above him, showering him with pots, tents and soiled clothing. Dragging a sleeping bag off his head, he slowly turned and shook his fist up at us with rage.

It was a great trip, but what was deeply frustrating was the fact that we were only hours from the spot where I hoped to look for the body. Then the next time I went to Mount Everest I was climbing from the south, Nepali side. And at last I succeeded in getting to the top.

12

High Mountains, Cold Seas

The north and south sides of Mount Everest are very different in character. My generation of climbers has been lucky to be allowed to climb on both sides, whereas the pre- and immediately post-war British expeditions had to make do with either Tibet or Nepal, not both, for political reasons. Air travel has been cheap and fast for us, too, whereas our predecessors had to spend five weeks or more at sea.

For me there are no ethical doubts about visiting Tibet, an occupied country with a terrible record of human rights violations. It is clear to see from the vast amount of resources ploughed into Tibet that China will never return her to the lamas. We, as concerned tourists, can do far more good by going to Tibet and reporting on any wrong-doing we see. For example, climbing friends of mine on Cho Oyu witnessed the shooting of fleeing Tibetan refugees by Chinese soldiers in 2006, and they published reports of this atrocity on the internet. I am convinced that closer ties with China are a good thing for everyone in the long run.

Because of the monsoon rain clouds that surge up from the Bay of Bengal and reach the wall of Himalayas every summer, it is rainy on the southern side, and dry on the north. The result is that the approaches from the south are a delight, with well-forested foothills sprinkled with colourful villages. There are many torrential rivers to cross on high, suspended footbridges, and there are fresh vegetables to buy in the markets along the way.

Mount Everest from the north, in a particularly dry year.

Mount Everest
29,028ft
8,848m

West Ridge

North Face

Norton's high point 28,126ft

Great (Norton) Couloir

Second Step 28,250ft

Somervell's high point 28,000ft

First Step 28,100ft

North-East Ridge

Oxygen bottle found here, 1991 27,800ft

Irvine's ice axe found near here, 1933 27,720ft

Changtse (Bei Peak)

Mallory found here, 1999 26,760ft

North Ridge

Camp VI 26,700ft

Odell's position at sighting 6 June 1924 26,000ft

Camp V 25,000ft

Ruth and George Mallory, soul-
mates who wrote to each other nearly
every day during their long
separations.

Mallory, painted by Duncan
Grant, 1912.

Mallory, photographed by Duncan Grant, 1911.
Mallory told Grant: 'I am profoundly interested in
the nude me.'

A gun crew photographed by the *Daily Mail* on 1 July 1916. Mallory wrote to Ruth lamenting their gun having been 'advertised'. It is possible that the officer in front of the sandbags (right) is Mallory.

Outside the Pen-y-Pass Hotel, North Wales, Easter 1919. Mallory, smoking a pipe, in the driving seat of his Studebaker, with Ruth in trousers (far left). By the braced figures and the hilarity it appears they are about to attempt a push-start.

Howard Somervell: according to Bruce, 'an absolute glutton for hard work . . . extraordinary capacity for going day after day . . . a wonderful goer and climber'.

'Irvine, our blue-eyed boy from Oxford, is much younger than any of us, and is really a very good sort; neither bumptious by virtue of his "blue" nor squashed by the age of the rest of us' (Somervell).

Mallory and Irvine, together from the very beginning of the 1924 expedition, on the deck of the SS *California*.

Somervell (with pipe) and Mallory.

John Noel used to illustrate his lantern-slide lectures with this bird's-eye view of the proposed route to the summit of Everest.

Mallory seemed to delight in removing his clothes at every available opportunity. Here he is about to ford a river on the approach to Everest with George Finch (left) and Arthur Wakefield (centre).

Mallory head-wrestling with Somervell just as the shutter clicks. General Bruce (seated, left) seems bemused.

Morshead, Norton, Somervell and Mallory
(left to right), after their near-fatal first attempt
to climb Everest in 1922.

George Finch. In Bruce's estimation, Finch
was 'probably the best snow and ice man on the
expedition, but has a curious constitution. On
his day can probably last as well as any man,
but apparently very soon shoots his bolt.'

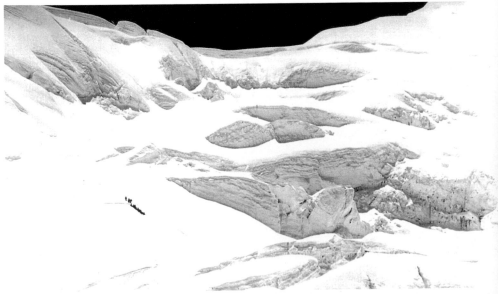

Seconds before the disastrous 1922 avalanche. Somervell wrote:
'. . . with a subdued report ominous in the softness of its violence, a crack
suddenly appeared about 20 feet above me. The snow on which I was standing
began to move, slowly at first then faster.' The photograph possibly shows
the beginning of the avalanche (seen as the fracture between the climbers).
Three climbers survived, and seven Sherpas were killed.

The 1924 expedition members, with George Mallory larking about for the camera as usual. Back row: Irvine, Mallory, Norton, Odell, John Macdonald (acting trade agent); front row: E. O. Shebbeare (transport), Geoffrey Bruce, Somervell, Beetham.

Somervell sketching – a familiar sight in camp.

'Everest is, on its northern aspect, rather a cubist mountain, and to one who, like myself, is of a modern tendency in artistic appreciation, it offered constant satisfaction as a subject for numerous sketches' (Somervell).

Mount Everest from the Pang La pass. This would have been Somervell's first proper view of the mountain, and the first of his many depictions of it.

'Past the 8oft-high ice pinnacles shaped like shark's fins, and then up Norton's Via Dolorosa.' Mallory and Irvine resting on the East Rongbuk glacier.

Mallory, Irvine and three porters. I love this image for so many reasons.

Norton approaching his high point, 28,126ft on Everest's North Face. Note his axe is in the wrong, downhill hand, perhaps a sign of exhaustion.

'When Mallory set off on his expedition he borrowed my camera, and of course it never came back. If ever Mallory's body was found I wonder if the camera will still be in his pocket. If so we may find out whether or not he reached the top' (Somervell in a BBC interview). The last known photograph of Mallory and Irvine alive, taken by Noel Odell.

Dear Noel,

We'll probably start early to-morrow (8th) in order to have clear weather. It won't be too early to start looking out for us either crossing the rockband under the pyramid or going up skyline at 8.0 p.m.

Yr ever

G. Mallory

Mallory's last note to Noel, showing his indecision as to choice of route.

'No trace can be found, given up hope ...' Noel's telephoto photograph of the signal from Camp IV, with sleeping-bags laid out in the snow.

The cairn of 1924, commemorating the dead of three expeditions. The memorial stones, so laboriously inscribed by Beetham and Somervell, have now all been stolen.

The members of the expedition return to Darjeeling without Mallory and Irvine.

A Vest Pocket Kodak, similar to the one that
Somervell lent to Mallory.

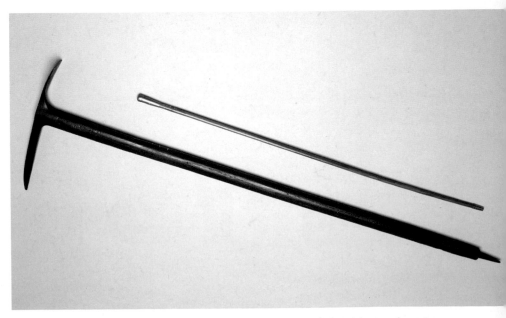

Irvine's ice axe, with his swagger stick beside it, showing
the three notches on each that suggest his ownership.

Mallory's climbing rope, found wrapped around his body, and the 1924-vintage oxygen bottle discovered just below the First Step.

Mallory's goggles, altimeter and penknife.

BASE CAMP (Cont'd).

Date. 1924 May	Barometer.	Temperature. 8.30.	12.	4.		Max.	Min.	Fur.	Hour for fur.	Kata. Noon.
24	16.20	31	38	36	4	49	+12	69	4 P.M.	17"
25	16.25	32	39	42	1	56	+13	65	4 P.M.	24"
26	16.26	42	49	42	3	54	+14	No sun		25"
27	16.25	36	49	42	4	68	+15	102	4 P.M.	26"
28	16.10	35	50	43	1	69	+16	No sun		20"
29	16.30	42	52	50	1	64	+14	102	4 P.M.	31"
30	16.30	39	52	51	1	66	+12	Sun obscured		28"
31	16.30	42	57	55	1	68	+10	120	4 P.M.	30"
June 1	16.25	41	54	53	1	66	+13	106		27"
2	16.30	39.5	56	53	1	69	+13	105.5		26
3	16.375	35.0	55	50	1	64	+12	98		32
4	16.275	38.5	56	55	1	67.5	+11	102		29
5	16.225	40.0	58	55	1	68	+12	99		65
6	16.50	45.0	60	57	1	72	+21	No sun		86
7	16.15	48.5	60.5	59	1	73	+22	88 (½ sun)		53
8	16.25	51.0	58	55	2	-	+25			
9	15.98	-	59	53	3	70	+26	124 at noon		
10	16.43	42	64	49	1½	63	+21			
11	16.36	41	57	53	1	60	+23	123	4 P.M.	28
12	16.38	37			1	63	+14			
13	16.35	43			2		+20			
14					4					
15					3					
16					4	monsoon bad				

The meteorological readings supervised by Somervell. Note the dramatic fall in barometric pressure between 8 and 9 June. By then, Mallory and Irvine were probably dead.

The author on the summit of Everest, 1993.

Russell Brice (left) and the author comparing new
and old Everest clothing.

John Doncaster Hoyland, whose climbing career was cut short on Mont Blanc in 1934.

Brian Blessed was a hugely entertaining addition to any Everest expedition.

Brian dressed as Somervell, sketching Everest from the north.

In contrast, much of Tibet is high-altitude desert – spectacular but hardly comfortable. Mallory loathed the country and its inhabitants. The difference in precipitation is seen on the mountain itself, as on the north side yaks are driven up the relatively dry East Rongbuk glacier to Advanced Base Camp at 21,300ft (6,450m). That is the height of Camp II on the south side, where you have a very active flowing icefall to contend with just after Base Camp.

In 1993 I was employed to guide Brian Blessed on his second attempt to climb the mountain, at an unusual time of year. Because of the difficulty of getting permission from the Nepali authorities we had to go post-monsoon, aiming to summit in early October. This isn't usually a recipe for success. There are few post-monsoon ascents because of the extra snow deposited during the summer, and the less stable weather patterns make climbing extremely difficult.

Unlike the north side in 1990, where Base Camp was pitched on gravel, on the south side of the mountain in 1993 we were camping on a stream of ice. Here's the description from my diary:

It is a stunning location. We are surrounded by the world's highest mountains, and just above camp the infamous Icefall tumbles its way down from the upper slopes of Everest. This vast ice-stream pours over a 600-metre cliff, and its jumbled maze of tottering ice blocks and yawning crevasses is threatened by avalanches from the mountain slopes either side. When the Icefall reaches the valley bottom it becomes the Khumbu glacier, and that's where we are camped.

My tent is bright orange, and therefore seems sunny inside. It is my home for the next two months, and is pitched on pure ice. Inside I have a thick mat between me and the glacier, and there is a double down sleeping bag, which I will use up the mountain. Otherwise, all I have is some clothes, a few books and climbing gear in two plastic barrels. I have an ice axe, a harness and a few bits of hardware to attach me to the mountain.

During the night the slowly flowing ice cracks and groans its way downhill. If you've ever broken a pane of glass by standing on it you'll know exactly what this sounds like. Last night the temperature inside the tent dropped to −12°C, and both the water-bottle and pee-bottle froze solid. The pee-bottle is vital because you really don't want to get out of your bag in these temperatures during the night, particularly high up.

In the morning the Sherpas arrive with bed tea. When the sun hits the tent the frozen condensation from my night's breath melts and it starts to snow – inside the tent. Very soon, though, the temperature shoots up to around 30°C and it is impossible to stay in it. You can see these extremes of temperature on the washing line outside; at one end is a frozen sock in shadow, and at the other end is its companion steaming in the sun. Further up the mountain, above the Icefall, camp life is going to become even more extreme.

Things have changed since 1993. The romantic picture of climbing Mount Everest that I had as a boy has largely been destroyed by the sheer numbers that climb it now. There weren't plastic flowers and hot showers at Advanced Base Camp commercial expeditions provide now – just a tarpaulin stretched over a couple of rubble walls. Nor was there a line of fixed ropes stretched all the way to the summit to climb up. We escaped three huge avalanches by the skin of our teeth. One of them swept down the Lhotse Face, gathering up all the oxygen, food and ropes we had deposited at Camp III, and burying them under thousands of tons of snow. We had carried the loads there a couple of hours earlier, and I counted that there had been 28 climbers on the route that day. It could have been an appalling disaster. As it was, our Camp III was completely wiped out, and we had to start again from scratch.

When I eventually got to the highest camp, on the South Col at 25,940ft (7,906m), we didn't find the camp already set up by the Sherpas so I had to help the expedition leader put up four tents. As we put each one up, our fellow climbers gratefully slid inside. Steve Bell and I got into the last one, and I have to say that was my proudest moment ever on the mountain – helping to set up such a high camp. And to me that is mountaineering: solving problems and helping your companions to get to the summit.

It was two o'clock in the morning when we left the tents for the summit. There had been a full gale blowing across the South Col since we arrived, and I crawled out into the darkness of a blizzard. We were using oxygen masks, but my valve kept freezing up with saliva. Steve yelled, 'Lead off, Graham!' Stepping forward in a pool of head-torch light we all entered into our own private nightmares.

A couple of figures – Sherpa or Westerner, we couldn't see which – dropped back and gave up during the night. Looking to my left down into Nepal I saw one tiny glimmer of light from the monastery at Thyangboche, down there in the real world. My torch was just giving up when I noticed a faint glow on my right, away towards Tibet. It was the dawn, the most welcome dawn of my life. I sat down on the Balcony – a ledge with a stupendous view at about 27,500ft (8,380m) – and tried to pull my oxygen mask off for repairs, but it was stuck to the beard I had unwisely grown during the expedition. I needed to get it off, though, and so had to pull off mask, beard and a large patch of skin. I then tried to have a drink, but to my astonishment and dismay the boiling water I had poured into the insulated bottle in my rucksack had somehow frozen into a block of ice. On we climbed, and I was surprised at just how steep it became.

The Sherpas are notorious smokers, and as I reached the South Summit I smelled tobacco smoke. There, leaning against a boulder, was one of the Sherpas, taking alternate puffs on his oxygen mask and his morning ciggie. I plodded around the

South Summit to see the final obstacles – the summit ridge, the infamous Hillary Step, and then, in the far distance, the summit itself.

The step is a 30ft rocky hiccup on the narrow summit ridge, first climbed, to his eternal credit, by Edmund Hillary. It is a very exposed place, and I had been worrying about it since I was a boy. Just as I reached its foot my oxygen valve became completely blocked and I actually lost consciousness for a few moments. But I managed to get the mask off again and gasp my way up the faded and frayed ropes that weren't hanging there when Hillary climbed his step. Three years later Bruce Herrod, a friend of mine, was to die on this very spot, and hung from those very ropes for months. As I jumared my way up them I wondered what they were attached to. This is what I wrote in my diary afterwards:

Once above the step I just kept teetering along that narrow icy summit ridge between Nepal and Tibet, between life and death. The sun was intensely bright and the sky was that deep blue-black of very high altitudes. All around were the icy fins of the world's highest mountains. And somewhere along that ridge I experienced one of those existential moments that is the reason you gamble your life. The intenseness of the now, the sharp savour of living wholly in the present moment, no past, no worries. The chop of the ice axe, the crunch of the crampons, the hiss of breath – this is the very stuff of life. Eventually I saw a couple of figures just above me, a couple of steps … and I was there.

I can't remember much. Now it all seems some sort of vivid dream; bright sunlight, a tearing wind, a long flag of ice particles flying downwind of us. A vast drop of two miles into Tibet. We could see across 100 miles of tightly packed peaks, and we could see the curvature of the earth. Contorted faces shouting soundlessly, lips blue with oxygen starvation. Doctors prove with blood samples that climbers are actually in the process of dying up there on the summit, but I would say that is where I started to live.

Up there I had a weird awareness that our notions of time are all wrong, that future events become the past with no intervening present moment, which seems entirely a construct of consciousness.

I had finally climbed the mountain in 1993, becoming the 15th Briton to stand on that supreme summit. Little larger than a dining-room table, it seemed a strange reason for so many deaths. I had passed five corpses in the snow on the way up, dead from cold, exhaustion and avalanches. And a Basque climber I passed on my descent slipped a few moments later and was killed in a 3,000ft fall. He was a nice lad and we were all shocked by this event.

On the way down the Hillary Step, I managed to drop my abseil device, an aluminium figure-of-8, and as it bounced and rang down the slabs of the South-West Face I thought I was hearing my death-knell. My eternal gratitude goes to team leader Steve Bell, who helped me make an abseil device with a couple of karabiners, and so I got down the ropes. Brian Blessed managed to get up to the South Col, which was a superb effort, but I realised how frustrated he must have felt at not getting to the top.

Although ascents from the north and south are somewhat different, I learned two things relevant to the Mallory mystery. One was just how long summit day is – we were out for around 16 hours. The second thing was the power of summit fever. Once I had the summit in view I distinctly remember deciding I was going to carry on until I got to the top, or died in the attempt.

Climbing that mountain was certainly the hardest thing I have ever had to do, and for a long time afterwards it left a strange rage and emptiness that I don't really understand. At the very least it cleared up a bit of family business. It had taken me exactly 22 years and 8 months to do it, from the meeting between a 13-year-old boy and an 81-year-old hero. I vaguely remember looking down on the great North Face from above and thinking that I might have climbed this mountain, but I still had to find that camera. That was the next job.

After climbing Everest everything disintegrated in my life. I separated from my girlfriend of 12 years. My previous mental state had seemed to alternate between elation on expeditions and depression between them. Immediately after the expedition this wrought-up state seemed to rapidly unwind. Even though I was invited to Downing Street and met the prime minister, I still felt terrible, and just when people were saying 'You must be feeling amazing!' I was actually staring into the abyss. The achievement of a long-held desire had not made me happy, and in fact, for some reason, I felt ashamed.

I am not a psychoanalyst so I won't indulge in too much Freudian self-analysis. As British comedian Ken Dodd said, 'The trouble with Freud is that he never played the Glasgow Empire on a Saturday night.' Theories about human behaviour are all very well, but it is the knock-about course of your life that shows you who you really are. Suffice to say that a deep examination of what led me to that mountain pulled me through.

Becoming the 15th Briton to summit Everest (or perhaps the 17th?) gave me the credentials to get work on a BBC film on Mount McKinley in Alaska – these days usually called by its indigenous name, Denali – about the British marine Alan Perrin, who although severely disabled got most of the way to the top. He made a good point to me – at high altitude we are all disabled.

Denali is a very cold mountain, and I remember the camera-man refusing to work one morning until the temperature in our tent rose to –35°C. I managed to get to the icy top of the mountain, thereby achieving the second of my seven summits. Unfortunately, one of my companions took this opportunity to announce that he had just gone blind. I had to put a short sling on him and together we inched back along the icy crest, *à cheval* – like straddling a horse. He kept on wanting to lie down and rest, but I wouldn't let him. That is the way of death. To our relief his loss of sight resolved on descending to thicker air.

Also with us was one of the more colourful characters of British climbing, John Barry, and through him I met Rebecca Stephens, the first British woman to climb Mount Everest. Rebecca and I were partners for a while, splitting up after a rather fraught voyage in a yacht to Antarctica across the Southern Ocean in 1995.

In 1996 I moved to BBC Manchester for a new job and met Sarah Champion, the young woman who would eventually become my ex-wife and would even later become the Labour MP for Rotherham. I submitted the *Mallory's Camera* idea once again. This time, being an Everest summiteer gave me a little more persuasive power with my proposal.

Just before then I had got to know a photographer, Bruce Herrod, and we became friends. He asked me a lot about climbing Mount Everest, which was one of his ambitions. He wasn't, however, a hugely experienced climber. One day he called and asked if I would be interested in working with a South African expedition on the mountain, and I said I would. He telephoned again and again, checking to see what cameras I might use and which batteries survive in the cold. The next thing I knew was that he was booked on the expedition as cameraman. In view of what was to happen in 1996 I wish he had never called. When I heard the news of his death later that season a cold hand grasped my heart.

In the spring of 1996, David Breashears was in Kathmandu to make an IMAX film about Mount Everest. With him was Audrey Salkeld, and he rang me to see whether I was available to work with them on what became a hugely successful film. I was committed to a new job, and I am glad I missed the deadly season that has been immortalised in Jon Krakauer's book *Into Thin Air*.

My quest for answers to the Mallory mystery started to turn up respondents, and in April 1998 a 28-year-old German geology student, Jochen Hemmleb, contacted me with a list of questions about Everest. I replied, saying that we could meet up as by chance I happened to have a trip to Germany coming up. I met Jochen in the pleasant city of Stuttgart. He struck me as a nice lad, very serious about his subject, which was the attempt to locate the position of Mallory or Irvine's body, using photographs of the Chinese camp at which Wang Hong Bao had been staying when he made his find.

During the interview I began to feel slightly uncomfortable about the intensity of Jochen's interest. He quizzed me hard about what I knew, but I didn't mention the sighting of the body at the bottom of the scree slope. He said he would keep in touch. Then he sent me a document outlining his intentions. He had certainly done his homework on the Chinese photographs, and I found that some of what he wrote struck a chord:

> dreams can become like avalanches. First you marvel at the force slowly building up, almost enjoying it, until there is the frightful realisation that it might carry you away and you have to give in – which is often the point at which you learn to play the game anew, riding the tide rather than swimming against it.
>
> I am afraid of getting carried away by this game, that this time my obsession might drive me over the edge.

People have always used Mount Everest – and what it signifies – as a means to further their own agendas. One Englishman who mixed up religion and Everest in a deadly brew came to a sad end. In July 1935 Charles Warren of Eric Shipton's expedition found the body of Maurice Wilson lying near the site of Camp III. He had attempted to climb the mountain alone to prove the power of his religion founded on faith and fasting.

Wilson was another of those lost souls who had been through the First World War and couldn't settle down. He had been injured in the chest and arm by machine-gun fire at Ypres, and on his return home found life in Bradford too dull. The pain in his arm plagued him all his life. He emigrated first to the US and then to New Zealand, becoming successful as a businessman but never quite satisfied. Returning to England he was clearly approaching a nervous breakdown, but healed himself by a mystery cure that seemed to involve 35 days of fasting, and then praying to be well again. This regime seems to be one of his own invention, based on an encounter with Eastern yoga mystics on the boat home. He emerged from the cure a new man with a purpose in life: to spread the word of his new faith. Knowing that he would gain huge public attention for his ideas if he pulled off the stunt, he settled on the idea of climbing Mount Everest solo, despite never having approached a mountain in his life.

He resolved to crash-land an airplane on the East Rongbuk glacier, so bought a Gipsy Moth biplane that he named *Ever Wrest*, and learned to fly. Defying the British authorities, he gained a great deal of press coverage. On the day of departure from England, and distracted by the watching journalists and photographers, he took off down-wind instead of facing into the wind, but somehow made it into the air (I have noticed that the presence of a camera often distracts contributors trying to concentrate). He flew out to Lalbalu, near Purneah in India, which was the same airfield used by the Duke of Hamilton on his flights the previous year. Here the British Raj caught up with Wilson and his plane was impounded.

If only he had left it there he might have gathered some followers and built a cult following. But being the stubborn Yorkshireman that he was, he had to go the whole hog by recruiting Sherpas, disguising himself as a lama and trekking to the Rongbuk valley. Clearly a tough and resourceful man, he did it in ten days fewer than the previous British expedition. However, his total lack of mountaineering ability meant that he could not find a route up the East Rongbuk glacier to Camp III and had to return to the monastery. On his second attempt he appears to have got stuck under an ice chimney below the North Col. His last diary entry records his third attempt: 'Off again, gorgeous day.' His body was found the following year. In the end faith alone was not enough.

Maurice Wilson and plenty of other people subsequently have focused inappropriate amounts of attention on Mount Everest. I have, too. It might be a way of redeeming your perceived failures in life, or it might be seen as a ticket to success. I knew one thing from my own family's experience: an obsessive interest in mountaineering is dangerous. So although I was interested in Jochen's theories that the Chinese camp's position could be located, I didn't particularly want to go climbing with him. I suggested to Jochen that if I got a commission from the BBC to make the film he would be welcome to come along to Base Camp and help out.

Before I tried the BBC again with my *Mallory's Camera* proposal I thought I had better find out more about the object we were trying to find. In the account of the 1924 expedition Bentley Beetham wrote a section on photography. Because John Noel was busy with his cinema work the stills photography fell to the other members of the trip, using their own raggle-taggle collection of personal cameras.

> Our photographic outfit was most essentially of the tourist description – a battery of nine hand-cameras among ten men! These ranged in size from a spacious post-card down to the vanishing point in the V.P.K.'s. These latter are probably ideal for photography high up on the mountains, where every ounce of weight and every mechanical detail, bother, or intri-

cacy, are of importance, and it may be mentioned that it was with such an instrument that Somervell, on two successive Expeditions, took his wonderful pictures above 25,000 feet.[1]

The Vest Pocket Kodak was a folding camera made by Eastman Kodak from 1912 to 1926. They were very high-tech for their day, being the first to use the tiny 127 film reels. I have my own next to me and it is even smaller than a modern digital bridge camera, sliding into an inside pocket with ease. The 'Autographic' version even had a slide-out door so that the photographer could write notes on the paper backing of the film. This version was known as the 'Soldier's Camera' as a result of its popularity during the First World War, and I think this is the actual model Somervell owned.

In 1998 I wrote to Martin Wood at Kodak Professional for some more information on the camera and film that Somervell lent to Mallory. He pointed out that film recovered from Salomon August Andrée's balloon attempt on the North Pole was successfully developed years after the photographs were taken. Reconnaissance films from aircraft that had crashed into lakes or sea during the Second World War showed that film could survive remarkably well under adverse conditions. Martin thought that we might be in with a chance, as the film would have almost certainly remained frozen through the years. He advised placing the camera very carefully inside black bags such as those used for unexposed film, then developing the film at Base Camp.

This sounded a terrifying proposition, but on re-reading the Beetham account it was clear that they had a successful developing regime in place in 1924. Noel had brought a portable darkroom and they experimented with developing solution. It was heated by a yak-dung stove. Somervell found that he had to double its strength and double the time to get acceptable results.

I far preferred to get any recovered camera back to England and the experts at the BBC and Kodak. Avoiding the X-ray machines in airports would be fraught with difficulty, but I felt that the next approach might be to Her Majesty's Government for permission to place it in the diplomatic bag.

Who owns the camera and any image found? The camera belonged to Somervell, as did the roll of film, but who would own any image retrieved? This was important to me in 1998 as I wanted to make the film about Mallory's last climb, so I asked the BBC's lawyers for an opinion. They replied that copyright law in Tibet of the 1920s was somewhat obscure. However, as the participants were British – and the Royal Geographical Society and Alpine Club were also British – then British copyright law would probably obtain, even though the images were made in Tibet (please don't even think about the summit being half in Nepal). The act that was in force was the Copyright Act of 1911.

The lawyers concluded that John Noel, who had made the expedition possible by his payment of £8,000, signed a contract giving him all photographic rights. He died in 1989, so the material is in copyright for 70 years from then, until 2059. The camera and film, as Somervell's chattels, belong to his heirs and assigns. It is odd that Hinks's influence extends beyond even today. Even if the film were developed in the US – as was encouraged by one researcher with questionable motives – British law would probably prevail.

However, as greed for a big-dollar pay-out is high in some minds, expect a big legal battle. And who will win? Only the lawyers.

13
The Finding of
Mallory's Body

On 26 September 1998 the *Independent* published an article announcing my expedition to go in search of Mallory's camera. After years of trying, the BBC had finally accepted my proposal – but in a complicated way. The proposal had gone in under the aegis of BBC Manchester, but they had passed it on to BBC Bristol, where executive producer Dick Colthurst had become interested in it. Eventually, a producer named Peter Firstbrook called me to discuss the proposal. It would form part of a series of six, and he would be the executive producer.

I met Firstbrook and explained that the best way to mount the expedition would be to go as part of Russell Brice's annual commercial expedition to the north side of Mount Everest. That way we would buy into the best operator and the strongest Sherpas. Most importantly, though, I knew I could trust Brice to handle the subject carefully. We might have to deal with a corpse, and I knew that the families' sensitivities should be respected. My own family had been badly affected by John Hoyland's death, and I knew we could cause a great deal of pain by insensitive handling of the subject. On the other hand, we would be celebrating Mallory and Irvine's lives, and possibly proving that they had succeeded in their attempt.

I contacted both the Irvine and the Mallory families, and was able to go and see the Irvines in England. I asked if we found Sandy Irvine whether they would like a cairn built over the body and what committal service would be appropriate. They were most helpful, providing copies of Sandy Irvine's letters that sketched in his character for me. I knew that members of the Mallory family were going to be harder to track down as John, George Mallory's son, was living in South Africa. I wrote to him, asked permission to search for his father's body, and enquired what he would like done with the body, should we find it. He answered:

> Frankly, I query whether the recovery of the camera and possible solving of the 'mystery' is worth the risks always inherent to any venture on Everest. But that is, of course, for you to decide. If you do find a body, my father's or Irvine's, I really doubt you will either find suitable material even for a cairn over it, nor at that altitude are you likely to have much spare energy; but I think that would be best, if practical.[1]

I also tracked down Mallory's grandson, also named George, as I knew he had climbed the mountain in 1995 to 'complete family business', as he put it. We corresponded for a while and I asked for his permission to undertake a search. He answered:

> I'm really not sure you need my permission to look for the body of George Mallory or Sandy Irvine ... My main concern is that the character of my grandfather (and the others too) is not tarnished. I hope that, whether you find the camera or not, you will make use of the opportunity to point out, to those who want to know, the differences between those brave mountaineers and today's typical Everest 'wannabees'. Everest in the 1920s was on the cutting edge, these days it's a trade route.[2]

George's reply was in line with my feelings about the subject, which is why I was mortified at what eventually happened.

I had also contacted Peter Firth, an ex-BBC colleague who was at that time the Bishop of Malmesbury, and I asked him to write an appropriate committal service to read over the body of

Mallory or Irvine. As for the British climbing establishment, I wrote to Lord Hunt, leader of the first successful Everest expedition of 1953. I knew him through the Alpine Club, and explained that I was trying to find Mallory's camera, and that there would be an outside chance of changing mountaineering history, and thereby denying his status as leader of the first ascent. He was typically generous, and made it clear that success in 1924 was a possibility in his mind:

> I wish you well in your search for this important clue to the fate – success or failure – of Mallory and Irvine in 1924.[3]

Having received the blessing – or at any rate, the agreement – of everyone who might be upset, I relaxed a bit. I didn't realise that I was now risking my reputation on the actions of other individuals.

At around about this time, working hard on putting together a search for Mallory, I bought a house at Ford Hall, Chapel-en-le-Frith, Derbyshire, after selling my previous home in Somerset. It was a pleasant stone-built place, somewhat in the Arts and Crafts style. I don't expect anyone to believe this, but after I had agreed the purchase the owner said, 'Oh, by the way, the last owner was a cousin of that Everest chap, what's his name? Mallory.' It turned out that the Longridges, relatives of Mallory's nephew Ben, had indeed owned Ford House. I attach no significance to this; it just goes to show that England is a small place. Mobberley, where Mallory was born, is only a few miles away in the next county.

I also completed a novel I had been working on, an adventure yarn about finding Mallory's body. I little knew I was about to shoot myself in the foot, being responsible for finding the actual body, and therefore making the novel impossible to publish.

I met Firstbrook in Bristol and took him to a meeting with Brice near Wells, the Somerset town with its fine cathedral. I explained all the family contacts and arrangements I had made, and as far I as understood we were going with Brice. Young Jochen Hemmleb was invited to come along, too. Even though we were working closely together in a production team, without telling me Firstbrook had then gone to the US with a possible director, Matt Dickinson, to meet up with Eric Simonson, another commercial expedition operator, who was looking for business. ('Didn't I tell you?' Firstbrook asked later.) Firstbrook presumably wanted American climbers on the film so that he could co-produce it with an American TV company. Then the question arose of who would write the expedition book for the BBC. I wanted to tell Somervell's story and the background of my researches, and I submitted a chapter and the synopsis of this book I am writing now to my BBC bosses. To my disappointment, Peter Firstbrook won the contract. I began to feel that I was losing control of a subject I knew could potentially be very sensitive.

Many commercial expeditions are advertised without the acknowledgement that if the necessary funds are not raised, the expedition will not take place. Perhaps Firstbrook was concerned that there would be some kind of race to search for bodies from the two teams, but I knew very well that Simonson's trip was unlikely to happen unless he got considerable funding. Firstbrook's arrival with BBC money was a godsend. The trip could run. Then I discovered that Jochen Hemmleb was going with Simonson instead of our BBC team. And the next thing I knew was that Brice had been dropped, and that our precious BBC funding was going to pay for a large element of Simonson's expedition. I was very unhappy about this decision.

In the event Matt Dickinson opted out of the project and Firstbrook appointed me high-altitude director. At least my name was in the expedition prospectus as the initial founder of the Mallory project, but acknowledgements of my efforts were few and far between. We went out to Kathmandu in March 1999. I knew Firstbrook was a diabetic and promised his wife that I'd keep an eye out for him. As a non-climber he wouldn't be travelling far out of Base Camp. We flew out with 500kg of excess baggage in 44 bags of film gear (I remembered that the 1924 expedition had 1,000 cases of gear). We arrived in Kathmandu to hear some shocking news: a German newspaper report that a Japanese team had found Mallory's camera! It turned out to be a complete misunderstanding of a *Mail on Sunday* report, but it shows how jumpy we were.

We met the American team and they actually turned out to be a nice bunch: Conrad Anker, already with a fine reputation, on his first expedition above 24,000ft (7,300m); Dave Hahn and Andy Politz, both Everest veterans; and Jake Norton (no relation of Colonel Norton) and Tap Richards, two likeable young climbers. They didn't seem to know very much about Mallory, and they still mispronounce Irvine's name (which rhymes with Mervin). Liesl Clark (who was now David Breashears's girlfriend after his divorce) would film for NOVA, with Ned Johnston as camera-man. Breashears was giving input as executive producer back in the States. How I wished he was there to steer the expedition! Everyone was welcoming and I genuinely enjoyed their company. Eric Simonson I had already met in London, and we got on very well, although I could see he had a robust leadership style. Jochen I had already met, and we found we had a great deal to talk about.

Everything started well but went sour pretty quickly. Peter Firstbrook and Eric Simonson travelled through Tibet arguing over the contract and a final payment that hadn't been dealt with earlier. I note from my diary that in Zhangmu Hotel (which had improved noticeably) Eric told me, 'Do not expect any warm feelings from us.' As a result there was mutual distrust and the seeds of disagreement were sown.

I have now worked on many filmed expeditions, and I have learned that one has to work very hard to keep film-makers and climbers on the same side. In 2006 on the North Ridge and in 2007 on the South Col route I made sure that film-makers and climbers travelled together, ate together and climbed together, and the result was much more harmonious expeditions.

We travelled to Tingri, where Jochen said he felt unwell, so I volunteered to stay another night there with him. I felt we had much in common and my diary notes that 'I do like him – he's sweet and open + earnest.' I admitted to him that I had a bad feeling about the mountain this year, telling him, 'Whenever I come here I feel the ghosts of Everest all around.' In the event this ominous feeling was justified, but perhaps the remark gave him the title for his book.

On the plus side the expedition had had a good start, with none of the usual respiratory or gastric infections that often bedevil travel in Tibet. We arrived at Base Camp early in the season, on 29 March, to see Everest in the driest condition any one of us had seen. This was a very good sign for a search party. We were also an extremely strong team, with seven of the 12 Sherpas having summited at least once previously, as had four of the Westerners.

There was the usual puja ceremony before we started climbing, which we were invited to attend. We always make a big event of this on every expedition because we know how important it is to the Sherpas; the safety of the climb depending on a successful outcome of the service. We all put our ice axes and crampons on a roughly constructed altar that is laden with offerings such as butter, whisky bottles and Marmite. A lama was asked to come up from the monastery to undertake the ceremony. Juniper smoke wafted towards the mountain and rice was thrown into the air to placate the mountain gods. Long lines of prayer flags radiated from the altar like the spokes of a wheel.

During the rather lengthy service the climbers became aware that there was the sloshing sound of clothes being washed just next to the moraine. Then I saw Firstbrook, sleeves rolled up, manfully pummelling his underwear. There were mutters and sideways looks from the Sherpas. Poor Peter didn't realise his solecism, so I had to race down the side of the hill and ask him to stop. After this episode the scowls from Sherpas and climbers alike became more and more evident. Washing his dirty laundry in public had turned out to be a bad idea.

I was feeling more and more disturbed by the growing conflict between the camps, and I tried my very best to smooth things between them. I worked on assembling a camera crane and helped to get shots of the climbers walking through the camp. Things went well at first, with some beautiful filming by Ned Johnston using a yak-portable crane up in the *penitentes*. But then personal disaster struck. When we eventually headed up the Rongbuk valley I had to wait around in a cutting wind while Ned filmed me. Then there weren't enough tents to go around at interim camp and I got a chill. Approaching Camp III at 22,000ft (6,700m) I became aware of a spreading numbness in my face and in my foot. I realised I was having a TIA – a transient ischaemic attack. This is a temporary spasm of a blood vessel in the brain, cutting off oxygen to part of it. I still had symptoms in the morning, so I had a discussion with Eric Simonson, who was very sympathetic. He told me he'd had a similar but worse episode years before on Everest that left him without sensation down his left side for a couple of years. By continuing up the mountain I risked another episode, and Eric made it clear that I could not expect rescue from high on the North Face.

I found out later that these TIAs are fairly commonplace at altitude but clearly one should not continue upwards. I could have remained safely at Base Camp, and in fact I could have contributed to the interpretations of the eventual findings, but Firstbrook took the opportunity to send me home, despite the fact that his own condition was worsening. His book was coming along fast.

In *Ghosts of Everest*, Hemmleb and Simonson's book of the expedition, they have this to say:

> Though the crisis had clearly passed and he could certainly be of value even at Base Camp, Hoyland's boss, BBC series direc-tor Peter Firstbrook, hustled him off the expedition to

Kathmandu, an ignoble and, to the rest of the expedition members, unfair fate for someone who had been so central to the idea of the expedition in the first place.[4]

Later on Firstbrook became so ill that the expedition doctor, Lee Meyers, thought he would die. 'I thought it interesting,' commented Eric Simonson, 'that when Graham Hoyland got sick, Firstbrook insisted that he leave the expedition immediately, citing BBC rules. But when Firstbrook himself became ill – much more seriously ill than Hoyland – he simply refused to leave, despite our doctor's orders.'[5]

I turned my back on Mount Everest and walked the 12 miles down the glacier back to Base Camp. I got in a jeep to Kathmandu and returned to England to watch events unfold on the Internet and the satellite phone. In the end one of the climbers, Conrad Anker, found a body in just 90 minutes of looking, exactly where Smythe had seen it. Oddly enough there were times when I felt I knew more about what was happening on the upper mountain than my film colleagues at Base Camp, as although there was radio silence from Advanced Base Camp, their daily internet bulletins continued.

When I heard that in the course of the first search Conrad had found the body of George Mallory, not Sandy Irvine, I was surprised. We had assumed the body described by Wang was that of Irvine, because it was his ice axe above the body, and indeed that was the first reaction of the climbers on the spot. When I flew back to Kathmandu to pick up the film gear at the end of the expedition we all met up in the Rum Doodle bar, and I got the story at first hand from the man who found him. I wrote this interview up for *High* magazine on my return:

Conrad Anker is one of the world's boldest climbers – and a lovely guy – and it was entirely appropriate that he should be the one who found George Mallory. He told me how he and Andy Politz, Dave Hahn, Jake Norton and Tap Richards had left Camp V, at 25,700ft, at 5:00am on 1 May to go up to Camp VI. They got there at 10:00am and split up to look around the area where the 1975 Chinese Camp had been. He spotted a couple of modern bodies and then in the course of removing his crampons to climb up some rock suddenly saw a patch of white, a patch that seemed even whiter than the surrounding snow.

It was a body, bleached to an extraordinary degree by 75 years of sun. He radioed his companions with the cryptic request for 'a mandatory group meeting' and they began the lengthy process of identifying the body.

Dave Hahn broke in here and said that it looked like a white marble Greek statue. I remembered Lytton Strachey's gushing description of George Mallory's body as a sculpture by Praxiteles, and thought that it had come only too true.

It looked as though he had died from a fall. There was some trauma, but the body hadn't been beaten to bits so he probably hadn't fallen all the way from the North-East Ridge crest where the ice axe had been discovered in 1933. It was obvious that the birds had found him. There was a perfectly preserved hob-nail boot on his right foot and a boot top fracture of his tibia and fibula above that. This was the leg that he had broken in his youth. There was also a piece of white cotton rope around his waist which had snapped, and I was stunned when I saw the piece the team had brought back down with them. It was about ten millimetres in diameter, and frankly one wouldn't tie a dressing-gown with it. The rope was knotted with a bowline, and had caused severe crushing and bruising to the ribs consistent with a free fall to the *left* of perhaps 30 feet. There was a severe head injury above one eye. He was lying face down, and had arrested his fall with outstretched hands after sliding some distance down the snow slopes. Strangely, the hands appeared to be darker than the rest of the body, perhaps suggesting some frostbite before death – or was it the remains of a tan? All the witnesses felt that he had survived the fall, and composed himself to die, crossing his unbroken leg over the other to get some last relief.

They weren't sure whether to disturb the body, but wanted to see if he had succeeded in reaching the summit and so they started looking for a camera. At this stage they were still assuming this was Irvine, as the hair appeared to be blond. In cutting away some clothing, Jake came upon a label that said 'G. Mallory'. They all looked at each other and said, 'Why would Andrew Irvine be wearing George Mallory's shirt?' Then it finally dawned on their oxygen-starved brains that they hadn't found Irvine. They hadn't just found Wang Hong Bao's English dead. They had found George Leigh Mallory himself.

There were a number of artefacts removed from the body; some goggles found in his breast-pocket, an altimeter calibrated up to 30,000ft, some letters, a penknife, some scissors, a couple of monogrammed handkerchiefs with his G.L.M. initials on them and a watch.

After they had removed all the artefacts the climbers read a short Christian committal prayer that the Bishop of Malmesbury had prepared for them. They then buried the body, safe, I hope, from the birds and the souvenir-hunters.

Later in the expedition came a very creditable rescue of a Ukrainian climber by our climbers, and then a successful summit bid when Conrad Anker, accompanied by Dave Hahn, climbed the Second Step trying not to use the Chinese ladder. He had to place one foot on it as a rung was in the way. This he did partly to attempt a 'clean' climb of the North Ridge, without using artificial aids. They also wanted to see if it would have been possible for Mallory and Irvine to surmount this obstacle. I watched the BBC rushes of this climb, and

Conrad said at the top of the Second Step that he didn't think the pair could have done it. Later he revised this opinion. Then one of Mallory and Irvine's oxygen cylinders was found by Jake and Tap behind a boulder beyond the First Step, confirming a previous sighting of it by leader Eric Simonson. Thus ended an eventful expedition.

What can we conclude from all of this? We can speculate that Mallory and Irvine were descending, possibly in the dark or in poor visibility, when the fall occurred. This is suggested by the direction of the rope injuries (they were indicative of a fall to the left, which would be consistent with the direction of travel if descending this part of the route) and by the fact that the goggles were in his pocket. It was reported that Mallory was still carrying three or four coils in his right hand and it looks as though the rope snapped after taking the weight of a free fall – there was a clean break. This suggests that either it was deliberately hooked over a rock horn, or that it snagged. In this case, we are left with Sandy Irvine alive high up the North Face, possibly in the dark, alone. What would he do? Would he circle around beneath the fall-line, looking for Mallory? Or could it be that he sat down behind a rock and waited for a dawn that would never arrive for him?

So where was Sandy Irvine's body, and was Somervell's camera on him? Why was Mallory not carrying the camera, when Somervell distinctly remembered him putting it in a pocket? Was it because Irvine was taking a picture of George Mallory? And why would he do that? Either to record the highest point they reached, or maybe because they were on the summit together?

This whole discovery left me with more questions than it answered. At the very beginning of it all, I knew that we couldn't prove that they didn't summit, but with luck perhaps that they did. Therefore I hoped that we wouldn't damage the legend of George Mallory that has been so important to me all my life.

Even though we have now found his body, for me he still stands for the quality I most admire in our species: the triumph of the human spirit over apparent impossibility, and the triumph of the human spirit over the inevitability of death.[6]

But then events started spiralling out of control. Photographs of the corpse were sold around the world and the reputation of the expedition became tarnished. There was a big fuss about the way the photographs were sold to the press, which I think was largely a consequence of naivety on the part of the Simonson team. Unfortunately, John Mallory, the son, opened a newspaper at his home in South Africa and was confronted by a picture of his father's corpse.

I was mortified. I felt that if only we had stuck with Russell Brice we would have found the body, as we knew exactly where to look. We certainly would not have sold pictures of the dead body. This might have contained the press criticism. Once again money was calling the shots on Mount Everest. Firstbrook warned me to be 'very careful' when an article by Ed Douglas appeared in the *Observer*, in which Douglas wrote:

Close-up pictures of the body of Mallory, dubbed the Galahad of Everest, are reported to have been sold to *Newsweek* magazine for more than $40,000 by the expedition searching for clues on the mountain to prove whether or not Mallory had reached the summit before his death. Last night the picture agency Rex Features, which controls the copyright to the photographs in Britain, circulated warnings to national newspapers that they would face legal action if they published the photographs. Family members and leading mountaineers have condemned the sale of the photographs and accuse the American climbers who found Mallory of exploitation. 'Frankly, it makes me bloody angry,' George Mallory II, grandson of the climber – who reached the summit of Everest in 1995 via the same route his grandfather attempted – told the *Observer* from his home in New Zealand. 'It's like digging for diamonds, without having to do any of the digging.'

[T]he decision to sell photographs of Mallory's body has alienated leading mountaineers. Sir Chris Bonington, who led three expeditions to Everest and reached the summit in 1985, has lost several friends on the mountain. He said: 'I'm absolutely appalled by this. Words can't express how disgusted I am. It's a disgrace. These people don't deserve to be called climbers.' The Everest historian Audrey Salkeld, who has been acting as a consultant for Nova, the US television production company which is making a film about the discovery, said: 'I'm horrified it's got to this stage. I feel very uncomfortable about it.'[7]

I think the American team was surprised by the vehemence of the reaction from George Mallory's grandson, Bonington and others, but if they had paused for a moment and thought about it they might have desisted. Money was clearly tight but one has to balance gain against integrity. Imagine foreign archaeologists digging up Elvis Presley at Graceland and selling pictures of his corpse. Or excavating and photographing a war hero in Arlington Cemetery.

It appears that the body could have been treated with greater care during the process of extricating it from the ground. Footage existed that I was never shown, and Wade Davis describes the scene:

[T]he suggestion that the body was handled with deference is a matter of interpretation. For several hours the search party hacked and gouged the frozen ground with ice axes and knives, prying up the limbs, crudely tearing at the clothing, creating the very cloth fragments later so carefully catalogued as rare specimens at base camp. At one point a climber is seen standing on Mallory's left leg as he struggles to prop up the torso of the cadaver. 'He's almost free, let's go ahead and free him,' says one voice. 'There's still some more shit here,' comments another. 'This is something … I think it's frozen fucking closed,' ends another exchange.[8]

A rumour suggested that Mallory's axe was found at some later time near his body, but this has never been accounted for. It remains an open question, and I hope the axe has not been spirited away into a private collection. Using some future technology, Irvine and Mallory's belongings might give up more clues in the same way that present-day DNA testing has solved past murders.

I have to admit that I am not blameless in all this. I was guilty of being naive in thinking that involving the media in this story was a good idea. I made a great deal of money for my employers, though. According to *Broadcast* magazine, my film *Lost on Everest* became the BBC's most commercially successful single documentary, but it did me no good at all professionally. I lost the chance of writing a book about my experiences of the 1999 expedition, and my objections about the way my programme proposal had been handled ensured that I was marked down at the BBC as too troublesome to promote. That is the downside of working in a large, hierarchical organisation. Bosses are nervous of people with minds of their own.

I had learned that Mount Everest could bring out the very worst and very best in people. My proposal had been used to further other people's interests. As a BBC employee I had no redress, and it cast a blight on the rest of my career. I would warn anyone with a good idea to be very careful whom they speak to.

The climbing establishment in Britain judged me and seemed to decide I was relatively innocent of disrespect to Mallory and Irvine. In George Band's book *Everest: The Official History*, he acknowledges me as the inspiration behind the expedition that found Mallory, but suggests that I have an obsessive, enquiring mind. I hold my hand up to that accusation. However, I would have thought that he, the author of a historical book about a mountain, would be mildly curious about who first climbed it. Band was on the 1953 Everest expedition that claimed the first successful summit, and of course if I had proved that Mallory had climbed the mountain first there would be an awful lot of history to rewrite. I contend that a mild obsession in the right place is acceptable if it harms no one and adds to the sum of human knowledge.

After the unpleasant experience of the 1999 expedition I sat back and reflected that after all the fuss we hadn't actually found the camera we were looking for. However, the location of Mallory's body was very much a hard clue, and pointed to an accident at the ice-axe site. He was near but not actually on the fall line from that point, so the two hard clues tended to corroborate one another. Surely Irvine would be on the same fall line? Maybe further up?

First of all, though, I was curious about the comparative lack of injury to Mallory. Bodies that have fallen any distance tend to be badly damaged by the trauma of striking unyielding rocks, indeed they often disintegrate. But Mallory looked as if he had only slid a short distance. Did this square with a fall from the ice-axe site? That was at 27,720ft (8,450m), and the body lies at around 26,760ft (8,155m), a vertical height of nearly a thousand feet and a horizontal distance of rather more. I decided I needed an expert opinion.

I had met Professor George Rodway of the University of Utah College of Nursing on another Everest expedition and immediately took to him. George has a studious manner and a serious approach to evidence, but he is also a hard climber. He is a specialist in high-altitude physiology, and had worked as a search and rescue patrol medic on Denali, a mountain I knew to be a tough proposition. He had seen many bodies in the course of his rescue work on the mountain. I asked him what he deduced from the injuries.

The body had suffered obvious trauma, which suggested a fall. He had a boot top fracture of both the tibia and fibula on the right leg, a fractured or dislocated right elbow, and an obvious head injury above one eye. He was lying face down and had arrested his fall with outstretched hands after a slide of some unknown distance – his flexed fingers were dug deep into the frozen gravel surrounding him. The search team all suspected that he had survived the initial fall, as the unbroken leg was crossed over the other in a seemingly deliberate manner – very likely in an attempt to ease the pain while waiting for the inevitable.

Regardless of the injuries the team observed on Mallory, perhaps the most important clue as to the extent of fall itself concerned what *wasn't* damaged on his body. Long falls in mountain terrain such as that found on the North Face of Everest (e.g., from high on the North Face near the intersection of the NE Ridge where Irvine's ice axe was found) typically leave a body very battered, broken, and something rather less than intact – with death not surprisingly almost instantaneous. Mallory's injuries, however, do not suggest a fall of this nature. The position of the body implies that he was conscious throughout the fall, and for some time after the fall stopped. Because of the nature of the terrain on the North Face of Everest – slopes of approximately 45–55° punctuated by ledges and short vertical drops of several meters – it is in reality somewhat difficult to accurately estimate the actual distance of the fall based on Mallory's injuries. If one had to estimate what sort of *vertical* fall onto a rocky landing would have been required to sustain the observed injuries, a mere 7–10 meters might well be a reasonable estimate. Thus, it stands to reason that Mallory's fall was (very likely) not a tumble over an extremely long vertical distance.[9]

Clearly Mallory's body was a reliable clue, and an oxygen bottle, marked No. 9 and thought to be either Mallory or Irvine's, was another. Eric Simonson had found this in 1991 at 27,800ft (8,475m) and stowed it under a boulder. On his instructions it had been recovered by Jake Norton and Tap Richards. If the cylinder had not been moved (an important qualification), this would mark the highest point that the British pair had reached, and it suggested that Mallory had taken the ridge route.

Later, on the same 1999 expedition, Thom Pollard and Andy Politz returned to the body, disinterred it and looked for more artefacts with a metal detector. They found a watch in Mallory's pocket, but somehow the hour hand fell off between the search site and Advanced Base Camp. This is the problem with this sort of archaeology: observations are not repeatable, as they are in laboratory experiments. The watch glass was missing and the watch had been placed in a pocket, leading some commentators to speculate that Mallory had broken the watch during an attempt to rock-climb the Second Step. When I saw it the stubs of the hands appeared to point to somewhere between 1:30 and 1:55. The watch had remained wound, and had not run down. This was potentially something of a black-box recorder like those on an aircraft, and it reminded me of John Hoyland's watch, which seemed to have stopped at the moment of his death. However, as usual with Mallory's clues, it was tantalisingly ambiguous. We do not know where the watch was broken, or if it stopped when it broke, as breaking the glass doesn't necessarily stop the movement. Nor did we know whether the time was am or pm. His altimeter exhibited similarly ambiguous rust-stains. Once again, promising clues turned out to be indefinite and vague.

Then Thom Pollard decided to have a look at Mallory's face. He crawled beneath the body as Politz lifted it. He reported to me that Mallory had stubble on his chin, that his eyes were closed and there was a hole over his left eye, with two pieces of bone protruding. Otherwise, his face was perfectly preserved.

Before I was removed from the 1999 expedition I had called my girlfriend on a satellite phone from Everest and agreed to her suggestion that we get married. This inversion of tradition was perhaps a hint that the marriage was going to turn out to be the biggest mistake of my life. On my return we had a romantic wedding. We kept a couple of horses at Ford House by then; mine was an ex-police horse, hers a thoroughbred. We rode Bebington and Mai Li down to the ceremony, and the deed was done.

I have noticed down the years that there seems to be a paradox in women's relationships with their male mountaineering partners. The very things that appeared to attract them when they were young, single women – adventure, risk-taking, a free spirit – would often come to be less attractive when they had to live with their partner. Or not live with them. Many of these men were away on trips for half the time and living on the bread-line for the other half. I have seen many male climbers either emasculated by their partners or divorced by them.

My repeated working trips on Everest did not improve my relationship with my wife, even though it brought home the bacon, and each time I returned from abroad she was increasingly distant. We followed the familiar old trajectory of criticism, defensiveness, contempt and finally stonewalling. In the end our selfishness finished off the marriage.

Then I heard from Audrey Salkeld, who had interviewed Xu Jing, the deputy leader of the 1960 Chinese expedition. The interview had taken place in 1998 under the watchful eye of an official interpreter, and Audrey realised he wanted to say much more than the interpreter would let him. It was clear to her that Xu Jing had seen Irvine's body, so in 2000 I returned to the mountain to look for him on one of Brice's trips, but came back with nothing but a tent pole with a brass sleeve and some faded green canvas from Mallory's last Camp VI, at 26,760ft (8,140m).

In 2001 I returned to the north side, post-monsoon, to film David Hempleman-Adams's attempt to hot-air balloon over the summit. This had been done in two balloons in 1991 by pilots Chris Dewhirst and Andy Elson, but Dave wanted to do it solo. We were ready to go on 10 September 2001, but events overtook us: the events of 9/11. The Chinese authorities told us that they would shoot down any aircraft near their border, so we had to leave. That year, 2001, Jake Norton had found an old woollen mitten at the exit from the Yellow Band at 27,690ft (8,440m). It was dense, with the appearance of felt, was over a foot long, and had probably belonged to Mallory or Irvine.

In a *Sunday Times* interview in 2003 Xu Jing then reported that he had seen a body lying in a sleeping bag at 27,300ft (8,320m).[10] This seemed odd, as two bags were found in the last camp, and no one in their right mind would carry that weight to the summit. Had he really seen Irvine? In 2004 I went alone to Beijing to film an interview with him for the BBC in the hope of getting a more accurate description of what he had actually witnessed. Mr You Liang Pu did the translation.

Xu Jing said he was going badly on 5 May and turned back after just 300ft (100m) at around 28,000ft (8,510m). On the way back down he took a more direct route. It was dawn when he found Irvine's body:

> His body was in a crack one metre wide, with steep cliffs on both sides. As if he was taking shelter, and fell asleep and never woke up. He was facing upwards; his body was blackened but intact. I felt sad and I wanted to cover him. I was at my limit and it was a difficult crack. I couldn't do anything.[11]

Here was another nebulous clue. This time Xu Jing denied the sleeping-bag report. In addition, he said that another climber on the same expedition had noticed something like a rucksack on the side of the route and Xu had investigated, whereas the *Sunday Times* had reported that Xu was alone. Xu said that Irvine had not been found previously because 'people don't go that way anymore.' This is a convincing detail – the Chinese followed the same route as the early British attempts, straight up the North Ridge without the modern traverse westwards. He didn't think an avalanche could have swept the body away since 1960 as there was a step just above it. He didn't think Mallory and Irvine could have climbed the Second Step, as it took four Chinese climbers five hours. He also said that there were some belongings with the body.

Xu's report suggested that the body was on the left of the route. Could it be that Irvine survived the fall, traversed east (leftwards viewed from Base Camp) towards the safety of the top camp, and had overshot it in the dark? And so, when the terrain began to 'cliff out' above the North Ridge, he sat down to try to survive the night? It was interesting to discover that these early Chinese expeditions had studied the British expedition books closely and had used the original route that went further east, straight up the ridge.

After this interview I travelled to Mount Everest to join Brice for another search for Irvine, which again proved fruitless. I climbed the North Col with Mark Whetu, and watched while Phurbar Sherpa and several colleagues criss-crossed up the Yellow Band. They could move over that ground as fast as deer stalkers in Scotland, 25,000ft lower. Others from the 1999 trip were also there; I bumped into Dave Hahn and Jake Norton that year. The press tried to make something of this; in the *Observer* there was a headline declaring 'Rivals race to solve Everest's final secret'.[12] In fact we shared our knowledge, sitting up there on the North Col. I took some flak for this, but in the end we found nothing. Other interviews with Xu have shown some discrepancies in the altitude of his find. It seemed to me that, as with Odell's sighting, one had to treat this clue as less than reliable.

On the way out of Tibet after this expedition I managed to get myself arrested at the Nepal–Tibet frontier. We had all arrived from Base Camp, ready for fun and games in Kathmandu, and shambled into the hut that serves as the Nepali frontier post. I didn't have a passport photo to stick on my entry form, so I looked at the guide next to me and asked if I could borrow one of his. Unfortunately Chris has a huge, black, Frank Zappa moustache and looks Mexican. I am free of facial hair, and have blue eyes and fair hair. The resemblance was not striking.

The office *babus* are terribly self-important in Nepal and the immigration officer was not amused. He looked long and hard at the photograph, then long and hard at me. 'This is not you,' he said with chilling accuracy. I protested that high altitude does terrible things to a man but he was not buying it. 'Lock him up,' he said to the armed guard. I was thrust into a cell to reflect on my sins for a couple of hours, while he worked through the rest of the queue.

Then in 2006 I helped Dick Colthurst, who was now working at Tigress Productions, to sell a series to the Discovery channel about Russell Brice's commercial trips. The working title was a comment on the situation that has developed in recent years – *Everest: No Experience Required*. In addition to filming, I was on a private mission to test replicas of the clothing Mallory had been wearing when he fell. It was on this expedition that we were all in proximity to a tragedy that seemed to epitomise the modern scene on Everest: the lonely death of David Sharp.

14

When Did Everest Get So Easy?

The queue of brightly suited climbers shuffled forward a few steps. 'For God's sake, move!' someone yelled from the back. They had already been there for an hour, waiting in the highest traffic jam in the world, just below the Second Step. On many of their faces, between goggles and oxygen mask, you could see that the silent fingers of frostbite were beginning to leave their mark. First, the skin was turning white and waxy; later, these marks would turn purple and swell, forming blisters. But these were just superficial injuries.

Shivering in the freezing blast of the jet stream near the summit, each of the climbers was effectively dying. They were well into the Death Zone, the height at which it is impossible to live for long. Their blood, already the consistency of syrup after weeks of acclimatising, struggled to pump through the capillaries in their fingers and toes. As a result, muscle, bones and tendons were slowly freezing. Ice crystals were forming inside the cells, growing by extracting the vital fluids and freeze-drying the tissues. Later on, we would see the results: first their digits would appear normal, but blackened beneath the skin. Then blisters would form, filled with bloody fluid. Finally, doctors would decide which fingers and toes to amputate, and which to try to save.

Another shuffle forward on the foot-wide ledge. The bottleneck was caused by the aluminium ladder that surmounts the Second Step. The problem was that a Chinese climber appeared to be trying to learn how to use his ascending device while balanced on the ladder. Some of the guides in the queue became exasperated by his incompetence and started to push past. The traffic jam started to move. And somehow, everyone in that queue had walked past a dying man without rescuing him – a 34-year-old Briton called David Sharp.

Sharp, who had given up his engineering job for the expedition and was due to start teaching in the autumn, was on a low-budget attempt on the mountain. Instead of spending $60,000 on joining a well-resourced commercial expedition he had chosen to spend $6,200 with Asian Trekking, which supplied some logistics only up to Advanced Base Camp. He climbed up the fixed ropes put into place by Sherpas employed by other, better-resourced teams, primarily Brice's, and probably reached the summit on 14 May at around 2:30pm. That is when his troubles really began.

I could see that Brice was worried in 2006. Four Sherpas had died on the mountain in April, but of course we didn't yet know that there would be seven further deaths that season. In the event, Brice attempted to avoid the crowds of lemming-like climbers by sending his clients to the summit much earlier than usual, in mid-May instead of towards the end of the month. Word slipped out, though, and as usual the other teams copied what he was doing, leading to the queues below the summit. David Sharp was one of those queuing.

Sharp had previously climbed Cho Oyu, an 8,000m peak often used as an introduction to Mount Everest. Like Mallory, he was on his third attempt to climb Everest. As such, he was more experienced than many who are guided to the summit every season.

At the outset, he had been offered a far better-resourced trip than the Asian Trekking offer. For an extra $1,000 he could have gone with his friend Jamie McGuinness, a New Zealand climber and guide who was leading a commercial group, Project Himalaya. But Sharp was something of a loner and wanted to climb the mountain on his own.

This is where it starts to get complex. Reinhold Messner had done exactly that in 1980 and had won universal acclaim. What was the difference? Sharp had no Sherpa support and no radio, and Asian Trekking could not have mounted any form of rescue even if he had called for help, so you could say that his was also a solo attempt. But the big difference from Messner is that Sharp climbed up fixed ropes put in place by other people, on a well-trodden trade route, and perhaps he felt more secure, being surrounded by other climbers. Little did he know how illusory that feeling was.

The first question to ask is this: when the mountain resisted seven pre-war expeditions with multiple, highly skilled climbers, how can someone climbing alone on the same route manage to get to the summit of Mount Everest in 2006? As so often, the answer can be found in the past:

> It has frequently been noticed that all mountains appear doomed to pass through the three stages: An inaccessible peak – The most difficult ascent in the Alps – An easy day for a lady.[1]

The quote is Mummery's, and he refers to a process that many previously impossible objectives seem to go through. A friend of mine, Brian Hall, who was on Everest's West Ridge in 1980, asked the question I had been ignoring for years: 'When did Everest get so easy?' Now complete amateurs who cannot walk straight in crampons or even tie knots stagger to the summit every May.

One answer is precedent. When three friends and I went to attempt the unclimbed Kellas Peak in a rarely visited part of Sikkim we struggled the whole way. The bureaucracy took three years to penetrate. We couldn't get enough yaks or porters. We ran out of food. In the end we attempted the wrong mountain and ignored the right mountain, which was standing next to it. And yet we had rough maps, GPS receivers and satellite photo-

graphs. We weren't that stupid and we were experienced mountaineers. We simply didn't know where to go.

Now amateurs can be driven in minibuses to Everest Base
Camp, led through all the early difficulties and guided through
any technical passages by following fixed ropes that are strung
all the way up the mountain. They can eat luxury food and
breathe through oxygen masks. Mount Everest is not a particularly technical mountain. In fact, it's sometimes called the highest trekking peak in the world, and therefore if you have fixed
ropes from bottom to top, ladders and good guides, you will
probably get away with it. I liken it to walking across a relatively quiet motorway blindfolded; the chances are that you will
survive, but if you are hit it will be the end of you.

Then there is the case of Geoffrey Bruce, who was on the
1922 expedition with Somervell. He and Finch made an oxygen-
assisted attempt on the summit on 26 May. On the first climb of
his life he climbed higher than anyone else had done before. In
other words, he set a world record in a sport completely new to
him – a unique achievement – and proved that to climb high on
Mount Everest doesn't take a lifetime of Alpine experience. Just
a good guide.

The precedent of others gives rise to another factor: you
know it can be done. The fear of the unknown is hugely
inhibiting to adventure, and plodding in the footsteps of a guide
who has been there before is far easier than striking out on a
new route. This can, of course, lead the inexperienced into
danger.

The advance of technology is another factor that leads to
countless advantages. In the 20th century we went from the first
powered flight to a landing on the moon in just 66 years.
Mountaineering technology has also improved. Better clothing
keeps us warmer, better boots and crampons make it easier to
climb, better nutrition and hydration keep us healthier. Small,
powerful radios keep communications open at all times, unlike
the written notes Mallory et al. had to send by runner. And

accurate weather forecasting by satellite communication makes a huge difference to success on summit day.

When Somervell made the first attempt to climb Mount Everest, even though he was a physician, he had no idea of the effects of high-altitude dehydration. As a result his companion Morshead was severely frostbitten. Now climbers know that they must drink copiously, and they also have drugs such as acetazolamide (Diamox) that help with acclimatisation, and steroids such as dexamethasone, which is used to treat cerebral oedema.

There is much more to come in this pharmacological area. In 2011 I tested Viagra (sildenafil citrate), as I'd heard it could improve the speed of ascent at altitude by up to 30 per cent. It works by relaxing the arterial wall, decreasing pulmonary arterial resistance and pressure. Despite the jeers of my colleagues ('Everest the Hard Way', etc.), I tried timed climbs up the slopes of the North Col. The best result I got was an improvement of 12 per cent, but I'm sure there are further gains to be made with other, as yet untried drugs.

Another reason for Mount Everest becoming easier that I believe has not yet been appreciated relates to air pressure. As a result of warming in the region,[2] there has been a corresponding increase in summit barometric pressure.[3] This, in effect, has made the mountain slightly lower. Although a climber may be breathing supplementary oxygen from a mask, a large component of the oxygen being breathed comes from the atmosphere. As I will discuss in Chapter 19, a climber nearing the summit is also nearing the limits of human physiology, and the tiniest drop in air pressure can make a considerable difference.

Climbing Mount Everest is never easy. I found myself vomiting with exhaustion the last time I went up to Advanced Base Camp in one day. But it is much easier than it used to be. So, unbelievably, in May 2010, a 13-year-old boy from California, Jordan Romero, climbed to the summit (realising my own dreams at that age). On the same day Apa Sherpa, somewhat older at 50, broke another record, reaching the summit for the 20th time. All the Everest books and TV films that people like me have produced have made non-climbers realise that they, too, can climb Everest.

The upshot of all these factors is that nearly any fit, healthy person with enough cash can now climb the mountain. Many of the people who now go to Everest are wealthy businessmen or people who are successful in some other arena of life. They want the cocktail-party trophy; they want to tick the box. They are treating the mountain more as an extreme bungee-jump than a potential killer. You can spot them around Base Camp, the rich guys with the suspiciously new-looking gear. If they go with one of the best commercial expedition organisers and pay the fee of $60,000, they might be lucky. By acclimatising for the statuary nine weeks or so, by obeying instructions to the letter and by investing a fair amount of physical exertion, they will probably top out and get the summit photo. But where is the romance? Where is the mystique?

There is a great deal of vanity driving this, just as with the big-money trophy hunters who paid to shoot big game in the past. In 2007 I went back to the south side of Everest and saw some of the boasting that now goes on. On the walls of the lodges are the vanity posters.

These posters are quite simply boasts from the climbers who pass through, and they don't appear to advertise anything except the egos of those who have commissioned them back in their hometowns. Our hero with the obligatory thousand-yard stare is usually striking a pose, and there's often some flattering text beneath. My favourite was the Canadian climber who lists his accomplishments as: 'International Adventurer. Tour Guide. Speaker. Filmmaker. Writer. Humanitarian.' I liked that last epithet. No surprise this man is now a politician. And no surprise that all these boasters are men.

However, there are funny ones: an 81-year-old Japanese man whose photograph features him swimming in an ice-encrusted glacier pool – two years running. Then the mysteries: a photo-graph of a Russian nuclear submarine. Presumably the crew came climbing for a breath of fresh air.

What is far more worrying is the fact that Mount Everest has now become a trap for the unwary. If you don't have that much money, it is tempting to go with one of the cheaper expedition organisers. As a result, people with frighteningly little ability are finding themselves far, far too high on the mountain. In the past the weaker climbers would drop out low enough to get back safely. Now it is relatively straightforward to ratchet your way up the fixed ropes to the North Col, up to Camp I, II, III ... and then on to the summit. The danger is that you don't know how little you have left in reserve. In his briefings Brice tells his clients that they must have 25 per cent of their strength left when they get to the summit. He monitors them on the radio and has strict turn-around times. If they haven't reached the top by the set time – usually around 1:00pm – he demands that they turn back, no matter how close they are. By far the most fatalities happen on the descent. Sometimes you will just run out of oxygen, and sit down in the snow and wait for rescue. The chances are that rescue won't happen.

So the mountain has become easier but is just as dangerous. This is the trap that David Sharp walked into. There is more to it, however, than that. It is extremely difficult to stage a high-altitude rescue, and the guides from the commercial teams are concentrating on looking after their paid-for clients. Money talks.

I listened to the whole David Sharp episode on the team radio, and I watched what happened on the cameras worn by the Sherpas. After probably summiting on 14 May, Sharp descended the mile-long North-East Ridge heading for the Exit Cracks that would have led him back to his tent. Night would have fallen before he got there, and so he crawled into the cave where the dead Indian climber known as Green Boots has lain as a sign-post since 1996. The first climbers to see him were a Turkish group making the next day's summit attempts. One of the Sherpas told him to get up and get moving, but he waved his arms to say he was all right. Later, groups of Turkish climbers saw him motionless, and the Turkish leader, Serhan Poçan, was convinced that Sharp was dead. Two Sherpas agreed, saying they would identify the body after they descended.

The next to arrive were Brice's climbers. Some did not see him at all, but New Zealanders Mark Woodward, one of the guides, and Mark Whetu, who was filming for our Discovery film, both saw him at around 1:00am. Quoted in the *Sunday Times*, Woodward said he was

> sitting almost on top of Green Boots, curled up in a foetal position. His nose was black with frostbite and he had very thin gloves on and he had no oxygen. Whetu kind of yelled at him, 'Get going, get moving,' that sort of thing.

When Woodward shone a head torch into Sharp's eyes,

> There wasn't even a flinch of his eyelids. I was just like, 'Oh, this poor guy, he's stuffed' ... We pretty much considered that he was, if not dead, then not far off it. We all looked at him and realised he was pretty close to death and continued on.[4]

The night passed, then an hour after dawn the returning Turkish climbers saw Sharp's arm move. They tried to give him some-thing to drink, but had their own problems. The next to arrive from the summit was the Lebanese climber Maxime Chaya, who was on our team and who was going well. He tried to speak to Sharp but couldn't get a response. In a radio call he spoke to Brice, who was watching events at the North Col at

23,000ft (7,010m). Unlike other leaders Brice prefers to observe events through a telescope from a tent equipped with a radio.

The context is important in this very complex story. Brice had two clients near the summit who he had been trying to turn around by calling to them on the radio. One of them, 62-year-old Gerard Bourrat, was badly frostbitten because he had taken his gloves off and was clearly in a confused state. With limited resources, Brice had the prospect of having to organise a rescue for both of these clients. Then, at 9:30am on 15 May, he suddenly had this other problem on his hands. I heard and recorded the whole exchange between Chaya and Brice on the radio.

I heard Chaya weeping as he tried to administer oxygen to Sharp: it was one of the most harrowing things I have ever heard. He did his very best to help, and he was with him for around an hour. I watched the footage from our cameras and saw the bad state David Sharp was in.

Both Mark Whetu and Mark Woodward saw Sharp on the way up. I have worked with them on several trips on the mountain itself, know both men well and consider them to be decent, moral people who enjoy helping others on the mountain. That is the nature of their work. For example, Mark Whetu nearly died trying to rescue his client Mike Rheinberger from the summit in 1994.

Mountain guides tend to be loyal to their own team on summit day. Everyone's mind is concentrated on their team's welfare, like a platoon of soldiers on a battlefield. Rather like Somervell's triage experience with the wounded after the battle of the Somme, people who seem to have little chance of life tend to be ignored. However, if Sharp had been one of Whetu or Woodward's clients I think he would have survived.

This seems to me to be the moral turning point of this story. As in Mallory's day on Mount Everest, on just about any other mountain nowadays the people you encounter on the way up will be fellow climbers. They are part of your 'in' group, and as such are peers who you will go to enormous lengths to rescue. David Sharp was, very sadly for him, part of no one's group, and as a result of the enormous pressures on those walking past he was allowed to die.

The press had a field-day. Sir Edmund Hillary had been very vocal about the changes that had taken place around the climbing of Mount Everest in recent years, and he had this to say about the 2006 season:

> I think the whole attitude towards climbing Mount Everest has become rather horrifying. The people just want to get to the top. It was wrong if there was a man suffering altitude problems and was huddled under a rock, just to lift your hat, say good morning and pass on by.

He went on to say that he was appalled by the callous attitude of today's climbers:

> They don't give a damn for anybody else who may be in distress and it doesn't impress me at all that they leave someone lying under a rock to die.[5]

The scene has changed: in his day mountaineers had a code of conduct and only real mountaineers would attempt the big mountains. Climbers helped those in trouble. But now people pay money to climb Mount Everest. That is the difference.

But not all climbers behaved callously in 2006. Russell Brice, for instance, collected Sharp's gear and met his parents, even though he wasn't part of Brice's expedition. In fact it was completely ignored by the press that Brice's expedition had already rescued a fellow climber that season; indeed I have seen Brice's guides perform this kind of rescue every season that I've been with them, with no mention in the press. His team has performed around 15 rescues, Brice never gets paid for the oxygen (at $400 a bottle) and rarely gets any thanks. Yet when a dying climber is encountered high on the mountain there is a storm of criticism.

The simple truth is that it is very hard to rescue someone from near the summit. Everyone is very near their personal limit, everyone is self-absorbed, and it takes a huge effort of will to organise a dozen other people to carry the casualty, prepare tents and safeguard the route down. And let's be blunt; when people have paid $60,000 for a package holiday they are reluctant to turn away from their goal.

In my experience most professional climbers I meet are decent people only too willing to help. They have a code of ethics that they are proud to adhere to. But people who have not developed their climbing within this moral framework often seem to bring the ethics of the market place to the mountain: 'Screw you; I'm alright.' Near the summit of Mount Everest, up in the death zone, their moral being is stripped away and what's left is a self-preserving core. It is an ugly sight. Frankly, the situation on the north side of Everest is now disorganised and dangerous, and if it was located in the US it would be the subject of litigation. The Chinese authorities really ought to enforce the kind of vetting that is seen on Denali in Alaska, and discourage climbers who are not in a position to look after themselves.

There is an interesting study of the psychology of climbers on Mount Everest, published in the *Journal of Applied Behavioral Science*, and prompted by the 1996 disaster involving the adventure-climbing companies Adventure Consultants and Mountain Madness.[6] In it, the authors suggest that the switch to commercial expeditions from traditional skilled-climber expeditions such as Mallory's led to huge psychological pressures on the entrepreneur-leaders of these expeditions. Unlike General Bruce, they not only have to make all the climbing decisions – they also have to turn a profit.

Furthermore, instead of skilled fellow-mountaineers on the climbing team, as was the case before commercial expeditions, the adventure climbing companies have had to attract paying clients with low climbing skills. The study claims that there was a dangerous personality type in some of these clients. The type is described as possessing pathologically self-inflated narcissism, with a higher potential for denial, rationalisation and self-aggrandisement, combined with feelings of self-entitlement. This heady brew, the authors suggest, would have been caused by inadequate mothering.

The result of this personality type getting high on the mountain was that in 1996 a number of clients abandoned responsibility for their climbing decisions and followed their guides like sheep. When the storm came in they were suddenly on their own. Certainly my experience of commercial expeditions bears a lot of this out, particularly the pressures on the leader and the type of clients they sign up.

There are difficult personalities in all walks of life, but the rise of the commercial expedition has brought more of them to Mount Everest. Money has perverted the spirit of mountaineering just as it has perverted so many other things. Real climbers follow their passion well away from Mount Everest.

I'm only sad that my boyhood dream of an impossibly remote Himalayan peak has evaporated like the clouds that embraced George Mallory.

15
Why Do You Climb?

Whilst giving a talk at the Smithsonian Institution in Washington, DC in 2000 I was approached by an elderly gentleman who had been a librarian at the House of Representatives. He told me that he'd had a friend who went to Mallory's talk in New York in 1923, and well remembered the quote attributed to him. When asked 'Why do you want to climb Mount Everest?' Mallory had replied 'Because it is there.'

This remark appeared in the *New York Times* the following day and has been laden with Zen-like significance ever since. It has been used to suggest that Mallory had a deeply philosophical approach to the sport.

This gentleman, though, was adamant. 'It was a brush-off,' he insisted. The questioner had been pushy, and it was not supposed to be a considered reply. In one of his articles Mallory wrote:

> In practice I find that few men ever want to discuss mountaineering seriously. I suppose they imagine a discussion with me would be unprofitable; and I must confess that if anyone does open the question my impulse is to put him off. I can assume a vague disdain for civilisation, and I can make phrases about beautiful surroundings, and puff them out, as one who has a secret and does not care to reveal it because no one would understand ...[1]

'Because it is there' is no answer at all, of course, and is suffi-
ciently vague, like the circumstances of Mallory's death, to have
all sorts of constructions placed upon it.

His reply reflects the difficulty of explaining why we climb to
those who don't. John Hoyland, in a mature piece of writing for
an 18-year-old, explained the love of hills in this way. He was
alone in the Carneddau hills of North Wales in Easter 1933,
gazing at Carnedd Daffyd:

> For some time I lay back, propped against a stone. The grand-
> eur of the view seemed to lift one out of oneself on to a higher
> plane, where one's only feelings were a profound peace,
> coupled with admiration and wonder. For one such moment
> as this all hardships are a thousand times worthwhile: in fact,
> without them one cannot experience to the full the tremen-
> dous elation which comes at moments such as this. It is one
> of the answers to the ever-lasting question of 'Why do you
> climb?'[2]

Inevitably the stories we bring back from the heights seem full
of horrors, but it is so hard to explain the intangible delights of
the sport. The views are stupendous. The surroundings are pristine. The battle upwards is absorbing. The summit is literally the
pinnacle of achievement, and Mount Everest's summit is the
ultimate pinnacle: you cannot climb any higher. For the pioneers
this must have been a heady mix. Add to this national and
personal prestige, and surely one can begin to understand the
fatal attraction of this mountain.

'There are only three sports – bullfighting, motor racing, and
mountaineering; all the rest are merely games.' This quotation
is attributed to Hemingway but cannot be substantiated. It may
not be his, as he called bullfighting a tragedy, not a sport. But
the meaning is clear: all these activities include the possibility of
violent death. Bullfighting and motor racing are now relatively
safe, but mountaineering remains an activity that can kill or

injure you. This puts it in an unusual place in the pantheon of human activities. So why do it?

Evolutionary psychology is the cruellest science, peeling away our apparently civilised skin to reveal a Stone Age brain beneath. It is not politically correct, and seems to reduce us to the state of amoral animals. As a result many non-scientists do not want to give it any credence. But Charles Darwin, who had a couple of good ideas about evolution, anticipated evolutionary psychology in his later work. Could it have an answer for us?

Our brains certainly evolved to cope with the environment in which early humans lived, but are we condemned to dwell for ever in a lost landscape? We appeared around two million years ago at the beginning of the Pleistocene, and many of our psychological mechanisms are adapted to dealing with the survival and reproductive problems encountered during that time. Since we first jogged across the African savannah, human beings have displayed overweening and ineradicable impulses for food, sex and highs. But human evolution is slow, and our brains haven't caught up with the extraordinary pace of technology. As a result we are imperfectly adapted to a world filled with easily gathered sweet and fatty foods, pornography and drugs. Those individuals who sought rare fats and sugars in a Stone Age environment survived to pass on genes that lead us to desire them at a time when their easy availability is killing us. Our brains lag behind in other ways: many of us are terrified of spiders and snakes when we ought to be more frightened of cars.

These observations, however, don't seem to explain phenomena that do not appear to favour breeding success, such as weeping over music, or feelings of spiritual uplift when seeing a high mountain.

Evolutionary psychology claims to help towards an understanding. After his work on natural selection, Darwin turned to the study of animal emotions and psychology. In *The Descent of Man, and Selection in Relation to Sex* in 1871 and *The*

Expression of the Emotions in Man and Animals in 1872 he dealt with what he had seen coming when he wrote in *On the Origin of Species* in 1859:

> In the distant future I see open fields for far more important researches. Psychology will be based on a new foundation, that of the necessary acquirement of each mental power and capacity by gradation.[3]

Darwin was curious about the peacock's tail. On the face of it this ludicrous appendage makes the male bird easier to be caught by predators, and costs a great deal of energy to grow and display. However, its attractiveness to the female means that these disadvantages are outweighed by the male's increased success in breeding. In a nutshell, this concept can be used to explain some human behaviour, such as why rich old men end up with beautiful young women. But can it really explain the phenomenon of mountain-climbers?

Darwin realised that in species such as ours females make a greater parental investment and are therefore fussier than males when it comes to choice of mate. The reproductive success of males depends on their ability to compete for the females either by displaying better resources, or fighting other males. This means that genes that favour risk-taking and competitive ability in males tend to survive at the expense of disease and parasite prevention, and repair capacity.[4] This is why the females of most animal species live longer. It also shows how Darwin's natural selection maximises the survival of certain genes rather than the survival of certain individuals. The thoughtful modern individual may deliberately practise contraception to improve her personal life, but she may still experience Stone Age impulses.

Could it be that mountain climbing is an activity that demonstrates fitness? Perhaps also mixed with quasi-religious feelings? Climbing Mount Everest does seem to be a predominantly male activity.

In the Scottish St Kilda archipelago, those young men wishing to marry first had to prove their ability to support a family with birds captured on the lofty cliffs. They demonstrated their mastery over vertigo by balancing across the edge of the Lovers' Stone, a rock protruding over a huge drop. They had to stand on the very edge with their left foot, put the right foot in front of it, bend down and place a fist over the foot which was now standing on thin air. This would appear to be taking Darwin's theory of the selection of the fittest rather too literally.

The 'costly signalling theory' suggests that women prefer physical risk-takers over risk-avoiders as long-term mates. However, just when I thought that I had found the reason why young men climb – to impress young women – along came another study. The article was titled 'Is risk taking used as a cue in mate choice?'[5] and the simple answer was no, not really. It seems that the young men in the study *thought* that their risky behaviour was impressing potential partners, but the young women in the study were actually not impressed if the behaviour was perceived as unnecessarily risky.

Another related study confirmed the theory for heroic acts that were altruistic, such as rescuing a child from a burning building (or collecting birds' eggs for food), but not for non-heroic acts that were brave but not altruistic (such as climbing mountains).[6] In other words, women's concerns about risk to their mates overrode any positive feelings about their men's risk-taking when these acts were highly risky and of no practical use.

But this all seems too reductive: we are not machines. Professor Steve Jones is sceptical of the way evolutionary psychology is trotted out to explain all human behaviour, and has suggested that the whole point of having a large, complex brain is to fine-tune our behaviour.[7] Our environment has always been changing, he says, and indeed we ourselves are still evolving.

Having known hundreds of mountaineers, my feeling about why people climb is that it is similar to the desire for fighting, or for competitive sports.

My personal guess is that men (and some women) need to fight, and when there isn't a war to fight they wage substitute war with tribal games such as football or mountain climbing. These games are addictive, and the high of surmounting a difficult obstacle is swiftly followed by the low of everyday life. For some of us the activity even becomes a substitute for religion. The fact is, we are very complicated creatures. In the same way that a footpath between villages becomes a cart-track, which then becomes a crowded motorway, so human characteristics that evolved on the savannahs of Africa may now look very different.

While we are on the subject of sex and Mount Everest, a Professor Ralph Pettman of Victoria University in New Zealand attempted to stop climbers and tourists having sex on the mountain. Pettman raised $2,000 to create a website he hoped would bring the issue to people's attention. Sherpas, he claimed, were bothered by people having sex at Base Camp because they consider it a sacred place. Some Sherpas alleged that it was the sexual antics of one famous socialite there in 1996 that brought on that year's disaster, although others among us think it was probably the bad weather. Orgasms are reported to be more intense at altitude, perhaps due to hypoxia. I had one girlfriend who claimed to have had successful sex on the South Col, thus setting a world record at five miles high. Knowing the lady (and gentleman) in question I have no doubt that this is true.

Our final thought on why we climb comes from John Hoyland. He is lying in his tent, which has collapsed on him under a weight of wet snow:

> Thus it always is in the mountains: at one moment life is too glorious to be described, at the next it is too miserable. One who has not tasted both extremes knows nothing of the mountains and the great sense of friendship they can offer. All who climb are convinced that climbing is the finest sport there is. A sport, and yet it is more than a sport. Most men need

some outlet for the fighting instincts; some fight mentally and some physically, and those who attack the most difficult climbs do not attack them to get to the summit or to see the view. They feel they must have something to fight against and find in the mountains something that will tax them to the uttermost and kill them if it can, and yet whose reward is great.[8]

16

What Does Mount
Everest Mean?

Borobudur is a man-made mountain in Java, Indonesia. It rises
from a volcanic plain and was built from one and a half million
blocks of stone in the 9th century. Java had come under British
administration in 1811, and its governor-general was Thomas
Stamford Raffles, who became fascinated by Javanese history
and culture. He knew India and her Buddhists well, and when
he was informed by the native Javanese of a great Buddhist
monument overgrown by jungle he commissioned an expedition
to find it.

Borobudur had lain deserted since the 10th century, possibly
as result of volcanic eruptions, and since the conversion of the
Javanese inhabitants to Islam in the 15th century it had become
a place of bad omen. Raffles would have none of that, and
ordered it to be uncovered and documented.

The builders were Mahayana Buddhists, who intended it to
be a place of pilgrimage and an architectural aid to spiritual
practice. Borobudur consists of terraced platforms topped by a
domed stupa at the summit. As pilgrims ascended this sacred
man-made mountain they climbed through the three levels of
Buddhist cosmology, represented by stone-relief panels illustrat-
ing the world of desire (*Kāmadhātu*), the world of forms
(*Rupadhatu*) and the world of formlessness (*Arupadhatu*). At
the summit stupa there is – nothing.

The pyramids of Egypt and Mexico are other examples of
man-made mountains with a spiritual meaning. The great
European cathedrals have strong vertical components in their

architecture and many of them, such as Paris's Notre Dame or Salisbury Cathedral, look like stylised dreams of fantasy mountain peaks. Even the 'Mersey Funnel', officially known as the Liverpool Metropolitan Cathedral, built in 1967, has white flanks and icy-looking pinnacles.

I am convinced that buried in our psyche is the feeling that high places are rich with spiritual significance. When nations have the leisure and manpower to indulge these feelings their rulers build pyramids or monuments such as Borobudur. If we are leisured individuals with ambivalent ideas about religion, perhaps some of us transfer our spiritual drives into climbing mountains.

The memorial window to Mallory in his father's church of St Wilfrid's in Mobberley, clinging to a Christian explanation for a pointless death, tells us this:

All his life he sought after whatsoever things are Pure and High and Eternal. At last in the flower of his perfect manhood he was lost to human sight between Earth and Heaven on the topmost peak of Mount Everest.

There is more at work here. We humans seem to need to make patterns and meanings out of the shapeless, death-dealing universe. We have already seen how Robert Burns seemed to ignore a view of the Isle of Arran that poets would now find beautiful. So perhaps mountains have no intrinsic meaning at all? Simon Schama in his *Landscape and Memory* offers a convincing explanation of the way we invent beauty:

Even the landscapes that we suppose to be most free of our culture may turn out, on closer inspection, to be its product … The brilliant meadow-floor [at Yosemite] which suggested to its first eulogists a pristine Eden was in fact the result of regular fire-clearances by its Ahwahneechee Indian occupants. So while we acknowledge (as we must) that the impact of humanity on the earth's ecology has not been an unmixed blessing, neither has the long relationship between nature and culture been an unrelieved and predetermined calamity. At the very least, it seems right to acknowledge that it is our shaping perception that makes the difference between raw matter and landscape … What lies beyond the windowpane of our apprehension, says Magritte, needs a design before we can properly discern form, let alone derive pleasure from its perception. And it is culture, convention, and cognition that make that design; that invests a retinal impression with the quality we experience as beauty.[1]

In the same way, the English countryside, with its chequerboard of fields and hedges that we find so beautiful and natural, is in fact almost completely artificial; the ancient Wildwood that our Mesolithic ancestors found here was cleared 7,000 years ago. Our culture tells us that the present landscape is beautiful, and that mountains are spectacular, and we find them so. This is challenging stuff; are our feelings merely products of our culture? I suspect that we have vague, powerful feelings and we attach them to forms such as gods, people and Mount Everest.

In my reading around the subject I have been struck by the spiritual language employed by the pioneers who first approached the mountain. Odell called the summit 'that most sacred and highest place of all'.[2] Younghusband said the summit was 'poised high in heaven as the spotless pinnacle of the world'. When I first saw the summit through the trees on the climb up to Namche Bazaar I remember lifting my eyes impossibly high and being struck by feelings of ethereal beauty, immaculate whiteness and purity. It seemed to me that if I could stand up there my spiritual self would be cleansed of worldly longing. In the event it did nothing of the sort, but perhaps I came to a kind of understanding.

There is danger in the worship of mountains. John Buchan, popular author of thrillers such as *The Thirty-Nine Steps*, as head of British propaganda during the First World War helped to hide the true horror of the war from the British public. After the war he urged support for the Everest expeditions. They would be 'a vindication of the essential idealism of the human spirit'. He saw warfare and mountain climbing as compatible spiritual quests.

The Nazis were fascinated with alpinism, and applauded Heinrich Harrer's conquest of the north face of the Eiger in 1938. There have been attempts to deny his membership of the party, but the facts are that he flew a Nazi swastika from his tent, and was photographed in his SS uniform at his wedding. This is not to denigrate one of the most remarkable climbers of the century. Hitler posed in front of his beloved mountains at his Berchtesgaden Berghof, and his favourite film-maker Leni Riefenstahl made mountain films. Audrey Salkeld writes of 'the usefulness of Alpinism to the Nazi cause ...' – the mountain films being 'a German equivalent of the Western, with their emphasis on tested loyalties, rivalry, struggle for homeland and the sheer power of nature'.[3] Alpine climbers were Nietzschean supermen, seeking purity in the high, thin air. But British climbers didn't engage with fascism, perhaps because they considered it ridiculous. Oswald Mosley, the nearest thing we had to a fascist dictator, wore the obligatory Nazi-chic military uniform. A Conservative MP, observing this, commented, 'I see jodhpurs. I see riding boots. But I see no horse.'

I have seen something of this seductive evil in mountaineering. Terry Eagleton in his book *On Evil* writes of

> the terrible non-being at the core of oneself. It is this aching absence which you seek to stuff with fetishes, moral ideals, fantasies of purity, the manic will, the absolute state, the phallic figure of the Fuhrer ... The obscene enjoyment of annihilating the Other becomes the only way of convincing yourself that you still exist.[4]

It seems to me now that many of the Mount Everest climbers I meet are pilgrims, and the lengths some of them go to achieve summit nirvana are quite extraordinary. Just one example is 53-year-old Australian Mike Rheinberger, who died near the summit in 1994 on his seventh attempt to climb the mountain, despite his guide Mark Whetu's best efforts to save him.

I mentioned Mark Whetu's story in Chapter 14, and it is worth a closer look. I have worked with the New Zealander guide on Everest for a number of years and I heard from him first hand the extraordinary story of his attempts to save his client. Mark had advised Rheinberger to give up as he was climbing so slowly, but he continued and the two men reached the summit at dusk. With no chance of reversing the route in the dark they dug a snowhole just 20 metres below the summit and sat down to try to survive the night. It was the highest bivouac attempted at the time. The next morning they started climbing down, suffering appallingly. Rheinberger started to lose consciousness and Mark had to leave him to try to find more oxygen. In the end Rheinberger died, and Whetu, who had made heroic attempts to save his client, lost his toes to frostbite. It was a terrible experience for Mark, and the whole episode leaves one astounded that people can value this goal so highly.

The question for me is whether climbing a mountain is something worth risking your life for. I think it's a question of maturity. When one is young and full of romance and pizzazz like John Hoyland, the fables are very appealing. You never imagine for a moment that *you* will die or be injured, or that *your* family will grieve for you for so long. When you are older, if you survive like me through a mixture of cowardice and luck, you might realise that you can still encourage the spirit of adventure without actually killing anyone. Rock climbing is nowadays safer than horse-riding, but it still feels stimulating. So my answer is, no, Mount Everest is not worth dying for, but I had to risk my life to understand the question.

Not only does Everest inspire spiritual thoughts, it seems to provoke supernatural experiences. Somervell felt the presence of a divine companion in the mountains, and just before his sighting of imaginary flying saucers on Everest in 1933, Frank Smythe had another paranormal experience that has been described many times before by explorers at their limits. He was climbing alone up to his high point of around 28,000ft (8,510m):

> All the time I was climbing alone I had a strong feeling that I was accompanied by a second person. This feeling was so strong that it completely eliminated all loneliness I might otherwise have felt. It even seemed that I was tied to my 'companion' by a rope, and that if I slipped 'he' would hold me. I remember constantly glancing back over my shoulder, and once, when after reaching my highest point, I stopped to try to eat some mint cake, I carefully divided it and turned round with one half in my hand. It seemed almost a shock to find no one to whom to give it. It seemed to me that this 'presence' was a strong, helpful and friendly one, and it was not until Camp VI was sighted that the link connecting me, as it seemed at the time, to the beyond, was snapped, and, although Shipton and the camp were but a few yards away, I suddenly felt alone.[5]

Another Everest man, Sandy Wollaston, was on a desperate return from his second attempt to climb Mount Carstensz in Indonesia. Again, he was at his last gasp from exhaustion and malaria when he saw a fellow European leading him safely through the jungle. But there was no other white man in the area. Afterwards, in London, he glanced at himself in a mirror while being fitted for expedition clothes. It was the mystery guide.

A climbing friend of mine, Dr Jeremy Windsor, experienced this phenomenon on Mount Everest in 2007 during our medical-research expedition. For six hours during his successful summit attempt he was accompanied by a ghostly presence who even came with a Sheffield accent, and a name: Jimmy. Windsor later wrote, 'Without his support and guidance I don't think I would have reached the summit.'

He became fascinated by the phenomenon and wrote a monograph on the subject.[6] He discovered that over 50 per cent of climbers above 8,000m experience something along these lines. He also found an echo in Eliot's *The Waste Land*:

> *Who is the third who walks always beside you?*
> *When I count, there are only you and I together*
> *But when I look ahead up the white road*
> *There is always another one walking beside you*
> *Gliding wrapt in a brown mantle, hooded*
> *I do not know whether a man or a woman*
> *But who is that on the other side of you?*[7]

Eliot was probably referring to an account by Ernest Shackleton, written only a couple of years before the poem. It is the story of probably the most famous rescue mission in the history of exploration.

Shackleton was leading an expedition that aimed to make the first crossing of Antarctica. He obtained sponsorship partly because the British were still smarting at Scott's failure to get to the South Pole before Amundsen, and in 1914 the party set out for the frozen continent on HMS *Endurance*. This was just as the First World War was breaking out, and although Shackleton offered his resources to aid the war effort, the authorities allowed him to continue (an interesting reflection of the expectation that the war would shortly be over).

In the event, *Endurance* became frozen in the pack ice and had to be abandoned by the expedition members in October

1915. After a hellish journey across the ice the expedition took to their small boats and eventually landed on Elephant Island.

Shackleton did not hesitate, and took a small crew in the most sea-worthy boat, the *James Caird*, aiming for the most likely source of rescue, the island of South Georgia. This was 800 nautical miles away, and if they missed it everyone would perish.

In a marvellous epic of navigation and small-boat handling, they landed on the uninhabited western shores of South Georgia. But they still had to reach a whaling station across two unmapped mountain ranges. They set off exhausted and at the absolute limit of their endurance. On the way, Shackleton, Crean and Worsley all independently experienced a fourth man in the party. Shackleton wrote:

> When I look back at those days I have no doubt that provi-dence guided us, not only across snow fields, but across the storm-white sea that separated Elephant Island from our landing place on South Georgia. I know that during that long and racking march of thirty-six hours over unnamed moun-tains and glaciers of South Georgia it seemed to me often that we were four, not three. I said nothing to my companions on the point, but afterwards, Worlsey said to me, 'Boss, I had the curious feeling on the march that there was another person with us.' Crean confessed to the same idea.[8]

Worsley reported:

> Three or four weeks afterwards Sir Ernest and I, comparing notes, found that we each had a strange feeling that there had been a fourth in our party, and Crean afterwards confessed to the same feeling.[9]

Shackleton uses the word 'providence', and I think this is a clue. This phenomenon has been reported as a religious experience by some, and I would suggest it falls neatly into our theme of wishful thinking. When body and mind are under huge pressure, what would be more sensible than to conjure up a helpful supernatural companion who can point the way?

Windsor describes these experiences as 'extracampine', or hallucinations that are not sensory. They are a perception of a presence. However, they can also involve sensory hallucinations: Jimmy is audible and visible. Another Everest climber sensed the presence of a friend who had died there two years before and detected his particular smell. Stephen Venables felt Eric Shipton warming his hands – although he was long dead. And during a long bivouac near the summit Dougal Haston had a long conversation with Dave Clarke, although he was several thousand feet below in camp.

Windsor is a medical practitioner with a bent for research, and he examines the likely causes for the 'Third Man', as he calls the ghostly presence. First, he points out that before the hallucinations there is usually a period of sensory deprivation. In his case both of his head torches had failed, and his vision was obscured by his hood and oxygen mask. Shackleton's party was walking in a white-out. Second, help and comfort are desperately needed – and the Third Man is always a benign presence who provides this. Third, there is death – or the threat of death – nearby.

I would add that in the case of Mount Everest a degree of hypoxia and exhaustion seems to be a fourth factor, and I wonder if there is another clue in the out-of-body experiences of intensive-care patients near death. They often report a comforting presence.

Shackleton had no doubts: his was a religious experience. He spoke of a 'Divine Companion', and in an interview with a *Daily Telegraph* journalist said:

> There are some things which can never be spoken of. Almost to hint about them comes perilously near to sacrilege. This experience was eminently one of those things ...

Windsor seeks explanations from neuroscience, and explains that we have a parietal lobe that processes information about where our bodies are and what they are doing – standing, walking, running, and so on – and a temporal lobe that helps us distinguish ourselves from others. Disturbing the junction between the two lobes has been shown to cause problems similar to those seen by the Third Man. Researchers in Lausanne were treating a patient with epilepsy, probing her brain with electrodes to determine whether her symptoms could be reduced by surgery. When they stimulated the left temperoparietal junction, 2.5cm above and behind the ear, the 22-year-old woman, a student, turned her head to the side. When they did it again, she turned her head again. 'Why are you doing this?' she was asked. The woman replied she had experienced 'the strange sensation that somebody was nearby', when no one was actually present. When the researchers turned off the current, she said the presence had gone away. The electrical stimulation was repeated, and again produced a feeling of presence in the patient's extra personal space.[10]

It seems that there would be an evolutionary advantage for a stressed individual to sense a comforting presence that might provide helpful advice from a more rational part of the brain.

Windsor concludes with a question that I think he is actually answering:

> Perhaps in the 'Death Zone' the temporal and parietal lobes of healthy brains are vulnerable?

Could the combination of hypoxia, hypoglycaemia, malnutrition, anxiety, dehydration, hypothermia, exhaustion and sleep deprivation have an impact on the brain and cause the Third Man to appear?

It would seem to me with that collection of pressures, it would be a wonder if our Mount Everest climber up near the summit did *not* experience hallucinations. I would further suggest that the explanation for all supernatural experiences lies in the human brain, and not in some shadowy world beyond our ken. Having said that, I am sure there is more in the universe than is dreamt of, and discoveries of extra dimensions might give us future heavens to explore, and different mountains to climb.

After all this I am disappointed to admit that although I was so hypoxic that I passed out below the Second Step, I had no experience of the Third Man – and I never have.

Not only is Mount Everest an immensely desirable quest, but the Mallory myth is a dangerous and seductive fable. The dark, handsome Sir Galahad leads the blond, young acolyte up into unknown heights to do battle with the Goddess Mother of the World. They disappear into the whirling snows, perhaps touching the Holy Grail of the summit, and promptly evaporate in a cloud of stardust.

Our expedition of 1999 torpedoed that myth; instead, we found a broken corpse and evidence of a commonplace accident. More Icarus Fallen than Sir Galahad. I attracted criticism from some quarters for helping to destroy a perfect legend.

It is worth disentangling the elements of this story that grips us so tightly. Mallory was an attractive, admirable character. We do not know exactly what happened to him, so we can put our own construction on events. The virgin mountain is clearly a symbol of aspiration and success, an objective correlative. There is a small cast of characters in exotic surroundings. Add in storms, heroism and drama, and the whole mix becomes utterly compelling to anyone with an imagination. Everyone has a theory about what happened to Mallory and Irvine, and why not? If they can argue their case with accuracy and passion it all adds to the rich culture of mountaineering.

Mount Everest attracts the ambitious. It also attracts the unbalanced. Maurice Wilson knew that his odd philosophy would gain credence if he could only climb the mountain solo using his system of faith and fasting. It attracts the fanciful. Psychics – even recently – have been pressed into service to solve the mystery of Mallory's disappearance. And it attracts dreamers. Jochen Hemmleb explained the latter well in the document he sent to me.

He explained that dreams often come in three stages, with a decreasing degree of realism and an increasing degree of audacity. First is the Realist, which is what you can reasonably achieve within your capabilities:

> Standing on top of the North Col, in full view of Everest's North Face, watching the lads – Graham, David, or whoever – pressing on towards Camp Six.

Second is the Idealist, which is what you might achieve if things work out exceptionally well:

> Walking upwards in the footsteps of mountaineering's past, passing through the remnants of the 1924 high camp and on to the Snow Terrace, with the Mystery in our minds and the ghost of Andrew Irvine in the winds around us.

The third – and most dangerous – phase is the Dreamer, which is beyond the realms of possibility and is what you might lie in your bed thinking of at night:

> Stepping onto the ledge at the First Step and, after a long, hard look at the ground beyond, forsaking everything in an all-out effort – until you finally plod up those last few feet, grab the tripod and yell like Leonardo DiCaprio in James Cameron's *Titanic*, 'I am king of the world!' (or like a male version of Kate Winslet, standing on the bulbous cornice

overlooking the Kangshung Face, spreading your arms and crying 'I am flying!' with the spindrift banner streaming miles back from your feet).

But dreams can become like avalanches. First you marvel at the force slowly building up, almost enjoying it, until there is the frightful realisation that it might carry you away and you have to give in – which is often the point at which you learn to play the game anew, riding the tide rather than swimming against it.

I am afraid of getting carried away by this game, that this time my obsession might drive me over the edge.[11]

This is insightful and honest, and is an explanation of how one can go beyond normal, rational behaviour if you think obsessively about your fantasies.

T. E. Lawrence in his epigraph to *The Seven Pillars of Wisdom* warns us to beware of dreamers who dream during the day with their eyes open. It is all very well suspending our disbelief during a film such as *Titanic* – and indulging in a fantasy – as long as we know how to stop when we leave the cinema.

The Mallory myth has also attracted a coterie of experts who talk endlessly and anonymously on internet forums. They hold strong opinions, and change them regularly. They pick over the minutiae and are vicious towards anyone who disagrees with them. They generally don't know what they are talking about and thankfully they rarely appear on the mountain itself. I try not to get involved. Pope had it right:

> *A little learning is a dangerous thing;*
> *Drink deep, or taste not the Pierian spring:*
> *There shallow draughts intoxicate the brain,*
> *And drinking largely sobers us again.*[12]

What is interesting is that the Mallory myth attracts a certain type of obsessive personality. It also seems to attract men who had weak or non-existent relationships with their fathers. This may be a coincidence, or it may be that concentrating on a perfect man helps to satisfy a need within such men. Most boys start by idealising their father, develop through a stage of rebellion against him and his values, and then perhaps come to an adult acceptance of him. If this process is interrupted, then perhaps the adult boy has to find an alternative father figure to worship. Mallory fits the bill to perfection.

I also detect something in the Mallory myth of the Elvis Presley cult that is almost becoming a religion in parts of the world.

Between 2008 and 2009 I worked on a series for the BBC Religion and Ethics department during which we studied 80 religions all around the world. We filmed voodoo in Benin and found elements of Catholicism in it. I noticed that Tibetan Buddhism and Catholicism contained extraordinary parallels: a celibate priesthood speaking a language the laity couldn't understand, with idols, bells, music and swinging clouds of incense. Then there were inbred Samaritans in Israel who thought *they* were the chosen few, and an extraordinary religion in Iraq that was so mystical that even the practitioners didn't seem to understand it. What struck me forcibly is that man is indeed a religious animal, and wherever there is a mystery there is fertile ground for a religion to grow. Howard Somervell, the medical missionary, was pretty clear-eyed about this:

> Where man evolves a religion, he tends to do so in certain ways which are common to many countries and faiths. The most important and fundamental of these is the creation of a priesthood – a section of the community who are said to be in special contact with the gods, and therefore in a specialist's position with regard to ordinary men and women.[13]

I am not for a moment suggesting that a Mallory religion is arising. But certain elements of a cult seem to be there: the martyrdom of a saint-like figure, a mysterious death, appeals to the spirit world through psychic mediums and the rise of an expert priestly caste that rejects heretics. What is even better is that the facts surrounding his death, like that of Jesus Christ, are reassuringly vague. Anyone can place their own construction of events upon the story, and add to it any meaning and significance they want. I think my own fascination, which has cost me dear, is something to do with a desire for uncovering the truth and giving credit where it is deserved.

A healthy dose of realism is well overdue. So it is now time to examine all the clues, reliable and less reliable, and try to cut through some of the verbiage that has gathered around the subject.

17

The Theorists and Their Theories

Over the years more and more attention has been focused on the story of Mallory and Irvine. All the participants of the 1924 expedition had their own well-informed views, and the consensus among them was that the pair had made it to the summit, but had fallen or – kinder to their families – been benighted. Somervell had a strong hunch that they had made it. They generally agreed that Mallory had become obsessed with the mountain and that when close to the summit, but dangerously late, he had climbed on to take the prize.

It must be remembered, though, that these men didn't know of the difficulty of the Second Step, nor did they realise that the effects of foreshortening meant that the summit was further away than they thought. Modern theorists know more about the route just as the original participants knew more about the characters, so any intelligent analysis has to take into both views account.

Our finding of Mallory's body in 1999 threw fuel onto the flames. There was much wishful thinking from people – like me – who would love to prove that he had been successful, but woolly thinking abounded. All kinds of proofs were put forward, such as the absence of a photograph of Ruth Mallory in her husband's pockets. Family legend had it that George was going to put a picture of his wife on the summit but, as Audrey Salkeld has pointed out, in a letter to Ruth he chided her for not sending a picture. So we don't even know if he had a picture on him, let alone whether he left it on the summit or not.

I think it is important to distinguish between this kind of evidence and the more reliable evidence of body, clothes and axe. It is fine to have a theory – in fact the more the merrier – but to have any credibility it has to be substantiated with hard facts. The risk is that some of the theorists use selective quotation and imaginative exposition to support their case.

Tom Holzel is one of the more combative theorists. The son of a German Second World War army officer and an American mother, he is a naturalised American. He became gripped by the Everest story after seeing an article in the *New Yorker*. Holzel calculated oxygen consumption and climbing rates, and wrote an article in *Mountain* magazine in 1971 claiming that Mallory might have been successful in his attempt on the summit by clever use of oxygen. It prompted a series of letters to the *Sunday Times* from Wyn-Harris (who found the axe) and other British climbing luminaries, all of whom dismissed his theory. Holzel enjoyed baiting the British climbers and quoted the exchange with glee:

> The astonishing attack on my theory of what happened to Mallory and Irvine is as long as the original article, all of it written with the same intense fervour as the above finale, with the name of Holzel appearing 79 times![1]

In the two chapters of *The Mystery of Mallory and Irvine* that he wrote he also claims that Mallory did indeed get to the top, but in later published work he completely changed his mind. This makes his theories particularly interesting to analyse, as by considering both sides we may get some way towards the truth.

In his 1971 article Holzel believed that climbers could not reach the summit without oxygen, a theory that was proved wrong in 1978 by Reinhold Messner and Peter Habeler. So he had to invent a complicated sequence of events in which Odell sees the two climbers on the Second Step, which Holzel claims they climbed in five minutes. Mallory then takes Irvine's remaining oxygen and leaves him at the top of the Step. 'Splitting up at 1 p.m., Mallory quickly raced up the final pyramid.'

This is glorious stuff, and utterly silly. I don't think I've ever seen anyone quickly racing up anything at Everest Base Camp, let alone near the summit. Holzel has not climbed Mount Everest, but even he must have realised that walking very slowly and taking around ten breaths per step is the most you can manage on or near the summit. He has Mallory sitting out the night 'dressed in hacking jacket and muffler'. In fact, as I was to find out later, his gear was rather more sophisticated than that.

What is refreshing about Holzel is that he changes his mind when confronted with new evidence. When Mallory's body was found it was realised that he did not have a hole in his cheek, as was thought from Wang's testimony. There was, however, a hole in his forehead. This was reported by Thom Pollard, who as I mentioned above returned to the grave with Andy Politz, disinterred the body, and lifted it to search underneath. He told me Mallory had some stubble on his face, and there was a hole above his left eyebrow.

More recently, Holzel has Mallory killed with a blow to his forehead from his own ice axe, and then rolled by Wang from a face-up position with the ice axe sticking out of his forehead to the face-down position he was found in. This was to explain Wang's reported statement that his face had a hole in it. This seems unlikely, and once again too complicated to be believable. The head of an ice axe has a sharp pick and a broad adze. During self-arrest – stopping a slide on hard snow – the climber holds the adze in the uphill hand and presses the pick downwards into the snow. This is what Somervell did after he fell during the first attempt to climb the mountain. If Mallory was attempting to slow himself down in this manner the axe should not have jumped up and penetrated his forehead, and if it had the broad adze would have left a larger hole than that reported.

The irony is that Holzel regularly conjures up William of Ockham, an English monk active in the 14th century, and his famous Razor: *Entia non sunt multiplicanda praeter necessi-tatem* ('one should not multiply entities beyond necessity'). Ockham formulates it thus: 'For nothing ought to be posited without a reason given, unless it is self-evident or known by experience or proved by the authority of Sacred Scripture.'

This, however, is precisely Holzel's error. He has to invent a complicated sequence of events to explain a reported observation (Wang's reported testimony that he saw a hole in the body's face) that we cannot prove to be true. Mallory's body took five man-hours to dig out of the frozen scree he was half-buried in, so it is unlikely that Wang was able to roll him over swiftly enough to look at the face, then get back to the tent (200 metres up the slope) within the reported 20 minutes. In addition, his body was literally frozen stiff, and would have been unlikely to adopt a new, spread-eagled position. Again, an unlikely deduction is being made from dubious evidence.

What had Wang really seen? The Japanese climber Ryoten Hasagawa who heard Wang's testimony was interviewed in Japan for our BBC film of the find, *Lost on Everest*. Our English version of his Japanese account of a conversation with a man whose language he didn't understand might have lost something in the translation, but here is a verbatim transcription.

In the interview he explained that Wang 'had been a member of the Chinese attempt on the summit in 1975. On the way, at about 8,150 metres at the foot of a rock, he found the old remains of an Englishman. He was lying on his side. His clothes were very old and if you took a pinch [of them] you could blow it away. The remains were that old. There was a hole in the side of his face big enough to put your fingers in. He'd found the really old remains of an Englishman.'

There are a number of inconsistencies here. When found, Mallory was lying face down, frozen into the scree, and not lying on his side. There wasn't a hole in the side of his face big enough to place fingers in, as Thom Pollard reported that the hole was above the left eyebrow. And the body was not at the foot of a rock – there was a clear slope of scree around it. Had Wang instead found the body of Sandy Irvine? Again, his verbal testimony seems inconsistent with the hard facts, and I think it has to be treated with caution.

Holzel tries to reconcile Wang's reported story with the hard facts of the Mallory find and gets in a fearful tangle, in the same way as he did when he argued that Mallory had reached the summit. To explain how this occurred he had to invent a complicated sequence of events: climbing the Second Step, borrowing Irvine's oxygen, leaving Irvine behind and climbing alone to the summit. The problem with hierarchical theories like this is that if you pull out a brick at the bottom the whole edifice comes crashing down. Sherlock Holmes, our most famous detective, said this: 'It is a capital mistake to theorise before one has data. Insensibly one begins to twist facts to suit theories, instead of theories to suit facts.'[2]

Holzel's latest theory has Mallory and Irvine failing to climb to the summit, turning back at the Second Step, falling and separating at the ice-axe site during the squall, then Mallory falling again to his final resting place.[3] In arguing this, he comes dangerously close to agreeing with the old English buffers of the Alpine Club who found him so irritating. We can examine all the new clues in the light of this theory.

For me, Ockham's 'known by experience' is important here. If you look closely at what Mallory and Irvine's peers experienced you may get an idea of what might have happened. If you climb the mountain yourself you might be able to judge what is likely. My own mantra is less complicated, and it isn't in Latin. It's 'keep it simple, stupid'. They fell off and died. We have an ice axe, and below it we have a body. What's the simplest and most likely way this accident could have happened?

Before our 1999 expedition Jochen Hemmleb pored over photographs and deduced that the body seen by Wang Hong Bao would be found near Wang's camp. But neither he nor Holzel have climbed the mountain, and therefore they miss vital facts. For example, the Chinese climber was unlikely to have been on an evening stroll; he was probably answering a call of nature and scanning the terrain for a sheltered place to defecate, so we should look for places that would fit this bill. Also, on my summit climb the oxygen-demand valve froze up and didn't deliver the full flow, with the result that I had more oxygen left on the top than expected. The problem was that I couldn't get at it. Those early British oxygen sets were prone to leakage, so the climbers might have had more or less oxygen available to them. Therefore one cannot make such precise deductions with incomplete information.

As for Hemmleb's claim that he guided the searchers over the radio to the location of the body: he didn't. His prediction was that it would be found near his estimated position of the Chinese Camp VI. In fact it was found just where Frank Smythe saw it: at the foot of the Great Scree Slope. It took Conrad Anker's mountaineering savvy to figure out where falling bodies were likely to collect:

> Jochen had located the Chinese Camp VI higher than I thought it was likely to have been. I was using my mountaineer's intuition, not the research manual. I thought, Now where would I pitch a camp on this part of the mountain? I was coming at it fresh – I hadn't overanalyzed, projecting preconceived 'facts' onto reality.[4]

However, Hemmleb contributed much further work to the problem, calculating oxygen consumption and examining the detritus left by the British climbers in their high camps. Nothing conclusive was found. His latest conclusion seems in line with Holzel's latest theory: the pair was unlikely to have made it to the top.

More recently, Geoffrey Furlonger, a pension lawyer in Belgium and another non-climber, has come up with an intriguing theory. Citing a piece of metal found on the Kangshung Face by the American climber Sue Giller, he postulates that if it is a part of Mallory or Irvine's oxygen-cylinder carrying frame, it proves that one of the pair took off their frame on the summit and flung it down the mountain.

For me this is another example of wishful thinking. As much as I would love to prove that Mallory was successful, there are too many imponderables here. Was it part of a 1920s frame, or just another piece of the detritus that covers the mountain? Perhaps it was blown from the South Col. And where is it now? I was told by Breashears, who saw it, that it was stolen by a local man. Does the topography really support the claim that the piece came from the very summit? It seems unlikely.

Are there any more clues to come for future theorists?

How about rock fragments on Mallory's boots? The rocks of the final pyramid are unique to this part of the mountain, and it occurred to me that if one found microscopic quantities of this in the nails of Mallory's boots (which were recovered), one could establish where he had got to on the mountain.

I had met Professor Mike Searle one day fossicking among the rocks on my way up to Advance Base Camp, and subsequently had long chats with him about the geology of the Himalayas. A professor of earth sciences at Oxford University he is a recognised expert on the subject, so when I put the idea to him he gave me this reply:

> The summit rocks are Ordovician limestones with tiny fragments of crinoid ossicles, it's like a limey mudstone. The Yellow Band is a metamorphosed limestone, so marble, and Everest-series black schists are metamorphic – i.e. have biotite black mica, muscovite white micas and metamorphic minerals in. We have a good collection from the summit to the South Col. If there were tiny frags of pure sedimentary limestone in Mallory's boots I guess you could say he got over the Yellow Band (highest step on NE ridge).[5]

So there we have it. A forensic examination of the boots might just find something. I realise I am clutching at straws here, as the snow on his return would surely have wiped off all traces of rock, but murder cases have been solved on similar evidence.

And so the theories go on. I now find the motivations behind them far more interesting than the theories themselves, which nearly always discount the reality on the mountain. Mount Everest has always attracted a driven sort of personality, and most of us have used the mountain's reputation to further our own ends.

In the end history is written by the victors, and I did not feel free to write my account of the facts until I left the BBC. I tell the story as I experienced it, and will let you decide for yourself from among this fascinating bunch of theorists and theories. But Sherlock Holmes was right: we needed more data – particularly on the weather on that day, and on the clothes that the men were wearing.

18

Wearing Some Old Clothes

Later in the 2006 season I took a little time out from the Discovery series we were filming, and went for a climb in Mallory's old clothes.

My arm arched over my head, and the old wooden ice axe bit into the snow of Mount Everest's East Rongbuk glacier. Splinters of ice showered bright in the intense glare of the sun. I stepped up and felt the silk underlayers sliding smoothly beneath my Burberry jacket and plus-fours. 80 years old, and yet brand new, the clothes felt fine.

One of the tangible clues I felt that I hadn't examined properly was the clothing. Many pundits claimed that, as they were wearing only tweeds, Mallory and Irvine couldn't have survived the cold in the vicinity of the summit, and that it was therefore impossible for them to have reached it. But various members of the 1920s expeditions had got to 28,000ft (8,510m) in similar clothing. Holzel described Mallory's clothing as a 'hacking jacket and muffler'.[1] And yet the clothing recovered from Mallory's body didn't look like tweed. So what was it?

Because one of the 1924 group pictures showed the expedition members at Base Camp wearing ordinary clothes, it was assumed that this is what they wore to the top. George Bernard Shaw, for instance, saw a photograph of an Everest expedition and commented that the members looked like a 'Connemara picnic surprised by a snowstorm'.

In fact, we now know that their clothing was at the cutting edge of contemporary technology, and in some ways was better than what we now use, although, as we shall see, in one particular way it could have been a death sentence to those wearing it.

Most of the hard work on uncovering the whole Mallory story has been done by unsung heroes – researchers working in the background. Yet we climbers working on the mountain get all the glory. In 2005 I found out about an extraordinary project to replicate Mallory's clothing, dreamed up by Professor Mary B. Rose of Lancaster University and Mike Parsons of Karrimor, clothing manufacturers and suppliers to numerous expeditions. It was funded by the British Heritage Lottery Fund and organised through the Mountain Heritage Trust. People such as Joyce Meader, a replica maker, re-created every stitch of Mallory's clothing by copying the fragments recovered from the body. With forensic techniques the team replicated two suits, one to Mallory's measurements and one to mine.

From the start of the project it had taken three years and cost well over £30,000. The plan was to put one suit on exhibition and for me to test the other suit on Mount Everest to see if the clothing was adequate for a successful summit attempt. And so I found myself opening the aluminium flight case at Advanced Base Camp and taking out Mallory's new clothes.

First impressions were of a warm, pleasant smell, and the feel of natural materials: silk shirts in wonderful muted colours, hand-knitted socks and cardigans, and a jacket and plus-fours made of gabardine. This is a tightly woven cotton fabric, proofed against wind and rain, and in this case a shiny green. There were six layers of material around my waist and yet it all felt warm, light and comfortable.

Vanessa Anderson, of the University of Derby, who was responsible for making copies of the shirts and windproofs, had found that body shapes had changed over the intervening 80 years, as well as fashions. She commented:

The fit historically has always been a lot tighter ... and that generation were trained to stand very straight-backed and chest out from childhood, as seen in photos of the period. Our posture and sizing has changed. If you try on garments from the Second World War and earlier, the same size will feel a lot tighter.

Because of the hard work of the researchers on and off the mountain, we know exactly what Mallory was wearing. His upper layers started with a silk wool vest next to the skin, then a beige silk shirt, a Shetland-wool pullover, then another silk shirt, green this time, then a flannel shirt. His windproof jacket was a Burberry Everywhere jacket made of Ventile cotton, which was cutting-edge technology for the time. It featured an articulated pivot sleeve that had been patented by Burberry in 1901. This had a deep-cut, V-shaped armpit area, and when I tested the clothing I found one could reach up without pulling the jacket from up around the small of the back.

For his lower body, he had cotton long johns next to the skin, then green Shetland long johns, then brown Shetland long johns, and on top of all this he wore Burberry breeches, matching the jacket. On his feet and lower legs he had a pair of blue socks, then mixed Shetland socks, then Argyle socks and finally Kashmiri puttees. These fine-woollen bandages would have been familiar to all those ex-soldiers but I found them the devil to put on. The whole ensemble was topped off by a fur-lined flying helmet – pure Biggles – and weighed a trifle over 4.5kg, compared with 4.9kg for modern clothing.

There was not enough money to replicate the boots, but these were also high-tech for the day, and at 800g and with no additional crampons they were less than half the weight of the boots and crampons I wore to the summit in 1993. They were to George Finch's design, and Parsons and Rose found that 'the thick wool felt boot was overlaid with calfskin and had a 10mm felt mid-sole and a 3mm leather sole. Unlike conventional nailed boots, nails were pre-attached only as deep as the felt mid-sole to avoid heat being conducted by the metal.'[2] In fact, those old boots were ideal for the sort of easy-angled mixed ground that lay between Camp VI and the summit, the nails doing the same job as crampons for less weight. The one bit of climbing they would not have been any good for was the rock climbing necessary for surmounting the Second Step.

I asked expedition leader Russell Brice to put on the clothes that he wore to the summit, and he came out of his tent looking like a polar bear. He had fleece underwear and a huge, hooded down suit, several inches thick. As he said: 'The main problem with climbing Everest nowadays is pissing through a six-inch suit with a three-inch penis.' But Brice exaggerates; his suit is only four inches thick.

We climbed up on to the glacier near Advanced Base Camp and did some tests. First, I cut some steps with the 1920s ice axe. I immediately found that the layers of silk that I was wearing slid easily against the wool layers, giving me great freedom of movement. Then I reached up and hacked out a hold in the ice above my head. The patented pivot sleeve of the Burberry jacket allowed me a full reach without dragging my shirt-tails out of my breeches. Before too long I was feeling too hot. Not for nothing was this gear developed for polar expeditions. Oddly, these clothes follow the latest fashion for super-lightweight gear.

Brice pointed out that in some ways this outfit, and the nailed boots that went with it, would have been better for climbing the mixed ground of the North Face than today's clumsy down gear and plastic double boots. Otherwise, modern boots are the greatest clothing advance we now have over our predecessors. Unlike the old leather boots they don't need to be thawed out in the morning, and during the climb they keep the feet reasonably protected against frostbite. Modern down clothing is around 40 per cent better at insulating, too.

But how would this clothing perform near the summit of the mountain? I had no money to fund an authentic climb using these clothes, and no time to test them more comprehensively. We should try an empirical test by dressing two climbers in this authentic re-created clothing and asking them to climb to the top (the clothes worn by Conrad Anker and Leo Houlding for the 2007 film *The Wildest Dream* were not true replicas). This real test of the clothing is something I would like to try in the future, if anyone is brave enough. After all, the last two men to try this didn't come back. So I looked at the science, instead.

At the same time as I was testing Mallory's clothing the BBC was reconstructing Scott and Amundsen's journeys in a series called *Blizzard: Race to the Pole*. Two teams of modern explorers were asked to travel along a snow route using the same resources and clothing available to Scott and Amundsen. Human thermo-regulation expert Professor George Havenith of Loughborough University was asked to compare the British team's woollen clothing with the Norwegian team's furs. Although the two sets of clothing had similar insulation properties there was a difference in the friction of the coarse woollens and the slippery furs. Scott's team, who were man-hauling their sledges instead of relying on dogs, would have expended much more energy simply walking in their gear.

Professor Havenith became interested in Mallory's clothing when he saw the Mountain Heritage Trust's display at a conference: 'I was amazed by the level of detail they had gone into to ensure the clothing was as close a match to that actually worn by Mallory in 1924 as possible.'[3] He approached the Trust, offering to assess the insulation and wind protection of Mallory's clothing, and provide them with further insight into whether what Mallory had worn would have prevented him from reaching the summit of Everest.

As we have seen, the outfit consisted of several different layers of silk, flannel, wool and cotton. The clothing was put on to a human-sized thermal manikin that simulates a human's skin temperature and is able to measure how much heat is lost through the material.

Through the tests I found that the insulation offered by the many layers Mallory wore was slightly lower than that offered by both Scott and Amundsen's clothing of 10 years earlier, though the insulative value per unit of weight was about 30 per cent better … If the weather conditions and wind speed on Everest had remained stable on the day Mallory set off for the summit, his clothing would have offered him enough protection from the cold – down to temperatures as low as −30°C – to enable him to reach the top … However the last person who reported seeing Mallory on the mountain commented that the clouds came in and obscured his view of the mountaineer, which appears to suggest that the weather was changing. If the wind speed had picked up, a common feature of weather on Everest, the insulation of the clothing would only just be sufficient to −10°C. Mallory would not have survived any deterioration in conditions.[4]

The professor was, however, impressed by one feature – the layering:

I had discovered through the research into Scott and Amundsen's clothing how important correct layering was for the energy cost. With Mallory, each time he wore a coarse layer, for example of wool, he layered it with a slippery fabric, such as silk. When you package these types of fabric together the clothing moves very easily which means the movement of the person wearing the layers is not restricted and energy cost is low. The way Mallory wore his many layers would have made climbing in the overall outfit very easy. If you compare

this to Scott's clothing, his outfit had a lot more friction inter-
nally which obviously has an impact on energy consumption
and would slow you down. Ergonomically Mallory's clothing
was very well designed.[5]

Professor Havenith was asked if his study of Mallory's outfit
enabled him to answer the question of whether Mallory reached
the summit of Everest.

> I think this is still impossible to answer. From the tests I
> carried out I know that his clothing would have offered him
> adequate protection as long as the weather remained stable
> and that Mallory remained active. Any deterioration in the
> weather conditions or the need to stop and bivouac overnight,
> and I believe he would have perished ... The main thing I
> think the Mountain Heritage Trust have succeeded in confirm-
> ing through this project is that Mallory was certainly no
> amateur. His clothing was advanced for the time and cleverly
> constructed.[6]

Tom Holzel claimed that Mallory's clothing was 'totally inadequate', citing the work of Professor Havenith.[7] He quotes him
thus: 'If the wind speed had picked up, a common feature of
weather on Everest, the insulation of the clothing would only
just be sufficient to −10°C (14°F). Mallory would not have
survived any deterioration in conditions.'
But this is selective quoting. As we have just seen, what
Professor Havenith actually said just before the quoted passage
was this:

> If the weather conditions and wind speed on Everest had
> remained stable on the day Mallory set off for the summit, his
> clothing would have offered him enough protection from the
> cold – down to temperatures as low as −30°C – to enable him
> to reach the top.

Is this clothing good enough for going to the top? I am sure it is – in good weather.

Mallory and Irvine were climbing on 8 June – late in the relatively warm pre-monsoon season – and at this time of year some climbers have been able to take off their jacket and part of their down suit, and wear a T-shirt to the top. In May 2007 Dutchman Wim Hoff reached 24,278ft (7,380m) wearing a pair of shorts, and in May 2006 a 25-year-old Nepali Sherpa, Lakpa Tharke Sherpa, took *all* of his clothes off and was the first to stand naked on the summit. Remember, too, that a few days before Mallory's attempt Norton and Somervell had come to within 1,000ft of the summit without suffering from hypothermia. Mallory and Irvine, however, did not have good weather. Odell reported 'a rather severe blizzard' coming in on the afternoon of 8 June.

I stood on the summit in a 20-knot wind in October 1993, with a lenticular cloud over my head. The temperature was well below –20°C. I was wearing a modern down suit and was barely warm enough. If I had been wearing Mallory's clothes I don't think I would have survived the day. Also, I am sure that the clothes of the pioneers – although good enough for climbing hard, when exertion keeps the climber warm – could not have kept Mallory or Irvine alive during a sit-down bivouac at night. Nor would they have survived a bad storm. Mark Whetu, wearing modern down clothing, barely came through his ordeal. And he lost all of his toes.

After the clothing test I felt I had learned a great deal: that the clothing would have been just good enough to wear to the summit in warm, windless conditions but probably could not have kept the climbers alive if bad weather had come in, or if they'd had to spend a night bivouacking on the slopes.

Clearly, the next thing I needed to know was what the weather was doing that day.

19

Perfect Weather for the Job

One thing Professor Havenith had been quoted as saying puzzled me. He said that we didn't have any weather reports for Mallory's summit day. I knew that we did, and I knew who had recorded them: Theodore Howard Somervell. He was responsible for the meteorological records on the 1924 expedition, and his work led me to the next vital clue.

One of the reasons Mount Everest is now becoming 'an easy day for a lady' is modern weather forecasting. Whereas the early British attempts relied on rough dates for the likely advent of the Indian summer monsoon, now an expedition leader has highly accurate satellite photographs and forecasting available by email. The requisite weather window for a summit bid can be predicted with reliability. But there is one variable that is literally invisible: air pressure.

If one tries to climb Mount Everest without supplementary oxygen some days are better than others. These are high pressure days, when there are more oxygen molecules in each lungful of breath. Conversely, a day with low barometric pressure can effectively make the summit nearly two hundred metres higher. On such a day, a climber nearing the summit without that extra oxygen is working at the absolute limit of human capacity, so a few millibars of atmospheric pressure either way can make all the difference. Somervell was aware of an invisible wall, an apt metaphor for the lack of oxygen that stopped him climbing further.

Even when one is using a standard open-circuit set the bottled oxygen is merely supplementing the ambient air, so low pressure will affect you, too. A recent study of fatalities on Mount Everest shows that deaths blamed on the weather are usually associated with a big drop in summit barometric pressure.[1]

In my reading of the 1924 expedition account I became curious about the unseasonably bad weather throughout May of that year. The expedition report states that tea planters in Darjeeling claimed 'that for at least twenty years no such weather had been known at this season'. Usually the cold winds of winter die down towards the end of April and we get a clear week or so around 17 May. But in 1924 they had such appalling weather between 9 and 11 May that they had to abandon Camp III below the North Col, something I have never known in recent seasons. I wondered if there was an outside event that might have influenced the weather, and in particular if El Niño was the culprit.

The phenomenon of El Niño has been much discussed in modern press weather stories. It refers to the periodic movement of warm water in the tropical Pacific from its usual home off Indonesia across to the coasts of South America. This happens around Christmas every few years, which gives the weather pattern its name (El Niño means 'the little boy', referring to the infant Jesus). La Niña is a corresponding movement of cooler water. Atmospheric pressure changes go hand in hand with this movement of warm water, an effect known as the Southern Oscillation, and this affects global weather; in particular drought in South Africa, increased Eurasian snowfall and a reduced Indian summer monsoon.

This fits the facts: the eighth-worse drought of the 20th century occurred in South Africa in 1924, and we know from the expedition report that not only was there unusually heavy snowfall in Tibet in May of that year, but also that the monsoon was overdue, enabling Mallory and Irvine to make a late attempt on the summit. What is interesting, in addition, is that this bad weather had similar characteristics to the storm that hit Mount Everest with such disastrous consequences in 1996, as recounted in Jon Krakauer's best-selling book *Into Thin Air*.[2] But not being a weather scientist, I didn't understand all of the implications of the bad weather in 1924 until later on.

In 2007 I collaborated on Mount Everest with Professor George Rodway in a study of hypoxia. We filmed arterial blood samples being taken from climbers who were near the summit and found how extraordinarily low oxygen saturation in the blood can become. During one of the inevitable bad-weather days I mentioned my El Niño theory to George and he drew my attention to the work of a Canadian physics professor, Kent Moore of the University of Toronto. So in 2009 I contacted Professor Moore and suggested El Niño might be considered the culprit for the events of 1924. In collaboration with John Semple, also of the University of Toronto, we wrote a paper that produced some surprising results.[3] Instead of having unusually good weather for their summit attempt, it turned out that Mallory and Irvine were climbing up into an invisible death-trap. Norton and Somervell, however, had enjoyed an invisible helping hand.

It was all to do with air pressure. The 1924 expedition was remarkable for collecting the earliest data on the meteorology of the Mount Everest region. This was done in a spirit of scientific enquiry, just as Scott had made measurements in the Antarctic. In 1924 there was particular interest in temperature measurements at heights of up to 23,000ft (7,010m), in other words up to Camp IV on top of the North Col. This was so that the environmental lapse rate – the rate at which temperature decreases with height – could be worked out. The air pressure (or barometric pressure) was also noted at Base Camp.

Somervell's meteorological data from the 1924 expedition was published as a table in 1926, but was not until recently analysed to provide information on the storm that Odell described as 'a rather severe blizzard'.[4] Somervell's data showed that there was a 10mbar drop in barometric pressure at Base Camp during the storm. This huge drop suggests that the conditions during Mallory and Irvine's summit attempt were much more severe than originally assumed, with the conclusion being easily reached that the appalling weather might well have contributed to their deaths.

72 years later another disaster was just about to happen. On the evening of 9 May 1996 a large number of clients and guides were poised to make summit attempts, having climbed from Base Camp in Nepal to the camp on the South Col at 25,940ft (7,906m). There had been high winds all day and the chances of summiting appeared low. The winds died down during the evening, though, and everyone thought it would remain calm for a while. As a result, the decision was made to attempt to summit. Instead, the weather was gathering itself up to deliver a terrible punch. During the afternoon of 10 May an intense storm – with wind speeds estimated to be in excess of 70mph, heavy snowfall and falling temperatures – engulfed Mount Everest, trapping over 20 climbers on its exposed upper slopes. Eight of the climbers died, the highest number to die during a single event near the summit of the mountain.

As I learned from a helpful meteorologist cousin in Arran, Daniel Mathew, the winter of 1995–96 was not itself an El Niño year but was sandwiched between the El Niño events of 1994–95 and 1997–98 (the latter being one of the strongest of recent times). Instead, 1995–96 is classified as a La Niña year. Daniel explained that anomalously cooler and wetter conditions over the Himalayas are actually a spring/summer teleconnection of La Niña. (A teleconnection is a linkage between weather changes occurring in widely separated regions of the globe.)

This is all very complicated, but suffice it to say that Mount Everest is occasionally prone to violent and unexpected storms that are connected to cyclical weather events on the other side of the globe. These storms come out of nowhere and they will kill anyone they hit.

David Breashears carried a barometer to the summit in 1997 and recorded a pressure of 336.6mbar on a fairly good summit day. If we look at Somervell's Base Camp barometric readings

– other expedition members continued to take readings while Somervell was on the mountain itself – and extrapolate and convert them to millibars to find the pressures on the summit, the minimum summit barometric pressure was approximately 331mbar during the 1924 storm.[5] This is the same figure as during the 1996 storm described in *Into Thin Air*.

A decrease in summit barometric pressure of just 4mbar is enough to trigger hypoxia (lack of oxygen).[6] Clearly both storms were associated with summit barometric pressures and pressure drops that were sufficient to drive the climbers into a hypoxic state.

The pressure drop was larger and occurred more quickly for the 1924 storm, suggesting that it might have been even worse than the 1996 storm. In 1924 the summit barometric pressure fell from 341mbar on 6 June to 331mbar on 9 June, a drop of approximately 10 mbar, equivalent to an increase of roughly 600ft/180m in effective altitude. This suggests to me that Somervell and Norton had a Camp VI night and a summit day of high pressure, which could partly explain why they got so high without oxygen. The 1996 storm saw the pressure fall from 337mbar on 7 May to 331mbar on 12 May, a drop of approximately 6mbar. So, contrary to Holzel's claim that Mallory and Irvine had 'unusually benign circumstances'[7] for their climb, they were in fact climbing up into a dead-end. Because of the low pressure, they effectively had a higher mountain to climb.

I was stunned by these results, and racked my brains for any way in which they could be wrong. Checking the expedition records, however, confirmed the results. I went to the Royal Geographical Society archive and drew out the 1924 Everest Expedition Camp III diary. As I carefully unwrapped it from its paper package, I hesitated. There, 86 years later and in the middle of London, I got a strong whiff of smoke. Yak-dung smoke.

Inside, the diary had been filled in by various members. Here is Somervell on 11 May: 'The bloodiest day I have ever seen anywhere – wind, snow, no sun to speak of, almost impossible to live outside.' Certainly they had rotten weather in 1924. But I was reassured. The way the dates were recorded seems to be unambiguous.

The pressures actually recorded at Base Camp at 8:30am over the crucial days in 1924 were:

June 3: 16.375 inches of mercury. Norton and Somervell at
  Camp VI.
June 4: 16.275 inches of mercury. Norton and Somervell's high
  point.
June 5: 16.225 inches.
June 6: 16.5 inches.
June 7: 16.15 inches. Mallory and Irvine at Camp VI
June 8: 16.25 inches. Mallory and Irvine's attempt. The air
  pressure would have dropped steeply when the storm hit.
June 9: 15.98 inches of mercury.

In the weather reports for Mallory and Irvine's summit day we have:

June 8: *Base Camp*. Fine morning, but clouds constantly all
  around Everest.
Camp III. Misty morning. Mountain only occasionally in view.
Camp IV. Cloudy, occasional gusts of wind. Mist, mountain
  almost entirely obscured, calm and very close. 12.00, calm
  and very close, 16.00, calm, clouds inclined to lift, patches
  of dew, etc.

The barometric pressure is recorded under a table headed 'June' and '8' and is recorded as 16.25 inches of mercury, taken at 8:30am: before the storm hit. The next morning it is at its lowest since early May, at 15.98 inches, and the monsoon had clearly set in:

June 9: *Base Camp*. Dull sky; very monsoony. Everest clear.

Camp IV. Clouds and mist, occasional gusts from W. 12.15 clouds and wisps of mist blowing from the W.: close and fairly calm. Mountain occasionally clear. 16.30 clouds, clear to E. Snow on mountain. Wind from W. appears to be of high velocity. Mountain clear. Camp sheltered but wind can be heard above occasionally. Cloudy E.

By then Mallory and Irvine were almost certainly dead.

Although the pressure readings at Base Camp on the mornings of 4 and 8 June were almost the same, what is most important is what happened next. For Norton and Somervell, the pressure remained relatively stable, but for Mallory and Irvine, there was a large and rapid drop in pressure. This led me to realise there was an even more seductive and invisible danger at work. Mallory had seen Norton and Somervell get to within 1,000ft of the top on 4 June using no oxygen equipment. It would therefore have seemed reasonable to him to assume that it was possible to reach the summit with the apparatus. What he didn't know was that the rapidly falling air pressure was effectively making the mountain even higher, and that the incoming blizzard was going to make his clothing very marginal indeed.

20

Utterly Impregnable

Which way did Mallory and Irvine go? Ever since Holzel suggested that they quickly surmounted the Second Step in the time that Odell described, all other Mallory experts have followed suit. After all, it is the way everyone goes today, right? What they forget is that a 15ft (4.6m) ladder was attached to the step by the Chinese in 1975. You have to ask why they did this, if it was so easy that two men wearing 30lb of oxygen equipment could nip up it in five minutes. A combination of ignorance and wishful thinking has perpetuated this myth.

There were two options open to Mallory, which are reflected in his note to Noel:

> It won't be too early to start looking out for us either crossing the rock band under the pyramid or going up the skyline at 8.0 p.m.

So they could have followed the way that Norton and Somervell had pioneered, passing well under the First Step and traversing across the face of the mountain. As it is hard to regain the ridge after the First Step, this route forces climbers to cross to the Norton Couloir.

Or they could have bypassed the First Step by passing across its northern face and continuing on to the Second Step, which is what Mallory called 'the skyline'. This is the modern route. Mallory was known to favour this ridge route, which would have meant climbing the Second Step.

The note implies that he was keeping his two route options open. By the rock band he meant the rocks beneath the summit pyramid (not what is today called the Yellow Band). It was the way Norton and Somervell were heading when they ground to a halt. But if he hoped to get there in a couple of hours he was sadly mistaken; it can take modern climbers up to three times as long from a closer top camp, and using fixed ropes and lighter oxygen.

It is worth looking at the history of the Second Step, and what the pioneers made of it. The fact is that once they saw it from below, none of Mallory's peers considered attempting this feature. Every pre-Second World War climber took one look at the crag, traversed under it and followed the same route attempted by all the British pre-war expeditions: the Norton–Somervell traverse. Not one of these pre-war climbers even bothered to climb up to inspect the modern Second Step route: neither Norton, Somervell, Wyn-Harris, Wager, Shipton, nor Smythe, who wrote:

> There was never any doubt as to the best route. The crest of the north-east ridge, leading to the foot of the second step, was sharp, jagged and obviously difficult. As for the second step, now almost directly above me, it looked utterly impregnable, and I can only compare it to the sharp bows of a battle cruiser. Norton's route alone seemed to offer any chance of success, and it follows the yellow band beneath a sheer wall to the head of the great couloir.[1]

Only Jack Longland, the rock-climber, thought it might go, and even he wouldn't have tried to get young Irvine up it. Irvine had only climbed at V. Diff (5.7, using the US rating scale) level on Great Gully on Craig yr Ysfa with Odell. This, a wet climb at sea level, was rather different to the Second Step.

Furthermore, while on leave in Britain, Somervell met Frank Smythe to discuss the forthcoming 1936 Everest expedition and said that he thought it might be possible to place a camp in the

Great Couloir that Norton had reached in 1924. This suggests that even at that date they were still concentrating on the Norton traverse.

The Second Step was finally climbed by the Chinese expedition of 1960 in an epic ascent involving pitons (that Mallory did not have), five hours of struggle and badly frostbitten feet (when one climber took off his boots and stood on a companion's shoulders). It was considered so difficult that the British initially refused to believe that they had actually done it. When they returned in 1975 the Chinese brought their aluminium ladder.

In support of the argument that the Second Step might have been surmounted in 1924, we might mention the fact that Oscar Cadiach, a Spanish climber, free-climbed the Step in 1985, although in that year there was the aid of a convenient snow ramp, which Mallory did not have. So too did Theo Fritsche, an Austrian climber, taking an hour in 2001 in dry conditions similar to those of 1924. But the Chinese ladder was standing there, providing at least moral support.

On our expedition of 1999 Conrad Anker climbed the step but had to use one rung of the ladder. I watched the rushes of his climb, and he was only forced to use the ladder because that rung blocked the only available foothold. He graded it 'a solid 5.10', far beyond what was being achieved by Mallory's contemporaries at sea level, and at that time he thought it was beyond Mallory's abilities. In his 1999 book *Last Explorer* Anker made it clear that he didn't think the pair had got to the summit, citing the extreme difficulty of the Second Step, their lack of crampons and a fixed rope, oxygen sets that weighed twice as much as modern ones, no climbing aids such as pitons, and inadequate clothing.

And what about rock-climbing capabilities of the boots that the two men were wearing? They were large, leather, alpine monstrosities, only lightly nailed to avoid too much heat loss from the feet. David Breashears said to me: 'Look at his boots. There's no way he would have tried the Second Step wearing those.'

Others disagree. In Anthony Geffen's *The Wildest Dream*, a 'documentary' film made in 2007, you will see Conrad Anker and Leo Houlding, both top rock climbers of the modern era, climbing the Second Step without the Chinese ladder in place. The film set out to prove that Mallory and Irvine *had* climbed the mountain, perhaps because it is a far more sensible commercial idea for a film of this type to represent success rather than failure. The problem is that if the 'reconstructed' events are twisted to make a film sell, audiences can become confused about historical truth. That said, as a film-maker myself I do understand the financial temptations to tell a good story.

Some of the reconstructions in *The Wildest Dream* are not signposted as such, for example the model of Mallory's dead body, so it is sometimes unclear what is real and what is faked. The modern climbers are seen wearing old-style clothes, but they are not the exact replicas that I had worn on the mountain the previous year. This is an important point in film-making, where drama-documentary begins to blunt the sharp edges of truth. Even if the Second Step had been climbed in the way portrayed in the film, then I still cannot see Mallory and the unskilled Irvine getting up it laden with 30lb oxygen sets in the weather that Odell described. And there is a hidden reason for this.

In the course of preparing for the filming, Houlding and Kevin Thaw had removed the ladder from the Second Step and attempted it without any aid – just as Mallory and Irvine would have done. Later, Houlding graded it 5.9, or Hard Very Severe in the grading used by Mallory: distinctly difficult with 1920s heavy oxygen systems and lightly nailed big expedition boots at extremely high altitude – but perhaps just possible.

However, the film-makers missed a crucial point in their study of the rushes. Houlding and Thaw reported to mountaineering historian Ken Wilson that there was no belay point for Mallory to fix his rope below the Step to protect himself on the hardest part. In other words, there was no place where Irvine could have secured their thin cotton rope to safeguard Mallory if he had fallen off while climbing the Step – and if Mallory had fallen it risked taking Irvine off, too, meaning certain death for the pair of them.

Mallory was a married man with children, and the question is this: would he have pushed his luck with a novice with no solid belay below him, even with such a glittering prize above him? The consensus among traditional climbers who know the old style of climbing seems to be no, he wouldn't. One of the cardinal rules of climbing at the time was 'The leader must not fall.'

Unfortunately there is not one scintilla of evidence to prove that the Second Step route was climbed in 1924, and the fact is that all the pre-war expeditions followed the lower route. I think the likelihood is that Mallory would have done the same as his peers, or perhaps turned back after examining the possibilities of the Step.

As a footnote to the Second Step controversy, I suggested in a Royal Geographical Society talk after my clothing tests in 2006 that the Norton–Somervell route might have had more going for it than was realised. After all, Reinhold Messner took this route when he made his extraordinary first solo ascent of the mountain in August 1980. Messner was an admirer of Norton and Somervell's alpine-style attempt, and he proved that the route could be done without oxygen.

From the position on the ridge where their oxygen bottle No. 9 was found, Mallory and Irvine could have struck off across the mountain on the same traverse that Bill Wager and Wyn-Harris had taken, and arrived at the Norton Couloir in much the same place as Norton and Somervell. There is good evidence from book annotations that those early pioneers thought that there was an exit from the Couloir onto the Third Step. This is not a direct route, but it would have avoided the Second Step.

Perhaps the consummate route-finder Mallory found a way around the puzzle that eventually took a Chinese ladder to solve but, as we have seen, he had more against him than he realised.

21

What Was in His Mind?

What were Mallory's thoughts in those last hours? This is perhaps the hardest question of all to answer satisfactorily, and the waters have been muddied by those who have sought to portray him as emblematic of some kind of quest. An answer has to be attempted, though, if we are to make sense of him as a man.

We have seen something of his upbringing, his character, the achievements of his peers and the effect that the First World War had on him. We know that he was on the brink of pulling off a feat that would have made him famous and ticketed for life. We also know that he was a family man who was leading a novice, and that he was probably not inclined towards performing a suicidal stunt. On the other hand he had a record of leading others into danger when success was near; Geoffrey Winthrop Young had warned him that he was prone to sweeping 'weaker brethren' along, beyond their abilities. Then there was the guilt of the disaster of 1922 still preying on his mind, and the frustration with the bad weather that had led to ill-considered dashes in 1924.

All in all there would be many competing motives pulling in different directions, as well as the supreme struggle of the climbing itself. So how would these various tugs have resolved themselves in his mind?

For more on his psychology I turned again to Audrey Salkeld, the most tireless chronicler of the Mallory years, and the person most likely to know what drove the man. In her monograph

'George Mallory: where was he going?' she makes a number of points.

The first is that when he died, his sisters suspected that even his parents didn't understand who he really was. His death was so symbolic that it was swiftly hijacked by the mystery-makers and his true nature was quickly obscured. The memorial service for Mallory and Irvine at St Paul's Cathedral in London on 17 October 1924 was the first and only time British mountaineers have been honoured in such a way. King George V and the Prince of Wales attended, and the Bishop of Chester intoned these words:

> that last ascent, with the beautiful mystery of its great enigma, stands for more than an heroic effort to climb a mountain, even though it be the highest in the world.

A beautiful mystery indeed, and you can almost hear the angels' trumpets. We might be criticised for trying to destroy a wonderful fairy tale, but the truth is surely more important. In our favour is the perspective given by the passage of time. We also possess just about every word that Mallory wrote, and it is in his writings that we get a glimpse of his true hopes and interests.

Salkeld points out that although his name is now inextricably tied up with a mountain, George Mallory was not exclusively a mountaineer, and indeed compared with modern-day career climbers his climbing was episodic. He had wide-ranging interests, and had big plans for the future. As we have seen, he was something of a late developer, and went up to university as a rather innocent idealist, probably expecting to follow his father into the Church. Cambridge, however, changed all of that. He fell headlong into a whirl of free thought and freer lovers, and got to know some of the foremost thinkers of the day, such as the Keynes, the Stracheys and other members of the Bloomsbury set, whose liberal views appealed to his sense of fair play.

From his tutor A. C. Benson he imbibed the value of a wide-ranging education, freed from the shackles of compulsory sport and classics, and he arrived at Charterhouse as an idealistic young schoolmaster eager to try out his ideas. Ideals collided with reality – for example when his pupils sat on his head – but he steadily learned how to be an effective master and, just as Graham Irving had done when Mallory was his pupil at Winchester, he started to take some of the boys climbing. This was a key moment. Salkeld says:

> George began taking selected boys to Snowdonia in the school holidays to join Geoffrey Winthrop Young's 'Hill Company'. Young saw himself as a kind of missionary, dedicated to converting some of the greatest brains and sportsmen of the age to a love of mountains. After energetic days on the hills, evenings would be for theatricals, singing and competitive feats. The idea of introducing teenagers to adventurous activity, combining this with personal expression and wide-ranging conversation formed the kernel of a new kind of school George, Geoffrey and David Pye were keen to promote. Geoffrey in time would help Kurt Hahn set up Gordonstoun, based on a similar ethos, but by then of course George had been dead for almost a decade.

The Downs School, run by Geoffrey Hoyland, and where young John Hoyland, my uncle, taught briefly in 1934, realised some of these same ideals. From their colleague Auden's writings, we can understand how exciting it must have been for Mallory to see the possibility of sweeping away the philistine old public-school system of Greek and rugger. In all of this, his other interest of climbing was seen as a means towards realising his ideals, rather than an end in itself.

After the Armistice, back home with Ruth and again teaching at Charterhouse, he became restless, finding the teaching of children too slow compared with the training of adult soldiers that he had undertaken at the end of the war. One gains the feeling that he was casting around for a cause that might save the world. He became interested in the League of Nations, and a letter of application to Gilbert Murray, Regius Professor of Greek at Oxford and a Vice President of the League, reveals how he chose to present himself at that time:

> How shall I tell you about myself? ... I believe that I am not without some gift for lecturing – partly from some little experience I had in France when we set about educating the Army, and partly because one can't be a schoolmaster for long without developing such talent of expression as he may be endowed with. I am to some extent a student of history – that is 'my subject' here; in a second rate sort of fashion no doubt as is almost inevitable, apart from mental gifts, in the case of a schoolmaster; still, history is an interest and a foundation which might be helpful. I have also a very great interest in literature and in writing on my own account but I expect that is not much to the purpose. Perhaps the most important thing about me which I ought to tell you is that I think and feel passionately about international politics ...[1]

Soon afterwards Mallory went on some kind of fact-finding mission for the League to Ireland during 'the Terror', just before Partition, but it led to nothing. Again, there is a sense of casting around for something to do. After Mallory's death Geoffrey Winthrop Young said that Mallory had worked out a scheme for promoting international understanding by geography teaching, and Howard Somervell told of his 'wonderful schemes for doing something to draw classes together and thwart the appalling scourge of class-consciousness being thrust upon the present generation'. Benson, writing in his diary after Mallory visited him in 1923, remarked that his friend was 'a bright gallant figure, possessed of much personality', who was 'absorbed in the League of Nations'.

Marriage and the war had re-directed his interests, rather than blunting them. Towards the end of the war Mallory felt that, when he was training young soldiers, he had found his true vocation in the teaching of adults. Hinks – in one of his few positive actions – had met Revd David Cranage, the Secretary of the Board of Extra-Mural Studies at Cambridge, on a train and suggested Mallory for a position teaching workmen. Mallory seemed ideal for the job as it appealed to his socialist ideals and training, and he was appointed. Soon, however, he asked for leave from his new job to take part in the 1924 expedition and, under great pressure from Hinks, Cranage relented and let him go.

Mount Everest must have seemed a heaven-sent opportunity to further Mallory's cause to make the world a better place. He was right to believe that success on the mountain would give him an attentive audience. If he had survived he could perhaps have enjoyed a long BBC career like Jack Longland, another Everester and pedagogue, or he could have been directly involved in setting up a new kind of school. I think he had a strong sense of destiny, which sometimes made him clutch at straws.

Audrey Salkeld, among others, has noticed how his feelings towards Mount Everest developed. In 1921 he was excited by the reconnaissance, but in 1922 his pleasure was overshadowed by guilt at the death of the Sherpas. Then, in 1923, when he was lecturing and planning the next Everest climb he became obsessed with climbing the mountain. In 1924 bad weather forced Norton's abandonment of his scheme, and Mallory's last-ditch climb was an attempt to snatch victory from the jaws of defeat. His state of mind in 1924 could be characterised by: 'This is it, at last I've found my vocation, and if I climb this mountain now I can get on with my real life's work.'

This is a very dangerous approach to a mountain that – more than any other – demands patience. I, too, caught summit fever near the top of Everest, and I know just how seductive it can be.

In those last hours it must have seemed that a great prize was slipping from his grasp. Exhausted by bad weather and oxygen starvation, the constant stream of decision-making that is the lot of the high-altitude mountaineer would have slowly trickled to a halt. For some climbers it then resolves into the mantra 'Summit or die. Summit or die.' However, Mallory was a better climber than that. I believe he went too high for the conditions, led on by the seductive prospect of success, but that he did make the decision to turn back when the weather became impossible. Then the lethal relaxation of vigilance during descent made one of the pair slip, and the rest was up to gravity and contingency. The brutal wreck of a fine mind and much-loved man swiftly followed, and all those ideals evaporated in the whirling blizzard.

22

Weighing the Evidence

By now, after studying the evidence for some 30 years and visiting the mountain on nine expeditions, I thought I ought to able to make a fairly accurate guess about what happened to Mallory and Irvine. If we evaluate each clue, then take the climb hour by hour, we might reach some reasonable conclusions.

Mallory had returned from his first attempt with Bruce in 1924 a frustrated man. His party had only reached 25,000ft (7,620m), when porter trouble prevented any further ascent. His swift abandonment of this oxygen-less attempt suggests that he thought it was a waste of effort. Returning to Camp III he fished out the gas sets to make a last-ditch attempt with Irvine. Turning them on, they climbed swiftly up the North Col slopes at record speed, which may have reinforced his belief that the oxygen would prevail. After a night on the Col they left for their summit attempt.

If Mount Everest were in the dock, standing accused of killing George Mallory and Sandy Irvine, the prosecution and the defence would stand or fall on the evidence. I would like to lay out that evidence as follows:

Reliable evidence:
- Mallory's body and where it was found. That he was not directly on the fall line from the ice-axe position suggests that there were two falls, not one.
- Mallory's injuries. As we have seen, George Rodway's evidence suggests these were not consistent with one long fall. In

addition, the severe bruising around his waist would have taken time to form. It is possible, in the case of a really severe accident, to have bruises start to form within 20 to 30 minutes of injury. So, if Mallory only fell once, he had to live at least that long post-fall for the bruises around his ribs to form. The bruises were pretty extensive – Rodway's best guess is that they might have taken at least an hour to form. So, again, we might have two falls.

- The clothes that Mallory was wearing. They were studied, replicated, tested in the field and the laboratory, and found to be adequate if the weather remained good, dangerously inadequate if it did not.
- Mallory's belongings taken from his body: sun goggles from an inside pocket, a broken watch, an altimeter and some letters.
- The weather. We now know there was dangerously low air-pressure that day, which was associated with a blizzard. The barometric readings were taken from calibrated instruments by men at Base Camp.
- The ice axe found in 1933 by Percy Wyn-Harris and Bill Wager. It is beyond reasonable doubt that it belonged to either Mallory or Irvine. It is probable that it was Irvine's, as it had identifying marks that tallied with his swagger stick.
- The approximate place where the axe was found. We know this by marked-up photographs from the 1933 expedition.
- Smythe's sighting of a body in 1933. We can give weight to this clue as Mallory was found exactly where Smythe reported a body to be.
- The oxygen cylinder first spotted by Simonson on the North Ridge in 1991, and brought down to Base Camp in 1999. Its unique markings established that it came from Mallory or Irvine in 1924, and it is identified in Mallory's jotted note on the back of a letter as cylinder No. 9. It had contained 110 atmospheres. Its exact original location is uncertain, though.
- The position of their last camp, Camp VI. This was found in 1933 and excavated in 2001.

- A woollen mitten found in 2001 by an American searcher on the exit from the yellow rock band.

Less reliable evidence:
- Odell's sighting. He was a credible witness, and his eyesight was good. He drove a car without needing spectacles well into his 80s. However, visual witnesses are notoriously unreliable, as many studies have shown.[1] The so-called 'forgetting curve' effect means that visual memory is already disappearing within twenty minutes, and Odell did not make his diary entry until a long time after his sighting. The effects of high altitude and stress have also been well documented by Jon Krakauer, among others. The problem is that eyewitnesses are generally given a great deal of credence in courts of law – and by wishful thinkers. Odell changed his story so much, however, that his evidence becomes too unreliable to support a whole series of events.
- Mallory's intended route. Our examination of this suggests that if Mallory had looked at the difficulties of the Second Step he would have rejected it as a route for its lack of a belay at its base. It's also unlikely that he would have attempted it in the worsening weather with an inexperienced second man. Moreover, all of the expeditions in the 1920s and 1930s followed the Norton–Somervell route. The likelihood is that Mallory would have done the same as his peers, or perhaps turned back when he examined the dangers of the Step. There is no hard evidence until someone discovers an oxygen cylinder above the Second Step, or a photograph in Somervell's camera.
- Mallory's state of mind and motivation. This was his last chance, and we have seen how his contemporaries were getting ahead of him in worldly success. We have seen that he was a man of high ideals, and that it is likely he would have had a receptive audience had he climbed the mountain. In addition, there was a culture of self-sacrifice after the First World War among its survivors, and Mallory was clearly in the grip of an

obsession. These factors might have predisposed him to take a risk on what was his last attempt at Everest's summit. On the other hand, he had a climbing novice in tow whose life depended on him. He was also a married man with children, and a close examination of his previous climbs does not suggest a reckless nature. He himself wrote: 'No mountaineer would be content to reach the top and not get down,'[2] so I think we can discount any notion of a one-way suicide mission.

- In the end it is unclear how all of these factors would have affected his decision-making, and so his state of mind has to go in the less reliable pile of clues.

- The fact that Mallory's sun goggles were in a pocket might suggest that he was climbing in poor visibility. However, Norton had also removed his goggles in good visibility on the same part of the mountain. And Mallory may have carried two pairs, as all sensible mountaineers should.

- The position of oxygen cylinder No. 9. Although in 1991 Simonson spotted one or two bottles about 600ft (160m) before the First Step at around 27,800ft (8,475m), the one recovered in 1999 may have been moved from somewhere else. Dave Hahn remembered seeing an old cylinder sticking out of the snow below the Yellow Band that was picked up by a Sherpa and cached somewhere on the ridge. Alternatively, the cylinder could have been moved down from somewhere higher by Chinese climbers, who were known to move oxygen sets around the mountain. If it was found in the place where it was dumped by Mallory and Irvine, it is the highest-lying evidence of their passage. But we cannot be sure.

- The calculations of oxygen usage. If oxygen cylinder No. 9 was found where Mallory or Irvine left it, and if their oxygen consumption was continual and consistent, Hemmleb calculates that the pair might have arrived at that point some time around or after 8:30. This depends on too many unknowns, and so unfortunately it is unreliable, like all calculations of heights reached that are dependent on calculations of oxygen consumption.

- The absence of a photograph of his wife Ruth from Mallory's clothing, suggesting that, as promised, he had left it on the summit. Mallory's notorious absent-mindedness is a more likely explanation, as he had even forgotten to bring his camera, compass and torch.
- Wang's sighting of a body, and his gestures suggesting it had been pecked by birds. As Wang and Hasegawa did not share a common language, something about the damage to the face may have been lost in translation.
- Xu's sighting of another body, possibly that of Irvine. The story has changed so much that it is not yet a tangible clue. Several searches have so far turned up nothing.
- The quantity of oxygen carried. Two cylinders each, or three? In a letter to his wife, Mallory wrote: 'My plan will be to carry as little as possible, go fast and rush the summit. Finch and Bruce tried carrying too many cylinders.'[3] He could have changed his mind, but later he said that 'we'll probably go on two cylinders – but it's a bloody load for climbing'.
- Reports from psychics. These were fashionable in the 1920s, and one present-day Mallory researcher has consulted a psychic. Their reports are contradictory and unscientific, and I would suggest that they carry no weight at all.

If we concentrate on the reliable clues, there are two that appear to be contradicted by a third: the position of the ice axe and the position of the body don't seem to fit with the lack of injuries consistent with a fall of nearly 1,000ft. I went back to my witness George Rodway and asked if Mallory could have fallen twice, once from the axe site, then again, fatally, from somewhere below.

It's possible that Mallory might have fallen all that way from the site of the ice axe but since he was conscious enough to self-arrest and his body relatively undamaged, not likely. The fall line would have had to be very smooth and unbroken by any significant drop-offs, obstructions or other stuff that would have killed him outright or broken him to pieces.

What no one has ever proposed (to my knowledge) is that M&I might have taken a minor slip near the site of the axe, recovered somewhat (but gone too far down to go back for the axe) and continued down in their mounting fatigue ... then fallen again ... this time more seriously. There are variables like this that need to be considered in the mix, I think. The bruising from the rope makes me think he was alive for some time after all the pressure exerted by a roped fall – and I don't think he lasted too long after stopping from the 'ultimate' fall. Bruises like that don't form in minutes ... so he might have had the bruises develop between the first fall and the last fall while they continued descending.[4]

George Rodway goes on to say:

What else can one reasonably deduce from this find? It is likely that Mallory and Irvine fell while descending, possibly late in the day – Mallory's sun goggles were in fact found in his pocket so they may have no longer been needed as the daylight waned. Alternatively, they may have possibly been descending in a snowstorm, thus removing iced-up goggles in order to at least temporarily improve vision. No supplementary oxygen kit was found nearby, and the lack of such lends support to the suggestion that the climbers had cast aside the useless weight of empty oxygen cylinders to hasten their descent. Aside from the fractured leg and the position of Mallory's body, the rope injuries on his abdomen and torso support the scenario of a roped fall over a modest vertical distance ...

The climbing rope that remained around Mallory's body appeared to have snapped after taking the weight of a fall. This fall and subsequent parting of the rope may have left Sandy Irvine separated from Mallory by some distance. Could Irvine have survived this incident relatively unscathed and have been left alone in the growing darkness, possibly in bad weather, high up on the North Face with little in the way of alpine climbing experience to guide him? Regardless of the status of Irvine after Mallory's fall, he probably did not survive the night out – the clothing of the 1920s simply did not lend itself to safely enduring open bivouacs above 8000m.

So now that we have looked at what might have happened to Mallory and Irvine, let us try to reconstruct their last day.

23
The Last Hours

The last men definitely to see Mallory and Irvine alive were their four porters, who had carried their oxygen cylinders, sleeping bags and provisions up to Camp VI, a grandiose name for one tiny tent. Mallory and Irvine had come up in good style from Camp V, 'going exceedingly strong with oxygen', as the porters reported to Norton, and had arrived at around lunchtime. Hastily writing the notes to Odell and Noel that we have already seen, Mallory would have waved the porters goodbye, not realising that would be the last he would see of the rest of humankind.

As the four men clattered down the slope, there would have been time for perhaps a look at the beginning of the next day's route. The one thing we know for certain is that Mallory noted the pressures of five cylinders on the back of a letter that was found in his pocket. Oxygen equipment strewn around the tent suggests that Irvine might have called out the pressures one by one as he read them on the gauge while Mallory wrote them down. Edmund Hillary spent the whole of his summit day calculating the amount of oxygen he had left, and it seems plausible that our two climbers would have planned to do the same. This might also suggest that the two men slept using oxygen that night. There seems to have been enough gas, and we know Mallory was by then seeing supplementary oxygen as the key to the mountain. They would brewed up some of the loose tea on the stove, and eaten a last supper.

The moon set at midnight, and not much sleep would have been had that night. Mallory intended to get off early on his summit day of 8 June 1924. Remember that in his last note to the cameraman John Noel he had said:

> Dear Noel, We'll probably start early tomorrow (8th) in order to have clear weather. It won't be too early to start looking for us either crossing the rock band or going up skyline at 8:00 p.m. Yours ever, G. Mallory

Most authorities accept the '8:00 p.m.' as a mistake for '8:00 a.m.' Although this note has been quoted many times, no one seems to have questioned why Noel, although equipped with a powerful lens at Camp III, did not see the pair climbing that day. We are therefore reliant on evidence of artefacts taken from Mallory's body, and those unearthed at Camp VI by the 2001 search team, to guess what happened next.

None of the early British expedition summit attempts began before sunrise at 4:45am. In fact 5:30am was the earliest that anyone set off, and Norton and Somervell, leaving from the very same tent a few days earlier, left at 6:40am, having been delayed by a leaking vacuum flask. They lost an hour melting snow to replace the water. This, by modern standards, is dangerously late. Modern-day climbers start leaving their tents well before midnight, and my colleagues on an expedition in 2011 on the same route left at 10:00pm from a higher camp.

In another note, this time to Odell, Mallory said that they would 'probably go on two cylinders – but it's a bloody load for climbing. Perfect weather for the job. Yours ever, G. Mallory.'

There are three points here. First, if they did take only two cylinders, they were not going to have sufficient capacity to get to the summit and back safely. Second, three cylinders would have been an even bloodier load. And third, it was not going to be perfect weather for the job, as we have already clearly seen.

The sun rose at 4:45am. A candle-lantern and electric torch were found in their tent, so they had not left during the hours of darkness. At the earliest they would have left at 5:30am, by which time most modern-day climbers would be approaching the summit. They were already far too late.

We know what cooking stove they had, the one left in the camp by Norton and Somervell: a Meta solid-fuel burner. Oddly enough, I was given one of these by my grandmother in the 1960s and they were utterly useless. Using solid fuel, they took an age to bring a cupful of water to the boil, even at sea level. Trying to melt snow or ice to give them enough liquid to avoid dehydration would have been a lengthy process, even if they could supplement it with water from a Thermos flask. Imagine attempting to unfreeze two pairs of giant leather boots at the same time, crouched in a cramped tent. Our modern butane–propane gas stoves are far more effective.

We even know how the stove would have been lit, as a box of Bryant and May's Swan Vestas matches was discovered on Mallory's body. And the loose tea leaves were found stored in an Army & Navy Stores tin that had originally contained acid drops.

At Camp IV on the North Col their last breakfast had been cooked by Odell and Hazard: fried sardines, biscuits, tea and hot chocolate. It is unlikely anything so lavish would have been prepared at Camp VI. I ate a bar of chocolate just before crawling out of the tent for my own summit attempt, and I wasn't hungry. They may have had a little lukewarm tea, and perhaps biscuits or chocolate.

We know exactly what Mallory was wearing, and how his clothing would perform in the prevailing weather. We know that the suit would feel rather less cumbersome than today's down suits, and with no hood he would have had rather better peripheral vision. We also know what he was carrying: a thin 9mm white cotton rope, with a red tracer thread, and an extraordinary collection of junk in his pockets: a pair of nail scissors with a leather holster, a pencil, a tin of Brand & Co. Savoury Meat Lozenges (similar to modern-day stock cubes), and a selection of letters and bills. He had remembered sun goggles and petroleum jelly, but we know that he had forgotten to take his compass with him. As he set off from the camp his boots would have felt lighter and less cumbersome than today's better-insulated versions. Irvine's clothing was broadly similar, except that he had sewn zip fasteners into the pockets of his jacket. These were the latest thing in 1924, and might help future researchers to identify his remains.

The next we know of them is the mitten found in 2001 by Jake Norton on the exit from the rock band, which suggests they were using much the same route as present-day climbers. It might have been dropped on the way up or the way down. They then took the crest of the ridge to a point 600ft short of the First Step, where they left us their next clue: the empty oxygen cylinder spotted by Eric Simonson. This suggests that they took around four hours to get from Camp VI at 26,700ft (8,140m) to this point on the ridge at 27,800ft (8,475m). So they were already running slower and later than hoped. What took place over the next couple of hours is unclear. Believers in a successful summit attempt like to think Odell saw them on the Third Step at 12:50pm, but as I have suggested, this sighting seems unreliable.

They might have looked at the Second Step; they might have taken the Norton–Somervell traverse. I have explained why Mallory is unlikely to have risked attempting the Second Step with no belay and an inexperienced second man.

But what we do know for sure is that a storm started at around 2:00pm and, with the new evidence from the barometric readings, we can be confident in stating that the air pressure was as low as during the 1996 storm. It was not a minor, localised storm, as the optimists contend. I suggest that this shows that further upwards progress was going to be very difficult, and that a successful summit climb is extremely unlikely. From the ice-axe evidence it looks as though Mallory and Irvine descended the way they had come, a logical thing to do in poor visibility.

I think the pair reached the slippery slabs of the ice-axe site, that the slabs were covered with fresh snow, and that Mallory slipped and fell. Experienced climbers know that the descent is the most common time for this sort of accident to occur; exhaustion and hypothermia are setting in, concentration has been lost as a result of a false sense of security and, because of the slope, you cannot see your next step as clearly as you can on the ascent.

After Mallory fell, Irvine dropped his axe to grab the rope, but was pulled off in a similar way as occurred in the John Hoyland accident. I think they then fell together in the curious, alternating fall that is often the fate of roped men: one falls, pulling off the other. The first slows down briefly, only to be pulled off again by the continuing fall of the second. And so on and on. What we do know is that the thin rope snapped near Mallory and that he sustained severe bruising, which needed 20 minutes to one hour of continued circulation to form.

His injuries are not consistent with one continual fall down to the place where his body was found; his bruises needed time to form, and his body does not appear to be in line with a fall from the ice-axe site. It seems, therefore, that he picked himself up and staggered onwards towards Camp VI, only 900ft (275m) away. Blood stains on the left cuff of his blue and white flannel shirt suggest that he may have wiped a bleeding injury, then fell for a second, fatal time.

Now, this is all of course supposition, but it seems consistent with the tangible evidence that we have looked at, and with the experience others have had in the same place. I now think that Mallory and Irvine didn't get much higher than Norton and Somervell, and that they died in a double fall off the boiler-plate slabs.

It's very hard to prove a negative – that the pair *didn't* get to the top, but Occam's Razor demands that the more simple theory (that Mallory and Irvine fell off and died before reaching the summit) trumps the more complex theory (that they somehow reached the summit, beating the lack of oxygen, the dangerously low air pressure and their marginal clothing).

When I digested the results from my clothing, weather and route researches, I reluctantly had to change an opinion I had held for some 30 years. If these facts and figures were true, and if the 1924 blizzard was as serious as that of 1996, I'm afraid that in my opinion there is no way in which Mallory and Irvine, confronting the Second Step in their marginal clothing, could have reached the summit of Mount Everest on that fatal day.

For years I was a believer. I tried to prove that Mallory and Irvine had climbed the mountain, and I was driven by a romantic notion of what was due to them. When I found that Mallory's clothing was adequate for the job in good weather I was delighted.

But writing this book made me assemble and weigh the evidence dispassionately. You have to change your mind when confronted with new evidence, and a slowly growing realisation that Mallory and Irvine had too much against them was buttressed by the new weather data. Wishful thinking can only take you so far. It was difficult to let go of a faith that had sustained me for so many dangerous and uncomfortable expeditions, but I could see no other choice. So I am now quite sure that Hillary and Tenzing were the first to climb Mount Everest, and that Mallory and Irvine could not have succeeded.

Every May I pray that someone will find Irvine and the camera to prove me wrong. For now, though, in this matter I am an atheist. It was hard to give up the faith of a lifetime, but I feel better by acknowledging the truth of the evidence, and I feel even more admiration for those two pioneers. My failed quest to find Somervell's camera and prove Mallory's success was not a huge disappointment. I now realise I was seeking something else: a purpose to my life. That enlightenment might not have come had I been successful.

I have been on a trajectory of belief. A suggestion fell on fertile ground in my childhood, and I found the idea motivating and a focus for my energies. I strove to prove the suggestion true in the face of increasing evidence against it, but in the end I have had to give up and admit that I was wrong. My grandfather Jack and Uncle Hunch believed in the existence of a perfect God – and I tried to believe in the perfect adventure story.

Postscript:
Goodbye to Everest

What do you do after you've climbed Mount Everest? For most climbers it seems to mark a turning point in their lives, a point when things get better. Some use it to further their careers. Few relax. Edmund Hillary drove Ferguson tractors to the South Pole on one expedition after Everest. Bill Tilman, leader of the 1938 Everest expedition, took up sailing in his 50s.

Somervell decided that his life's work lay among the poor of India. He operated on thousands of people in his hospital at Neyyoor, and it is interesting to see what the most common cases were. The first was, unexpectedly, duodenal ulcer. He wrote:

> This is an agonising condition, which if not treated properly leads to continual vomiting and gradual starvation. Every meal, though it removes the pain for an hour or so, is followed with awful regularity by intense pain that lasts until something else is eaten.

Duodenal ulcers used to be treated by the local quack doctors by the application of red-hot branding irons to the stomach, which caused more agony and extensive scarring. Somervell started operating for the condition, cutting the anterior vagus nerve to the stomach, which reduced the flow of acid. It became known as the 'Somervell operation', and he performed it 2,500 times in ten years, usually watched by an audience of relatives of the patient from a gallery at the end of the operating theatre.

Although this relieved much suffering, Somervell would be amazed to learn that all along it was being caused by a bacterium. Australian scientist Barry Marshall suspected that most stomach ulcers were caused by *Helicobacter pylori* and not by the eating of spicy food, as previously thought. To prove this he drank a Petri dish full of the organisms and developed symptoms. His wife complained of his bad breath, but he won a Nobel Prize for the discovery. Suitable antibiotics would not have been available to Somervell, but it is interesting that one can labour over a problem for a lifetime and have the hidden answer in your hands the whole time. This is what happened to me with the Mallory mystery and the meteorological readings. And Sherlock Holmes was strangely blind to fingerprints.

What happened to our cast of characters?

After retiring to England from India, Howard Somervell became the Alpine Club president from 1961 to 1964. A pacifist all his life he died in 1975, aged 85, and was buried in his beloved Lake District.

Gandhi, a rather more famous pacifist, came to a violent end in 1948 when, on his way to address a prayer meeting, he was assassinated by a Hindu nationalist.

Jack Hoyland, his disciple, died at home in 1957, his arm held out and his hand clasped in the hand of Jesus Christ. He firmly believed that he would meet Billy, his favourite dog, in heaven.

Ruth Mallory brought up her three children on her own for a while, but eventually re-married. Unfortunately her new happiness did not last long, and she died of cancer in 1942. Her daughter Clare married an American climber who was killed in a climbing accident, and so, like her mother, she was widowed by mountaineering, and left with three children to bring up alone.

George Finch became Professor of Chemistry at Imperial College, London, and gave up climbing after an accident in the Alps in 1931 killed three fellow-climbers. He took up sailing instead.

In 2007 I finally came to grief on Mount Everest. I went back to the southern, Nepali side of the mountain to make a BBC *Horizon* film about a group of doctors studying hypoxia. The subject interested me, as I had often wondered over the years why some individuals did so much better at altitude than others. I was also interested in the physical changes to the mountain itself. Here is my diary entry for 21 April:

In the 21 years I've been coming to Mount Everest I've never seen the mountain looking so dangerous. The reason is the notorious Icefall. In the 1950 reconnaissance expedition Bill Tilman pronounced this obstacle unjustifiably dangerous, but since then thousands of ascents have been made through it, and this year we continue. It is the only way up the mountain from the Nepali side. Two days ago we in the climbing team climbed through the Icefall to spend a night at Camp I, and so we were able to reacquaint ourselves with this great natural feature.

The fact is that it has changed. The Icefall is a great frozen river pouring over a cliff. In the past it seemed to break off in great slices that were relatively easy to climb. Now, perhaps due to less precipitation, it seems to have collapsed in on itself so that the break point occurs further up the valley, and the great slices of ice seem to have fragmented.

As a climb it is full of interest. You start from your tent at Base Camp and put your crampons on as soon as the bare ice starts. Then, puffing hard in the thin air, you start climbing up and down the frozen waves of ice. You skirt round little ponds and haul yourself up icy crests. Soon you are hopping over crevasses in the ice, and then you will encounter your first ladders. Balancing over three ladders tied together across a bottomless crevasse is a nerve-wracking experience. Then the fixed ropes start. These are woven up the Icefall by a group of Sherpas, the 'Ice Doctors'. They are thin white ropes attached to the ice by stakes and ice screws, and the idea is to clip yourself in as a sort of extreme stair-rail. If you fall off the ladder they might just hold you. After the three ladders there is a collapsed section of ice we're calling Popcorn Alley, because the metre-wide blocks do look like a vast popcorn spillage down some giant staircase. It is very hard to find something solid to stand on in here. After this is The Hammer, a 50-tonne beam of cracked ice bridged across the route. As you try to rush under this you try not to think that one day soon it is going to fall. Unfortunately some joker has put a knot in the fixed rope right under the Hammer so you come to a twanging halt and have to unclip, then re-clip on the other side of the knot.

After this comes Happy Valley, a collapsed section of such terrifying insecurity you only dare whisper to your companion for fear of dislodging the tottering blocks around you. Some are extraordinarily like blocks of ice cream, except that they are the size of a house. Other parts of the ice are exactly like a Fox's Glacier Mint: hard and transparent.

Climbing as quickly as we could in air that contained only half the amount of oxygen at sea level we eventually came up to the Great Slices: the top of the Icefall. Here we relaxed a bit, but Camp I was still hours away. Base Camp radioed a warning of bad weather, so we pulled extra clothes on and climbed up into a snowstorm.

As we got out of the Icefall the terrain flattened out and we entered the Western Cwm, the huge valley under the peak of Everest. As we trudged along in the whirling snow I thought about my brother Denys, who is sailing around the Isle of Skye this week. I wished I was with him. Eventually ten tents loomed through the mist and we threw our gear into one of them. We dragged food out of the store tent and started melting ice to drink. One by one the rest of the climbing team came in to camp after us. After my worst night for years (the mats were hard and my sleeping bag soaked), we descended back to Base Camp. Running as fast as we could we got down in two and a half hours – half the time it took to come up. The Icefall is not a place in which to linger.

After this first climb I had an accident and had to be helicoptered off the mountain. I'd caught a virus at Base Camp after the person demonstrating the masks forgot to tell us he had a cold. I felt awful, but when we in the production team heard of a rescue going on further up the mountain I headed up the mountain instead of down, as I had to film what was going on. The pressures on programme-makers often lead to bad decisions like this. I climbed alone through the Icefall once again, then plodded up to Camp II through the wonderful silence of the Western Cwm and promptly collapsed from exhaustion when I arrived mid-afternoon.

Next morning I was just able to film the arrival of Usha Bista, the 22-year-old Nepali girl climber who had been found unconscious and alone at the Balcony. An old friend from my Mallory expedition, Dave Hahn, had discovered her after returning from his own successful summit attempt. Despite his weariness he gave her dexamethasone, a steroid that alleviates cerebral oedema, more oxygen, and organised her rescue. Members of our own expedition took over her medical care and looked after her evacuation. When I saw her she had some frostbite to fingers and toes, but what was upsetting was her rage at having been left to die by her teammates. We are very used to hearing stories about Western climbers walking past dying colleagues, but this was an all-Nepali expedition.

After I had filmed the overnight radio traffic from the successful summit attempt I filmed Pasang Sherpa arriving with the precious blood samples that had been taken to measure the oxygen levels in the summit climbers. He took just two hours to run down from the Balcony to Camp II – surely a record. The blood was duly tested and filmed.

Next morning, feeling terrible, I was told by the medical officer to head back down the hill. Usha was bundled up and brought down, too. As we approached the top of the Icefall one of my companions clipped into the fixed ropes. At that moment a huge block of ice fell off with a roar and a cloud of white ice smoke. It was no more than two metres from us, it took out a section of ropes, and my heart sank; of all days to have to start abseiling down the bloody Icefall! Ten seconds later and it would have killed all of us.

Eventually we got down and started to get proper attention. Thank God for the doctors on this expedition and particularly Mark Wilson, the medical officer. Wilson organised a helicopter rescue, paid for by the BBC, and Usha was going to come along for free. Her alternative means of descent was a horse.

Next day we were loaded into a huge Russian helicopter that was piloted by an interesting character named Sergei. Both he and his chopper looked like veterans of the Soviet war in Afghanistan. He was dressed in polyester slacks and shirt, as if he were ready for a spot of gardening, but he controlled a monster of amazing power and violence – the down-draft was enough to send stones spinning in all directions. We took off and in minutes had retraced the path that had taken us weeks to ascend. Usha slept through the flight, and when we arrived at Jiri we were off-loaded into the hot sun to wait for a Nepalese Army helicopter. Its pilot was under instruction, so we were treated to aerial versions of a three-point turn and an emergency stop. To cap a rather taxing day we had to endure a siren-screaming ambulance in the Kathmandu rush-hour that was even noisier than the Icefall.

I spent a terrifying three days in a hospital in Kathmandu from which I emerged very weak. When I got home the BBC soon made me redundant. Then my beloved sister Jane died. Then my wife, a pragmatical woman, divorced me.

It was clearly time for a major rethink. I wondered what to do next. Clearly life at 29,000ft *above* sea level was getting a bit tricky, so how about trying a new life *at* sea level, like Bill Tilman? As ever, I looked into books for answers to fundamental questions.

The Dangerous Book for Boys was that summer's publishing sensation, winning the National Book of the Year award. It's packed with information on how to make a bow and arrow, how to hunt and cook a rabbit, and how to build a tree house. It contains a list of 'Poems Every Boy Should Know', including *If* and *Invictus*, and it also tells you that you must expect to have the occasional accident – that's how you learn.

It reminded me of the sailing books that I had loved as a boy, and how they had influenced me. There was the *Swallows and Amazons* series by Arthur Ransome, wonderfully dangerous books for both boys *and* girls. Ransome was the kind of man I wanted to grow up to be. He was in turn a sailor, an enthusiastic first-hand observer of the Russian Revolution and then a British spy. Escaping from a loveless marriage, he ended up marrying Trotsky's secretary Evgenia in 1924 and took her to the Lake District, where he wrote the best-selling series for which he is remembered today.

But my favourite *Swallows and Amazons* book is set in a landscape much closer to London. Just 45 miles from the M25 motorway that encircles the city is a wilderness so deep, so remote, that you could travel across it all day and not see a soul. Immortalised in Ransome's book *Secret Water*, the flat islands, creeks and marshes to the north of Walton-on-the-Naze are a surprise to those who think that the county of Essex is all commuter belt.

Ransome's book deals with two groups of children – the Swallows and the Amazons – who are cast ashore for a week by over-worked parents to fend for themselves and map the area, in the process meeting a horde of savages (in reality, another group of children who call themselves the Eels). When I got home I pulled out my old copy of *Secret Water* and glanced at the inscription on the title page. It had belonged to my brother Denys when he was about ten years old. I started reading, and slowly a realisation dawned on me. In Ransome's drawings the yacht *Goblin* that had carried the children to the island looked curiously familiar. The Swallows' family were staying in a rented cottage at Pin Mill on the banks of the river Orwell ... wasn't that where Denys now kept his boat on a mooring? I knew that he had bought an old, wooden yacht, so I telephoned him and arranged for a couple of days sailing off the Essex coast. I had to forget about Mount Everest for a while, and think hard about something else.

When I arrived at the boat she looked the very image of *Goblin*, although my brother protested that he had little recollection of the book, and certainly wasn't consciously trying to re-create a childhood dream. A wooden, single-masted cutter, she had once been a rich man's fancy, and when built had cost the same as the house in which we grew up. Vastly more characterful than the plastic boats of today, these deep-hulled old yachts feel firmer and more stable in the choppy North Sea. Inside there is so much hand-carved joinery it's rather like sailing in a vast piece of furniture. Ransome had based *Goblin* very largely on his own boat, *Nancy Blackett*, named after one of the characters in the book, and as I boarded I felt that I was stepping back into an idealised version of the 1930s. Smells of varnish, cordage and tea rose from below, and the June sunshine made the teak decking hot underfoot.

We ghosted down the river past the last low hills of Suffolk, past the great cranes and gantries of the container port of Felixstowe, and past the disease-ridden cruise liner that had dominated the news that week following an outbreak of projectile dysentery on board. We felt lucky not to be with the cramped tourists aboard.

Soon the north Essex coast emerged from the heat-haze. After living under the world's highest mountain for months I felt almost dislocated by this landscape. An enormous sky met the North Sea with a pencil-thin line of land in between. Soon that too disappeared, and I found it very hard to steer a straight course in the featureless sea. Turning back towards the coast, we searched for the buoy that marks the entrance to the world depicted in *Secret Water*. The original tarred barrel has only recently been replaced, and I felt a creeping sensation of the fictional book merging with the factual reality. 'Ahead, the land seemed hardly above the level of the sea, just a long low line above the water.'

It is here that the third dimension of up and down can seem to disappear, as the water and the land lie so closely stretched together that they change places every tide. It is a fascinating sensation to glide between the two. The old Thames barges used to steer across these waterways until they touched the bottom and then tacked, or went about, hence the expression 'touch and go'. This captures exactly the trepidation you feel as you wring the last few feet of depth before you go about, and slide across the wind in the other direction.

Before long we found an anchorage for the night. Our chain rumbled into the water, and the anchor dug itself into the mud as the boat gently drifted back in the ebbing tide. Silence. We sipped tea. Somewhere across the marshes a curlew called a long, bubbling cry. Darkness fell.

Inside the warm, wooden cabin the gas ring hissed, and baked beans and sausages sizzled in the pan. The light made the outside very dark all of a sudden. We turned it off and ate on deck, listening to the bubble and suck of the tide. Out there great, glistening flats of mud were being exposed to the night. Land was emerging from the water in a slow, vegetable-like heave. But in 12 hours the water would be back.

In *Secret Water* the map is slowly filled in from the rough outline sketched by Commander Walker, the children's father.

The children explore and survey their domain in exactly the same way as much of the British Empire had been mapped on charts. Using small dinghies they reconnoitre creeks they call the North-West Passage and the Red Sea, names redolent of British endeavours long before their time. Somehow they know how to take bearings and draw maps.

We were anchored just to the east of the real-life Horsey Island, which in Ransome's book becomes Swallow Island and is the first to be mapped. After landing, the children unwrap their 1930s *Ripping Yarns*-style provisions: 'Three tins of pemmican ... Six tins of sardines ... One tin of golden syrup ... One stone jar of marmalade ... Six boxes of eggs.' In the centre of the island still stands the farm, which the children call a native krall. To the north lies Peewit Island, which becomes Peewit Land. The correspondences with the real landscape are close. To the south is the Wade, a causeway to the town that is submerged at high tide. The three youngest children find themselves trapped in the middle by the rising water and are only rescued in the nick of time by The Mastodon, another child who lives aboard a derelict barge. My brother and I found a few rotting timbers that we imagined could have come from *Speedy*, his ironically named residence. Because of the literary overlay – the fictional adventures that have been superimposed on these commonplace surroundings – I felt there was something quite magical about the landscape. This is what I felt when I saw Mount Everest for the first time – the shock of a long-imagined reality. Such is the power of childhood books.

Although adults are almost incidental to Ransome's tale, there is an underlying tension throughout the story created by the deadline for completing the map in time for their parents' return. It is as if the father – or indeed the author (Arthur Ransome had an extremely demanding father) – had very high expectations of his children. In particular, John, the eldest child, seems to be driven by nervous anxiety: 'The expedition had failed. They would be embarking that day with the map unfinished …' In the end, however, everything turns out all right, and the map is finished. The children are safely picked up by *Goblin*. The map – and the children – become completed entities.

In the morning my brother and I lifted the anchor and sailed back out to sea, leaving our childhood behind.

The ache of self-induced nostalgia is a pleasant pain, even when it is imagined nostalgia. Ransome's children never existed, except in his mind. But to me they are as real as the low-lying islands, the mud and the tide.

W. H. Auden called the 1930s 'a low, dishonest decade'. To adults, perhaps it was, but to Ransome's fictional children it seems an age of innocence. What parents would now leave their young children to camp on an island unsupervised? With small boats, campfires and marshes that flood at high tide, these children had ample opportunities to harm themselves, but what they succeeded in doing was to become self-reliant, confident individuals.

The last two lines of *Invictus* read:

> *I am the master of my fate:*
> *I am the captain of my soul.*

Then I thought: why not sail around the world?

Why not? No one had ever sailed the Seven Seas (that is, the seven oceans) *and* climbed the Seven Summits. Over 275 climbers have become Seven Summiteers, which means they've climbed:

Aconcagua (South America, 6,960m/22,834ft)
Carstensz Pyramid (Australasia, 4,884m/16,024ft)
Denali – also known as Mount McKinley (North America, 6,194m/20,320ft)
Elbrus (Europe, 5,642m/18,510ft)
Kilimanjaro (Africa, 5,895m/19,340ft)
Mount Everest (Asia, 8,848m/29,028ft)
Mount Vinson (Antarctica, 4,892m/16,050ft)

I didn't know if it was possible. I'd already climbed Mount Everest and Denali, the two hardest mountains on the list. I'd sailed across the Southern Ocean to Antarctica, certainly the hardest sea, so maybe it was possible.

Sailing does have similarities with mountaineering. Both activities involve uncomfortable battles with the elements, interspersed with short moments of pleasure, and both seem to attract similar personalities, although there seems little crossover between the two. George Mallory, for example, was not a natural sailor. Writing after his passage across the Indian Ocean on the way to Mount Everest in 1921, he states:

> The sea is as deeply evil as it is attractive ... There's an unquiet spirit in the ocean ... we seem to be pursued by the shadow of its brute nature, not allowed to forget the violence of which it is capable.

I have certainly been more scared at sea than on any mountain. It always seems to be out to get you.

Surely the most remarkable person to be both a climber and a sailor was Bill Tilman. He explored untrodden territory in the Himalayas and elsewhere at a time when there were still blanks on the map. In his 50s, realising that he couldn't any longer climb to high altitudes, he asked someone to show him how to sail. He learned quickly, bought *Mischief*, the first and most loved of his three Bristol Pilot Cutters, and undertook some astonishing voyages. His first took him across the Atlantic to South America, through the Magellan Straits to Peel Inlet, where he landed and made the first proper crossing of the Patagonian Ice Cap.

Tilman was a real explorer and, not being a peak-bagger, probably wouldn't have had anything to do with the Seven Summits. But to me it seemed a meaningful framework for an interesting journey.

Not having much money left after the divorce, I could only afford to buy a sunken boat. By the time I got to Florida the steel ketch had been lifted off the bottom of the canal in which she was submerged and was looking rather forlorn. But she was just what I was looking for. Built in a Dutch yard in 1976 she has a strong steel hull and a centre cockpit, so she can bump ice and protect her crew from heavy weather. She has two masts and a ketch rig, which means that the individual sails are small enough for one man to handle. I decided to name her *Curlew* after the bird that loves mountains and estuaries.

I spent three months in the summer of 2009 repairing the damage to the boat's electrics and engines, then sailed her to Cuba on a shake-down cruise with my girlfriend Gina that winter, which is where most of this book was written. We proceeded to sail across the Caribbean to look for the inspiration for Robert Louis Stevenson's *Treasure Island*. This is one of the British Virgin Islands: Norman Island. Real treasure was recovered there that had been stolen in 1750 from a Spanish treasure galleon, *Nuestra Señora de Guadalupe*.

As I write this, I'm still in the Caribbean, and the next leg of my voyage will be to sail to the South American mainland and attempt to climb Aconcagua, the second highest of the Seven Summits, near the Argentinean border with Chile. They've built a hotel at Base Camp since I was last there, so I hope to rest in comfort. Then it is down to the Patagonian Channels to ponder the next and most difficult leg of the journey, the voyage through the Southern Ocean to the shores of Antarctica. This is why I wanted a steel yacht, as we might be nudging growlers (small icebergs) on our way to Mount Vinson, the last continental summit to be discovered and climbed. This fact is hardly surprising as it lies well south, at a latitude of 80°. Oh, and Vinson is a long way from the coast.

Then across the Pacific to Irian Jaya for an attempt on Carstensz Pyramid, which was so nearly climbed by Wollaston of the 1921 Everest expedition. There is some very dense jungle here, inhabited by the Dani people, who still live in a Stone-Age world. The men wear penis gourds, and birds of paradise feathers in their hair, while the women wear raffia-grass skirts. Season-conscious climbers will ask: when do you climb Carstensz? Answer: any time, it rains constantly. After this, we'll head through the South Pacific and land in New South Wales,

The author aboard *Curlew* off the coast of
Cuba on his round-the-world voyage.

Australia, then continue west, cross the Indian Ocean and sail around Africa, passing through the South and North Atlantic. I've already climbed Kilimanjaro and Elbrus, so I don't need to stop off in Africa or Europe.

Keen geographers will notice the absence in our itinerary of the Arctic Ocean. This will have to be remedied, perhaps with an attempt on the North-West Passage.

It will be a long journey from Mount Everest. What has been learned? We may have destroyed a legend in 1999 with the discovery of Mallory's body, but Mallory was still beautiful in a way: the body breathily described by Lytton Strachey as resembling a statue by Praxiteles has now frozen into a white marble-like figure,[1] and he died trying his utmost to further the adventure of the human spirit. It doesn't matter to me anymore whether he got to the summit or not. His wife Ruth expressed it best:

> Whether he got to the top of the mountain or did not, whether he lived or died, makes no difference to my admiration for him; I think I have the pain separate. There is so much of it, and it will go on for so long. If only it hadn't happened. It so easily might not have.

The pain in her voice still cuts through the years.

I think George Mallory was a wonderful man and that his death was a tragic waste. His last employer, Cranage, put it well: 'In him we have lost not only a fine mountaineer, but "a very perfect gentleman", a man of high ideals, willing to spend himself in the service of others.' I believe he was seduced by Mount Everest, against his better instincts, and paid the price.

I now have mixed feelings about climbing Mount Everest. Is it really worth the destruction of all those lives? Wasn't

Somervell's life, with his relief of so much human suffering in India, more worthwhile in the end?

In spring 2011 I went back to the mountain for a final farewell. I wasn't trying to climb it again; my job was to help others to get to the top. I sat down with my diary at Advanced Base Camp – Mallory and Somervell's old Camp III – and thought about what I had learned in 21 years on the mountain.

As I write these words I can lift my eyes from the page up to the summit of Mount Everest 8,000ft above me. I'm sitting on a flat rock, in hot sunshine, at ABC. My friends from the expedition are climbing down from the summit as I gaze up to the tiny triangle of snow, so high in the sky. There has been another abortive search for Somervell's camera, and for me this is the last time I shall come to this mountain.

I feel partly a sense of exhaustion, and partly a sense of loss. Everest has been such a big part of my life for so long that it will leave a huge hole. If I do not move on, though, it will become a destructive source of longing and regret.

So, goodbye to Everest. Goodbye. Goodbye. Goodbye.

Chronology

1802
The poet Samuel Taylor Coleridge records the first rock climb in literature.

1846–52
Surveyors working for the Great Trigonometrical Survey of India calculate that one large Himalayan peak (which they knew at first simply as 'B', and later as 'Peak 15') rose to at least 28,000ft, making it probably the highest in the world.

1854
The height of Mount Everest is calculated as 29,002ft.

1854
Sir Alfred Wills initiates the Golden Age of Alpinism with his ascent of the Wetterhorn.

1857
The Alpine Club is founded in London.

1865
Pandit 001, Nain Singh, travels incognito to Tibet, secretly mapping as he goes. Efforts to find a universally accepted local name for 'Peak 15' are unsuccessful and the mountain is renamed Mount Everest in honour of Sir George Everest, who had superintended much of the work of the Great Trigonometrical Survey.

1886
George Mallory is born.

1890
Howard Somervell is born.

1903–04
'Diplomatic Mission' to Lhasa is led by Sir Francis Younghusband.

1912
Captain Scott dies on his return from the South Pole.

1914
Outbreak of the First World War.

1915
Somervell joins up as an army surgeon, Mallory as an artillery officer.

1921
Mount Everest reconnaissance expedition explores Everest's lower northern and eastern approaches and gains the North Col.

1922
Mount Everest expedition. Mallory, Somervell, Norton and Morshead make the first serious attempt to climb the mountain. George Ingle Finch and Geoffrey Bruce, the first to use supplementary oxygen, later achieve an altitude record of c. 27,300ft (8,320m). The first casualties on the mountain are suffered when seven Sherpas die in an avalanche on the slopes of the North Col.

1924
Mount Everest expedition. 4 June: Norton reaches 28,126ft (8,570m) on Everest without supplementary oxygen. This altitude record stands for 55 years.

1924, 8 June
Mallory and his young companion Sandy Irvine disappear into the clouds on their last attempt to climb Mount Everest.

1933
An ice axe belonging to Mallory or Irvine is found. The first flights over Everest provide good aerial photographs of the summit.

1934
Frank Smythe discovers John Hoyland's body on Mont Blanc.

1953
Everest is climbed by a British expedition, led by Colonel John Hunt. Climbers Edmund Hillary and Tenzing Norgay reach the summit via the South Col and South-East Ridge on 29 May.

1960
A Chinese expedition reaches the summit by climbing the Second Step.

1975
A Chinese climber, Wang Hong Bao, finds the body of an Englishman during a Chinese expedition.

1979
The first ascent without supplementary oxygen is achieved by Reinhold Messner and Peter Habeler.

1980
Messner makes the first solo climb of Everest, again without oxygen equipment. He uses the route pioneered by Norton and Somervell.

1990
The International Peace Climb. BBC film, *Galahad of Everest*.

1993, 6 October
The author reaches the summit, becoming the 15th Briton to climb Mount Everest.

1998
The author initiates a Mallory search expedition.

1999
George Mallory's body is found.

2000, 2001, 2004, 2006, 2011
Searches for Somervell's camera.

2007
BBC Horizon film of Caldwell Everest expedition.

2009
The yacht *Curlew* sets sail on the *Seven Seas, Seven Summits* expedition around the world.

Notes

CHAPTER 1: Start of an Obsession

1. Letter from Jack Longland to J. S. Hoyland, September 1934.
2. Everest Archives, Royal Geographical Society, Box 18.
3. Foreword in T. H. Somervell, *After Everest*, Hodder & Stoughton, 1936.
4. Letter from George Mallory to his sister Avie, August 1917.

CHAPTER 2: Getting the Measure of the Mountain

1. Letter from Samuel Taylor Coleridge to Sara Hutchinson, 5 August 1802.
2. Simon Schama, *Landscape and Memory*, Alfred A. Knopf, 1995, p. 502.
3. John Carey, *The Intellectuals and the Masses*, Faber and Faber, 1992.

CHAPTER 3: Renaissance Men

1. T. H. Somervell, op. cit.
2. Ibid.
3. Ibid.
4. Ibid.
5. Robert Bridges, *The Spirit of Man*, Longmans, Green & Co., 1916.
6. Wilfred Owen, 'Dulce et Decorum est', 1920.
7. T. H. Somervell, op. cit.

CHAPTER 4: Galahad of Everest

1. R. L. G. Irving, 'George Herbert Leigh Mallory, 1886–1924', *Alpine Journal*, November 1924, vol. 36, no. 229, pp. 381–5.
2. George Mallory in a letter to his mother, 22 August 1905.
3. Letter from Lytton Strachey to Clive and Vanessa Bell, 21 May 1909.
4. Geoffrey Winthrop Young, *On High Hills*, Methuen, 1927.
5. George Mallory, 'The mountaineer as artist', *Climbers' Club Journal*, March 1914.
6. E. F. Norton, *The Fight for Everest 1924*, Edward Arnold, 1925, p. 145.

CHAPTER 5: The Reconnaissance of 1921

1. Royal Geographical Society, 1920 presidential address.
2. J. B. Noel, *Through Tibet to Everest*, Edward Arnold, 1927.
3. Simon Schama, op. cit.
4. Everest Archives, Royal Geographical Society, Box 3.
5. C. K. Howard-Bury, *The Reconnaissance of Mount Everest, 1921*, Longmans, Green & Co., 1922.
6. Ibid.
7. Ruth Mallory, quoted in Wade Davis, *Into the Silence*, Bodley Head, 2011.

CHAPTER 6: The Expedition of 1922

1. Exhibition catalogue, year unknown (possibly 1935).
2. C. G. Bruce, *The Assault on Everest: 1922*, Edward Arnold, 1923.
3. George Mallory, 'Everest Unvanquished', *Asia*, no. 9, 1923.
4. T. H. Somervell, op. cit.
5. *Everest, Journey to the Third Pole*, BBC Radio 4, presenter Stephen Venables, producer GH.
6. T. H. Somervell, op. cit.

7. *Everest, Journey to the Third Pole*, BBC Radio 4.
8. E. F. Norton, op. cit.
9. Walt Unsworth, *Everest*, Baton Wicks, 1981.
10. David Robertson, *George Mallory*, Faber and Faber, 1999.
11. Email from Audrey Salkeld to GH.
12. Robert Graves, *Goodbye to All That*, Jonathan Cape, 1929.
13. T. H. Somervell, op. cit.
14. Ibid.

CHAPTER 7: 1922, and the First Attempt to Climb Mount Everest

1. T. H. Somervell, op. cit., p. 57.
2. *Everest, Journey to the Third Pole*, BBC Radio 4.
3. T. H. Somervell, op. cit.
4. Letter from Longstaff to Wollaston, 19 August 1922.
5. Email from Audrey Salkeld to GH.
6. Wade Davis, op. cit.
7. Report from Bruce to Hinks, 4 July 1922.
8. T. H. Somervell, op. cit.
9. T. H. Somervell, op. cit., p. 77.

CHAPTER 8: 'No trace can be found, given up hope ...'

1. Doug Scott, 'Ego Trips', *Summit* magazine, BMC, autumn 2011 (adapted from an article in the *Alpine Journal*).
2. Letter from George Mallory to General Bruce, British Library, BL 63119.
3. Cable, Somervell RGS Everest Archive, Box 34.
4. Julie Summers, *Fearless on Everest*, Phoenix, 2000.
5. E. F. Norton, op. cit.
6. T. H. Somervell, op. cit., p. 125.
7. T. H. Somervell, op. cit.
8. BBC interview used in *Everest, Journey to the Third Pole*, BBC Radio 4.

9. Ibid.
10. Ibid.
11. T. H. Somervell, op. cit., p. 132.
12. BBC interview used in *Everest: Journey to the Third Pole*, BBC Radio 4.

CHAPTER 9: A Pilgrim's Progress

1. H. Ruttledge, *Everest 1933*, Hodder & Stoughton, 1934.
2. Sir Percy Wyn-Harris, *Sunday Times*, 17 October 1971.
3. N. E. Odell, 'Mr. Odell's Story', *Alpine Journal*, November 1924, vol. 36, no. 229, pp. 221–5.
4. N. E. Odell, 'The Last Climb', *Alpine Journal*, November 1924, vol. 36, no. 229, pp. 265–72.
5. E. F. Norton, op. cit., p. 130.
6. *The Times*, 21 February 1980.

CHAPTER 10: John Hoyland and a New Clue

1. Letter from J. S. Hoyland, Chamonix, 20 September 1934.
2. F. S. Smythe, *Climbs and Ski Runs*, Blackwood, 1931.
3. *Journal of the Friends Historical Society*, 1989, vol. 55, no. 7, p. 220.
4. Letter from J. D. Hoyland to G. W. Young, Sheffield, April 1934.
5. W. H. Auden, *Selected Poems of W. H. Auden*, Faber and Faber, 2010.
6. Letter from J. Longland to G. W. Young, Durham, 2 October 1934.
7. *Alpine Journal*, 1934, vol. 46, pp. 415–19.
8. Letter from J. Longland to J. S. Hoyland, September 1934.
9. *The Badger* (Downs School magazine), autumn 1934.
10. Letter from F. S. Smythe to E. F. Norton, Joshimath, 4 September 1937.

CHAPTER 11: I First Set Eyes on Mount Everest

1. George Mallory, 'The Eastern Approach, 1921', in C. K. Howard-Bury, op. cit.
2. *Rubaiyat of Omar Khayyam*, trans. E. Fitzgerald, stanza 17.
3. Hilaire Belloc, 'The Yak', in *The Bad Child's Book of Beasts*, Duckworth, 1918.
4. P. Scheid and H. Shams, 'Birds over Mount Everest: extreme hypoxia tolerance', *Journal of Physiology*, 1997, vol. 499 (P).

CHAPTER 12: High Mountains, Cold Seas

1. E. F. Norton, op. cit., pp. 324–5.

CHAPTER 13: The Finding of Mallory's Body

1. Letter from John Mallory to GH, 10 August 1998.
2. Letter from George Mallory to GH, 29 September 1998.
3. Letter from Lord Hunt to GH, 17 February 1998.
4. Jochen Hemmleb, Eric Simonson and Larry Johnson, *Ghosts of Everest*, Macmillan, 1999.
5. Ibid.
6. Graham Hoyland, *High* magazine, August 1999, no. 201, pp. 20–3.
7. Ed Douglas, 'Everest row over photo profits from body of pioneer Mallory', *Observer*, 9 May 1999.
8. Wade Davis, op. cit., p. 569.
9. Email from George Rodway to GH.
10. *Sunday Times*, 27 April 2003.
11. Transcript of a filmed interview by GH, April 2004.
12. Ed Douglas, 'Rivals race to solve Everest's final secret', *Observer*, 16 May 2004.

CHAPTER 14: When Did Everest Get So Easy?

1. Albert F. Mummery, *My Climbs in the Alps and Caucasus*,
   Basil Blackwell, 1936.
2. K. Fukui, Y. Fujii, Y. Ageta and K. Asahi, 'Changes in the
   lower limit of mountain permafrost between 1973 and 2004
   in the Khumbu Himal, the Nepal Himalayas', *Global and
   Planetary Change*, 2007, vol. 55, no. 4, pp. 251–56.
3. G. W. K. Moore and J. L. Semple, 'The impact of global
   warming on Mount Everest', *High Altitude Medicine &
   Biology*, 2009, vol. 10, no. 4, pp. 383–5.
4. Woodward quoted in Peter Gillman's article, *Sunday Times*,
   24 September 2006.
5. Tom McKinlay, 'Wrong to let climber die, says Sir Edmund',
   New Zealand Herald, 24 May 2006.
6. Michael Elmes and David Barry, 'Deliverance, denial, and the
   death zone: a study of narcissism and regression in the May
   1996 Everest climbing disaster', *Journal of Applied
   Behavioral Science*, June 1999, vol. 35, no. 2, pp. 163–87.

CHAPTER 15: Why Do You Climb?

1. George Mallory, 'The mountaineer as artist', op. cit.
2. J. D. Hoyland, 'Partly concerning a leaky tent', extract from
   the Bootham School magazine, July 1933.
3. Charles Darwin, *On the Origin of Species*, John Murray,
   1859, p. 449.
4. Daniel J. Kruger and Randolph M. Nesse, 'Sexual selection
   and the male:female mortality ratio', *Evolutionary
   Psychology*, 2004, vol. 2, pp. 66–85.
5. Andreas Wilke et al., 'Is risk taking used as a cue in mate
   choice?', *Evolutionary Psychology*, 2006, vol. 4, pp. 367–93.
6. G. William Farthing, 'Neither daredevils nor wimps: attitudes
   toward physical risk takers as mates', *Evolutionary
   Psychology*, 2007, vol. 5, no. 4, pp. 754–77.

7. Professor Steve Jones, 'Aping evolution', BBC Radio 4, 9 November 2009.
8. J. D. Hoyland, 'Partly concerning a leaky tent', op. cit.

CHAPTER 16: What Does Mount Everest Mean?

1. Simon Schama, op. cit.
2. E. F. Norton, op. cit., p. 139.
3. Audrey Salkeld, 'The many faces of evil', *Guardian*, 28 November 2008.
4. Terry Eagleton, *On Evil*, Yale University Press, 2011, p. 100.
5. Quoted in Hugh Ruttledge, *Everest 1933*, Hodder & Stoughton, 1934.
6. Jeremy S. Windsor, 'Voices in the air', *British Medical Journal*, 2008, vol. 337, p. 1433.
7. T. S. Eliot, 'The Waste Land', *The Criterion*, 1922, lines 359–65.
8. Ernest Shackleton, *South: The Story of Shackleton's Last Expedition (1914–1917)*, Pimlico, 1999.
9. Frank Worsley, *Shackleton's Boat Journey*, Wakefield Press, 2007.
10. Shahar Arzy et al., 'Induction of an illusory shadow person', *Nature*, 2006, vol. 443, 21 September.
11. Jochen Hemmleb, 'Everest – of obsessions and confessions'.
12. Alexander Pope, *An Essay on Criticism*, lines 215–18.
13. T. H. Somervell, op. cit., p. 264.

CHAPTER 17: The Theorists and Their Theories

1. Tom Holzel and Audrey Salkeld, *The Mystery of Mallory and Irvine*, Pimlico, 1996.
2. Arthur Conan Doyle, *A Scandal in Bohemia*, Oxford University Press, 1999.
3. www.velocitypress.com/mallory_irvine.html.

4. Conrad Anker and David Roberts, *The Lost Explorer*, Simon and Schuster, 2000.
5. Email from Professor Mike Searle to GH, 18 July 2010.

CHAPTER 18: Wearing Some Old Clothes

1. Tom Holzel and Audrey Salkeld, op. cit., p. 291.
2. Mike Parsons and Mary Rose, *Mallory Myths and Mysteries: The Mallory Clothing Replica Project*, Mountain Heritage Trust, 2006.
3. 'Unravelling the mystery of Mallory', at www.lboro.ac.uk/service/publicity/publications/view/springsummer08/mallory.html.
4. Ibid.
5. Ibid.
6. Ibid.
7. www.velocitypress.com/mallory_irvine.html.

CHAPTER 19: Perfect Weather for the Job

1. P. G. Firth et al., 'Mortality on Mount Everest, 1921–2006: descriptive study', *British Medical Journal*, 2008, 337, December.
2. Jon Krakauer, *Into Thin Air: A Personal Account of the Mount Everest Disaster*, Anchor Books, 1999.
3. G. W. K. Moore, J. L. Semple and G. F. Hoyland, 'Global warming, El Niño and high-impact storms at extreme altitude: historical trends and consequences for mountaineers', *Journal of Applied Meteorology and Climatology*, 2011, vol. 50, pp. 2197–2209.
4. N. E. Odell, 'The last climb of Mallory and Irvine', *The Geographical Journal*, 1924, vol. 64, no. 6, pp. 455–61.
5. T. H. Somervell, 'The meteorological results of the Mount Everest Expedition', *Quarterly Journal of the Royal Meteorological Society*, 1926, vol. 52, no. 218, pp. 131–44.

6. J. B. West, 'Climbing Mt Everest without oxygen: an analysis of maximal exercise during extreme hypoxia', *Respiration Physiology*, 1983, vol. 52, no. 3, pp. 265–79.
7. Tom Holzel and Audrey Salkeld, op. cit., p. 1.

CHAPTER 20: Utterly Impregnable

1. F. S. Smythe, *Camp Six*, Hodder & Stoughton, 1941, chapter XV.

CHAPTER 21: What Was in His Mind?

1. Letter from George Mallory to Gilbert Murray, quoted in *Alpine Journal*, 2000, p. 161.

CHAPTER 22: Weighing the Evidence

1. M. P. Gerrie, M. Garry and E. F. Loftus, 'False memories', *Psychology and Law: An Empirical Perspective*, N. Brewer and K. Williams (eds), Guilford Press, 2005, pp. 222–53.
2. George Mallory, 'Everest unvanquished', op. cit.
3. Letter from George Mallory to his wife, 19 April 1924.
4. Email from Professor George Rodway to GH.

POSTSCRIPT: Goodbye to Everest

1. Quoted by GH in *High*, op. cit.

Credits

Text

The quotations from 'A Summer Night' and 'Johnny' by W. H. Auden on p. 123 are courtesy of the Estate of W. H. Auden. The quotation from 'The Yak' by Hilaire Belloc on p. 143 is courtesy of the Estate of Hilaire Belloc. The quotation from *The Waste Land* (lines 359–65) by T. S. Eliot on p. 209 is © Faber & Faber and courtesy of the Eliot Estate. All other quotations are as cited in the text.

Plates

Plate 1 © Bonington Library; Plate 2: top left © Salkeld Collection; top right © National Portrait Gallery; bottom © Tate Gallery; Plate 3: top © Imperial War Museum; bottom © Salkeld Collection; Plate 4: top left © *The Times* Picture Library; top right © Salkeld Collection; bottom left © Salkeld Collection; bottom right courtesy of private collection; Plate 5: top © John Noel Photographic Collection; bottom left © Royal Geographical Society; bottom right © Finch Family Collection; Plate 6: top left © The Alpine Club; top right © Finch Family Collection; bottom © *The Times* Picture Library; Plate 7: top © John Noel Photographic Collection; bottom left © Royal Geographical Society; bottom right, courtesy of private collection; Plate 8: top © The Alpine Club; bottom © Royal Geographical Society; Plate 9: top left © The Alpine Club; top right © John Noel Photographic Collection; bottom © The Alpine Club; Plate 10: top and bottom © John Noel Photographic Collection; Plate 11: top © Royal Geographical Society; bottom © Norton Everest Archive; Plate 12: top © Mark Thiessen, National Geographic Society; bottom © Julie Summers; Plate 13: top and bottom © Getty Images; Plate 14 © Royal Geographical Society; Plate 15: top © Steve Bell; bottom © Graham Hoyland; Plate 16: top left © Rachel Gilliatt; centre right © Salkeld Collection; bottom © Graham Hoyland.

Acknowledgements

No one ever reads the acknowledgements pages, do they? Only those who should have been thanked. It is a long list in this case, and I hope I have remembered everyone.

In no particular order, then, thanks to Audrey Salkeld, who with Tom Holzel reignited the whole debate about Mallory and Irvine. She has supported me through thick and thin, with letters, pictures and advice, and is the most tireless of all the Mount Everest historians. There is my cousin Jim Hoyland, who always supported my quest, and at whose house I met another relative, Howard Somervell. Thanks go to his son, David Somervell, who gave me two of his father's precious pictures of Tibet in the 1920s and shared his memories of him, and to John Doncaster Hoyland's sister – and my aunt – Rachel Gilliatt, for the photograph of JDH.

There are the writers: David Seddon, whose excellent monograph on Howard Somervell dealt with all the facets of that remarkable man, in particular his painting. The Gillmans and Wade Davis, for their extraordinary scholarship, and Tony Smythe for his help with his father's finding of John Hoyland.

Then there is a furnishing of professors: Professor George Rodway, who got this book published by drawing it to Collins's attention; Professor Mary Rose, who with Mike Parsons made the replica-clothing project happen; Professor Mike Searle, for his knowledge of Mount Everest's geology; and Professor Kent Moore, whose findings clinched the meteorological evidence for me.

The climbers: David Breashears, Russell Brice and Mark Vallance all belong to that hardy breed, and they all helped in their different ways.

The Mallory family, John, George and Virginia, were all welcoming and helpful, and so too was the Irvine family, in particular Julie Summers, Sandy's great-niece.

The readers: my cousin Bill Mathew, my girlfriend Gina Waggott, my aunt Rachel, brother Denys, and editors Myles Archibald, Mark Bolland and Tony Wayte all helped with sensi-tive and helpful criticism.

The equipment makers: Berghaus, Garmin, Henri Lloyd and Panasonic are all supporting my *Seven Seas, Seven Summits* voyage around the world with their excellent products.

Index

Index

Index

Index

Shamsherpun (Gurkha), 96
Sharp, David, 183, 185–6, 190–3
Shaw, George Bernard, 226
Shebbeare, E. O., 96
Shekar Dzong, 140
Sherpas: adaptations to altitude, 47–8, 144; breathing, forced, 135; compared with Tibetans; 'discovery' by Kellas, 47–8; 'Ice Doctors', 270; 1922 expedition accident, 55, 62, 79, 82–3, 250; Olympic medals, 90; puja ceremony, 168; rope-fixing, 99–100, 146, 185, 270; and sex on Everest, 201; smoking, 153; traditional culture, 48; 2006 season, 185, 190–1
Shipton, Eric, 92, 116, 158, 208, 211, 242
Sierra Leone, 20
signalling theory, 200
Sikkim, 44–5, 47–8, 52–3, 62, 64, 186
Silk Road, 140
Simonson, Eric: discovery of oxygen cylinder, 173, 179, 253, 255, 262; and 1999 Everest expedition, 166, 167, 169–70, 174
Simpson, Sir James Hope, 87
Skye, Cuillin traverse by Somervell, 24
Smith, Walter Parry Haskett, 16, 138
Smithsonian Institute, Washington, 196
Smythe, Frank: in Alps, 25, 88; on difficulty of Second Step, 242; hallucinations on Everest, 142, 208; on Kangchenjunga expedition, 47, 85; letter to Norton, 128–30; on M&I's fate, 125, 129–30; on 1933 Expedition, 116; search and recovery of J. D. Hoyland & Wand, 118, 125–7; sighting of body on Everest, 129–30, 148, 170, 223, 253
Snow Terrace, 214
snow-blindness, 105, 106–7
Snowdonia, 197, 248; Pen-y-Pass meets, 32, 34, 54, 69, 70, 122
Somervell, Billy, 88, 93
Somervell, David, 58–9, 89
Somervell, Howard (T. H.): coughing fits/frostbitten larynx (1924), 98, 99, 104, 105; death, 131, 268; divine companion on Everest, 208; search for his camera, 4, 100–1, 108–9, 130, 131, 160–2, 173, 264, 282, 286
acquaintances/friends on: Bruce, 3, 84; Longstaff, 83; Odell, 68–9; Younghusband, 3

character and faith: 3, 19–20, 24, 83, 84, 86, 89, 95, 216
early life and war: in Alps: 20, 24–5, 88–9; at Cambridge, 19–20, 59, 68; marriage, 87–8; in WWI, 20–3, 24, 35
interests and achievements: Alpine Club president, 268; artist, 19, 59–60, 64, 67, 127; climbing ability, 2, 20, 24; Cuillin Ridge traverse, 24; doctor, 2, 20–2, 35, 65, 86–7, 267–8; lecture tour, 87; musician, 2, 66, 87; at Neyyoor Hospital, 8, 86, 267; oxygen equipment testing, 88–9
writings: on Hazard, 96; to Hinks, 61; on Irvine, 93–4; on Mallory, 73–4, 93, 110, 249; on M&I's fate, 218; on religion, 216
see also individual expeditions
Somervell, Rachel, 119
Somervell, William (T. H.'s father), 58–9
Somme campaign (WWI), 20, 22–4, 35, 36, 192
South Africa, 164, 174, 235
South African Everest expedition (1996), 157
South Col, 50, 102, 141, 153, 155, 167, 201, 224, 237
South Col (Noyce), 133
South Face, 124
South Pole, 41, 63, 209, 267
South Summit, 153–4
South-East Ridge, 141
South-West Face, 155
Southern Ocean, 157, 278, 279
Southern Oscillation, 235
Sou'wester Slabs (Arran), 112
Speer, Stanhope T., 17
The Spirit of Man (Bridges), 22, 73
Stafford, Thomas, 203
Stanage Edge, 121
Stephen, Leslie, 17
Stephens, Rebecca, 157
Stevenson, Robert Louis, 279
Stopes, Marie, 42
Strachey, James, 31, 247
Strachey, Lytton, 31, 70, 171, 247, 281
Strutt, Lt Col E. L. 'Bill', 68, 90
Summers, Julie, 92
summit fever, 155, 250
Sunday Times, 181–2, 191, 219
surveying, early, 7–10, 11–13
Swallows and Amazons (Ransome), 273